FIGHTING AMERICAN

FIGHTING AMERICAN
ISBN 9781785862106

FIGHTING AMERICAN CREATED BY JOE SIMON & JACK KIRBY

WRITER: GORDON RENNIE
ARTIST: DUKE MIGHTEN AND PC DE LA FUENTE
COLORIST: TRACEY BAILEY
LETTERER: SIMON BOWLAND
EDITOR: DAVID LEACH

SENIOR EDITOR Martin Eden
MANAGING/LAUNCH EDITOR Andrew James
DESIGNER Russ Seal
SENIOR PRODUCTION CONTROLLER Jackie Flook
PRODUCTION CONTROLLER Peter James
PRODUCTION SUPERVISOR Maria Pearson
SENIOR SALES MANAGER Steve Tothill
PRESS OFFICER Will O'Mullane
COMICS BRAND MANAGER Chris Thompson
DIRECT SALES & MARKETING MANAGER Ricky Claydon
ADVERTISING MANAGER Michelle Fairlamb
HEAD OF RIGHTS Jenny Boyce
PUBLISHING MANAGER Darryl Tothill
PUBLISHING DIRECTOR Chris Teather
OPERATIONS DIRECTOR Leigh Baulch
EXECUTIVE DIRECTOR Vivian Cheung
PUBLISHER Nick Landau

TITANCOMICS

Published by Titan Comics, a division of Titan Publishing Group, Ltd. 144 Southwark Street, London SE1 0UP. Originally published in single comic form as Fighting American 1-4. FIGHTING AMERICAN © 1954, 2018 JOSEPH H. SIMON AND THE ESTATE OF JACK KIRBY. All Rights Reserved. With the exception of artwork used for review purposes, no portion of this book may be reproduced or transmitted in any form or by any means, without the express permission of the publisher, Titan Comics.

A CIP catalogue for this title is available from the British Library.

First edition May 2018

10 9 8 7 6 5 4 3 2 1

Printed in China

www.titan-comics.com
BECOME A FAN ON FACEBOOK.COM/COMICSTITAN
FOLLOW US ON TWITTER@COMICSTITAN

For rights information contact Jenny Boyce:
jenny.boyce@titanemail.com

FIGHTING AMERICAN

BRAVE NEW WORLD

GORDON RENNIE

DUKE MIGHTEN AND **PC DE LA FUENTE**

TRACY BAILEY

Titan
COMICS

FOREWORD

It's been 63 years since Simon & Kirby's Fighting American first leapt off the page to punch evil on the jaw and save freedom and democracy from the evils of communism and un-American activities!

Those woebegone days of the early 1950s seem like an eon ago and a lot has changed since Joe and Jack first created their uber-patriotic hero, Fighting American.

For one thing, today's superheroes have become a grim, brooding and angst-ridden bunch of anti-heroes more-often-than-not almost as dangerous as the villains and threats they fight... and to hell with collateral damage! Modern comics have turned into dark, melodramatic soap operas a million miles away from those bright, four-color, rip-roaring heroic romps of our fathers' generation.

They saw the wonder and joy in the notion of the superhero – of a garishly costumed hero with a lantern jaw leaping into battle to save the day with some two-fisted action. They could see the drama of it, the theater of it and, more importantly, the sheer unbridled fun of it.

This new *Fighting American* comic, written by Gordon Rennie and drawn by Duke Mighten, is a celebration of those 'old-fashioned' principles enshrined in the work of Simon & Kirby's original comic. It takes a hero from those more innocent times and sets him loose in the 21st Century to see how he copes, offering us a chance to see our world through his eyes. It's a glorious collision of attitudes, action and adventure and we could not be happier to see our fathers' work renewed and re-vitalized in this fantastic new comic!

Signed

Jim Simon

Gail Simon Reynolds

Melissa Simon Groben

Lisa Kirby

Lori Courtney

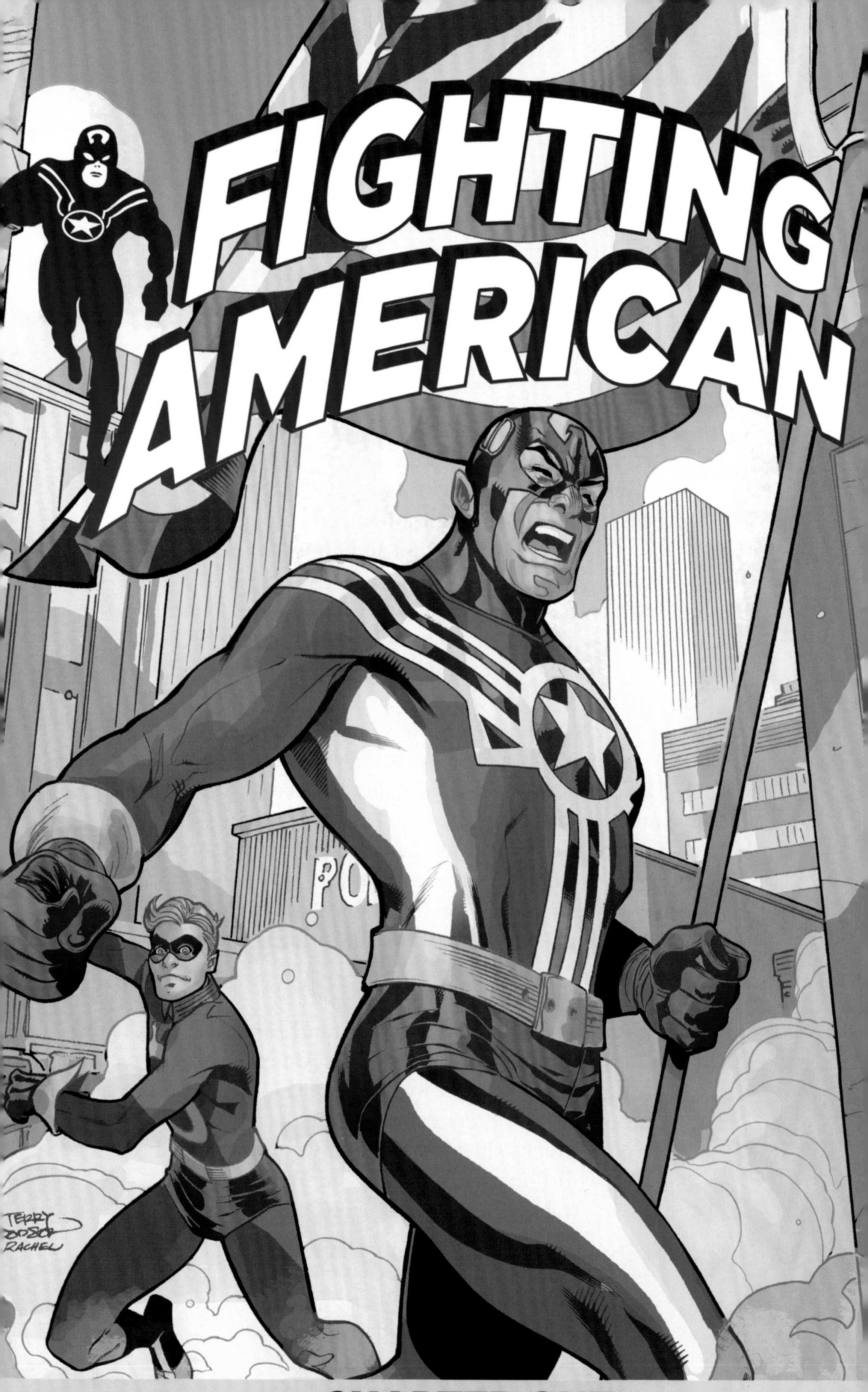
FIGHTING AMERICAN

CHAPTER ONE COVER BY TERRY DODSON

THE STORY SO FAR

"HELLO AMERICA! THIS IS THE VOICE OF FREEDOM!"

JOHNNY FLAGG'S OPENING MONOLOGUE FROM HIS SYNDICATED NEWS-CAST.

It was during the spring of 1954 when JOHNNY FLAGG, twice decorated war hero and crusading investigative television news journalist, was beaten to death by a murderous gang of fifth column Communists following his hard hitting expose of their criminal, un-American activities.

His kid brother, reporter NELSON FLAGG, vowed to Johnny as he lay on his deathbed, that he would spend the rest of his life tracking down the rats responsible…

Moments after Johnny's death, Nelson was approached by a super-secret American military program called PROJECT FIGHTING AMERICAN and was offered a chance to become a super-strong, almost indestructible Agent of the Future and bring his brother's killers to justice. He leapt at the chance. The experimental procedure saw Nelson's mind transferred into the body of his brother, which had been repaired, revitalized, enhanced and incredibly strengthened – and so was born the legend of FIGHTING AMERICAN!

For one glorious year, from April 1954 until April 1955, Fighting American fought for justice, truth and the American way, defending his country, and the free world, from enemies – foreign, domestic and extra-terrestrial – until one day he, and his young plucky sidekick, SPEEDBOY, disappeared whilst on a mission assisting Welsh time traveller and inventor PROFESSOR DYLE TWISTER. They were never seen again.

Until today…

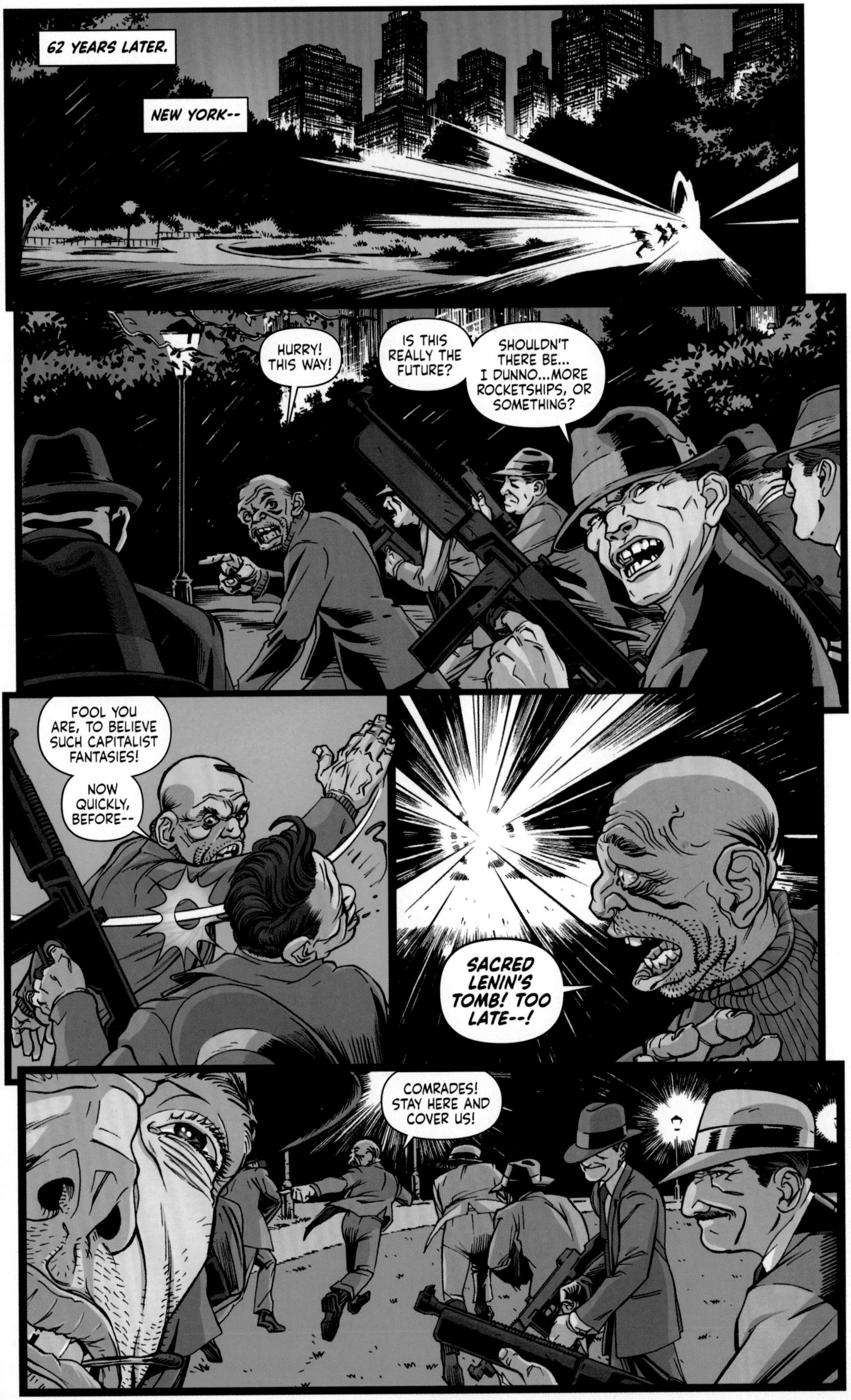
62 YEARS LATER.
NEW YORK--
HURRY! THIS WAY!
IS THIS REALLY THE FUTURE?
SHOULDN'T THERE BE... I DUNNO...MORE ROCKETSHIPS, OR SOMETHING?
FOOL YOU ARE, TO BELIEVE SUCH CAPITALIST FANTASIES!
NOW QUICKLY, BEFORE--
SACRED LENIN'S TOMB! TOO LATE--!
COMRADES! STAY HERE AND COVER US!

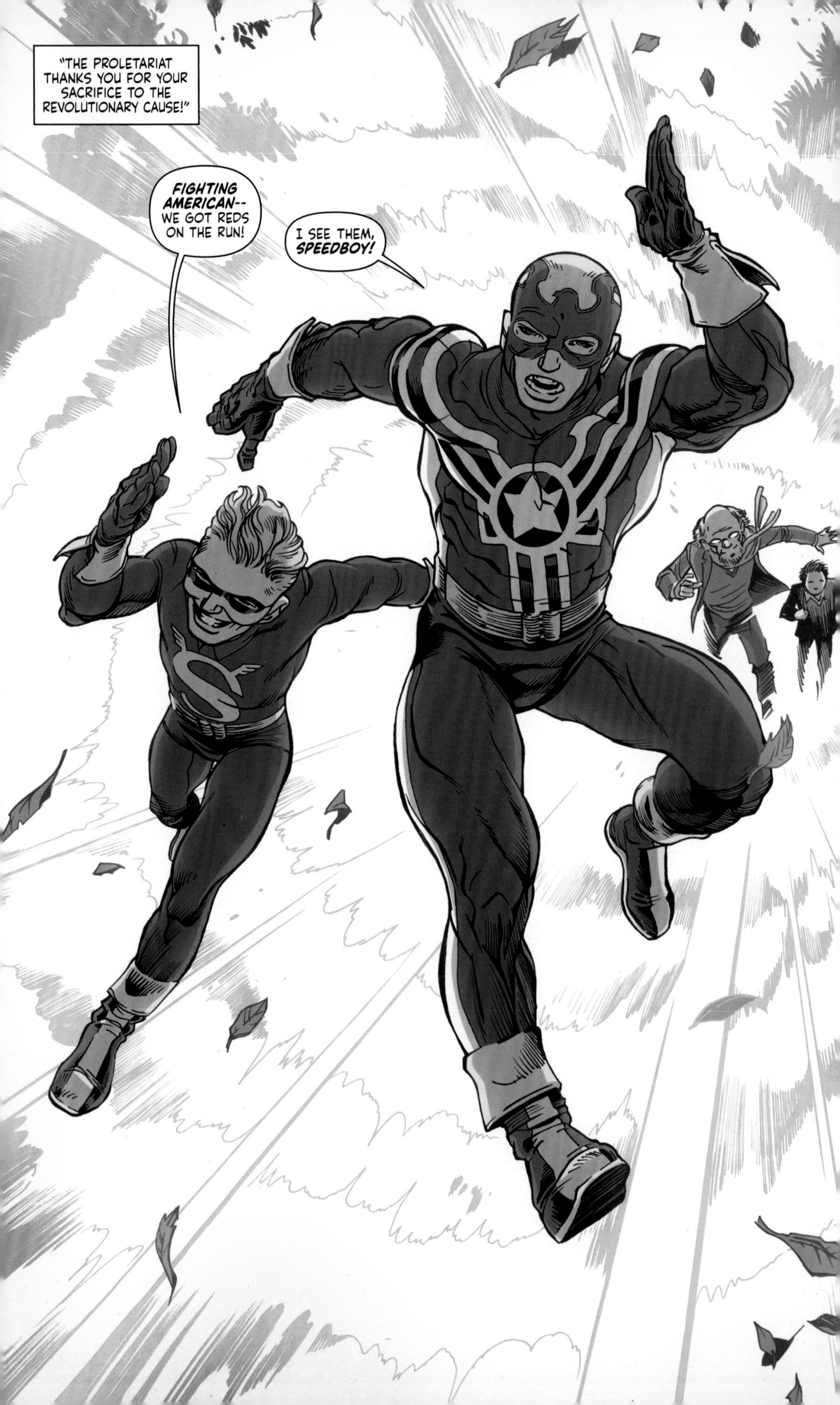
"THE PROLETARIAT THANKS YOU FOR YOUR SACRIFICE TO THE REVOLUTIONARY CAUSE!"
FIGHTING AMERICAN-- WE GOT REDS ON THE RUN!
I SEE THEM, SPEEDBOY!

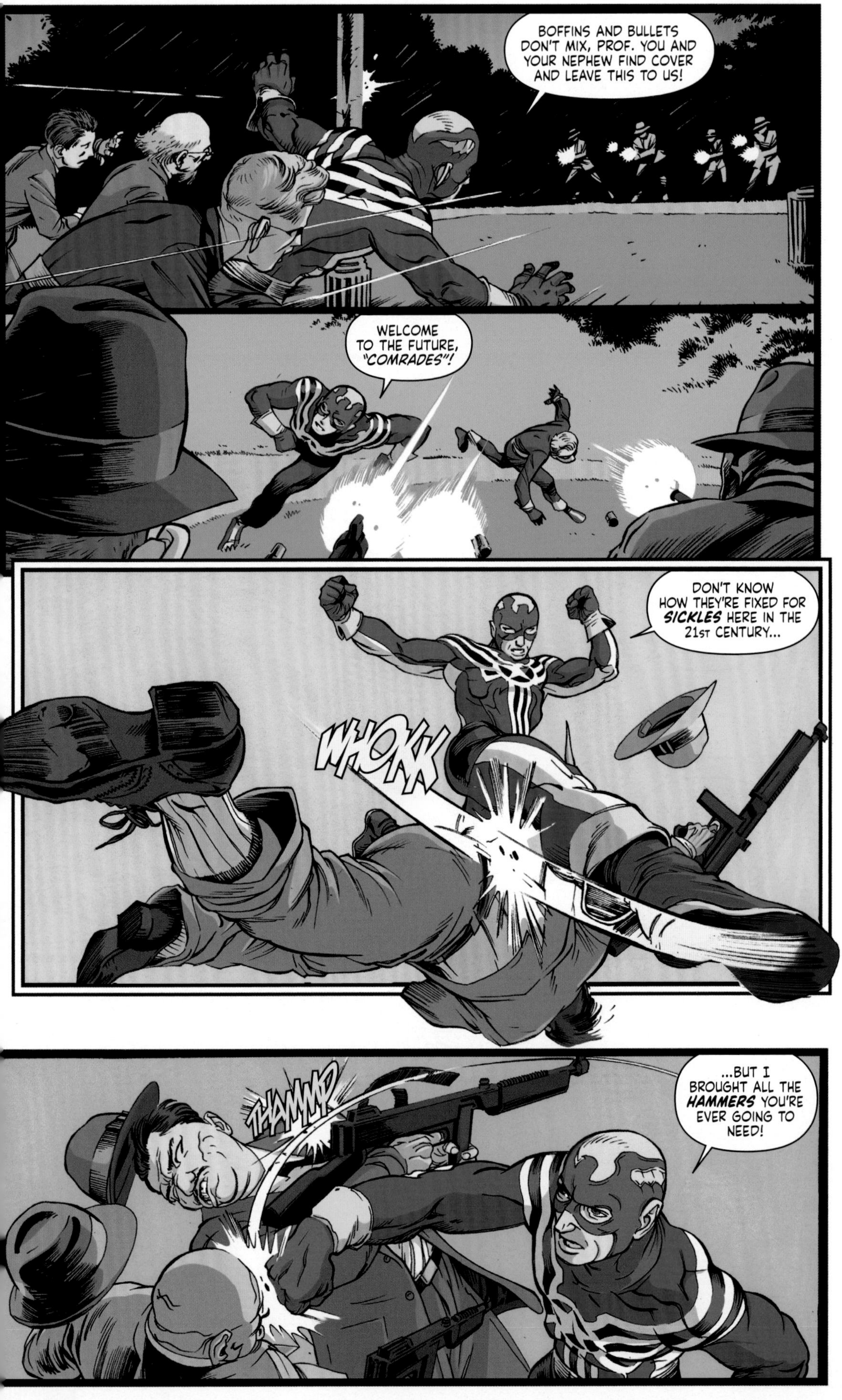
BOFFINS AND BULLETS DON'T MIX, PROF. YOU AND YOUR NEPHEW FIND COVER AND LEAVE THIS TO US!
WELCOME TO THE FUTURE, "COMRADES"!
DON'T KNOW HOW THEY'RE FIXED FOR SICKLES HERE IN THE 21st CENTURY...
WHOKK
...BUT I BROUGHT ALL THE HAMMERS YOU'RE EVER GOING TO NEED!
THAMMP

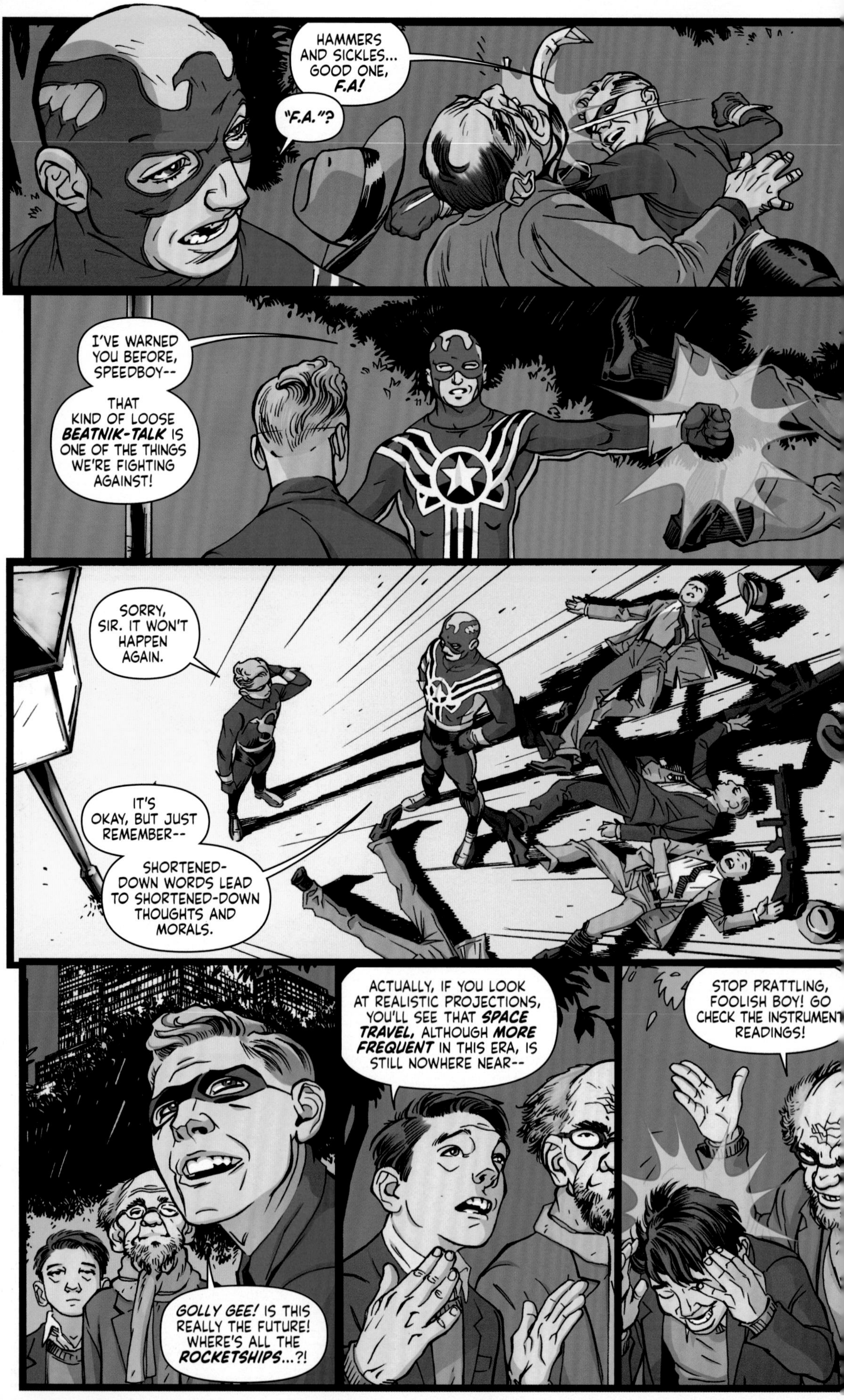
HAMMERS AND SICKLES... GOOD ONE, F.A!
"F.A."?
I'VE WARNED YOU BEFORE, SPEEDBOY--
THAT KIND OF LOOSE BEATNIK-TALK IS ONE OF THE THINGS WE'RE FIGHTING AGAINST!
SORRY, SIR. IT WON'T HAPPEN AGAIN.
IT'S OKAY, BUT JUST REMEMBER--
SHORTENED-DOWN WORDS LEAD TO SHORTENED-DOWN THOUGHTS AND MORALS.
GOLLY GEE! IS THIS REALLY THE FUTURE! WHERE'S ALL THE ROCKETSHIPS...?!
ACTUALLY, IF YOU LOOK AT REALISTIC PROJECTIONS, YOU'LL SEE THAT SPACE TRAVEL, ALTHOUGH MORE FREQUENT IN THIS ERA, IS STILL NOWHERE NEAR--
STOP PRATTLING, FOOLISH BOY! GO CHECK THE INSTRUMENT READINGS!

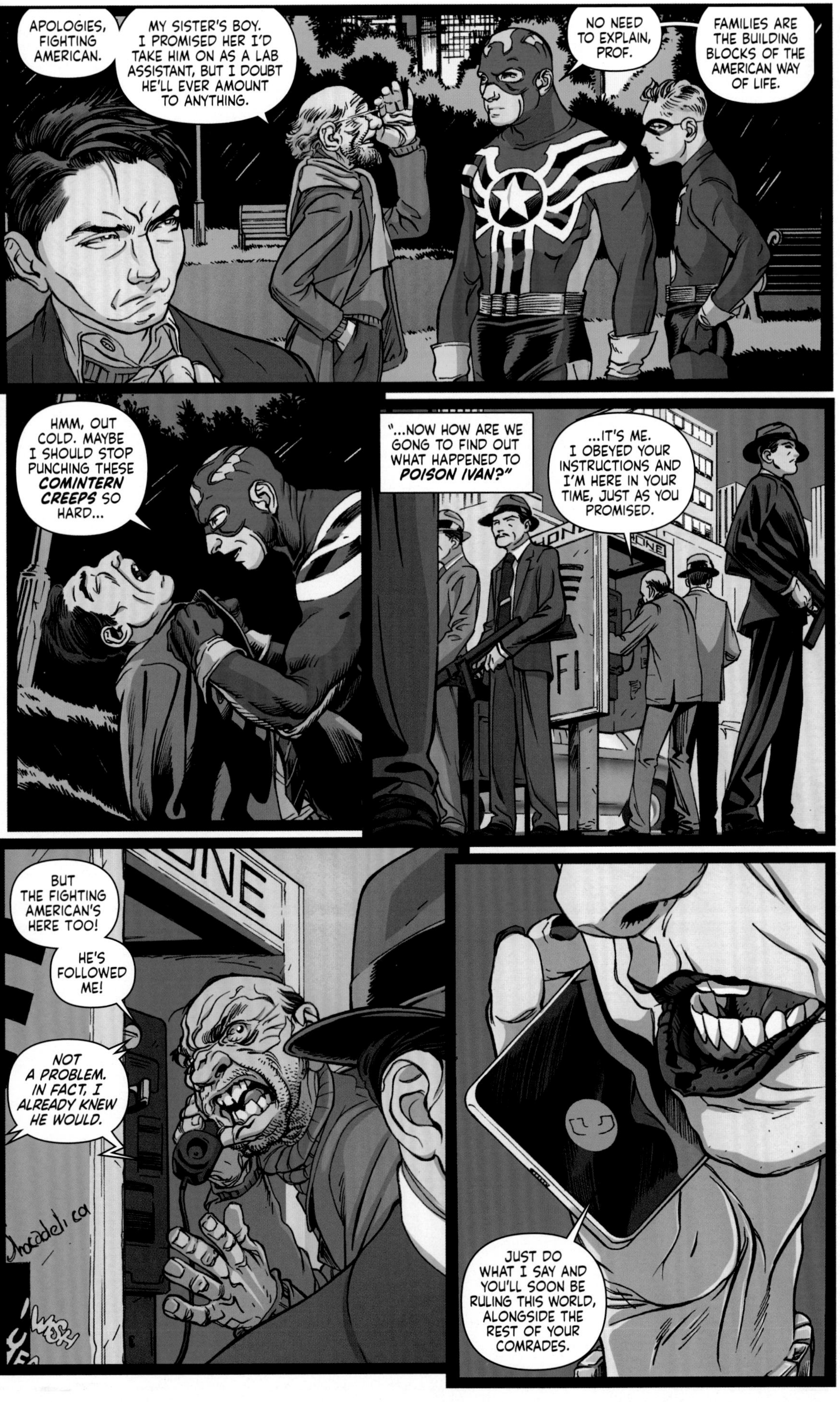
APOLOGIES, FIGHTING AMERICAN.
MY SISTER'S BOY. I PROMISED HER I'D TAKE HIM ON AS A LAB ASSISTANT, BUT I DOUBT HE'LL EVER AMOUNT TO ANYTHING.
NO NEED TO EXPLAIN, PROF.
FAMILIES ARE THE BUILDING BLOCKS OF THE AMERICAN WAY OF LIFE.
HMM, OUT COLD. MAYBE I SHOULD STOP PUNCHING THESE ***COMINTERN CREEPS*** SO HARD...
"...NOW HOW ARE WE GONG TO FIND OUT WHAT HAPPENED TO ***POISON IVAN?***"
...IT'S ME. I OBEYED YOUR INSTRUCTIONS AND I'M HERE IN YOUR TIME, JUST AS YOU PROMISED.
BUT THE FIGHTING AMERICAN'S HERE TOO!
HE'S FOLLOWED ME!
NOT A PROBLEM. IN FACT, I ALREADY KNEW HE WOULD.
JUST DO WHAT I SAY AND YOU'LL SOON BE RULING THIS WORLD, ALONGSIDE THE REST OF YOUR COMRADES.

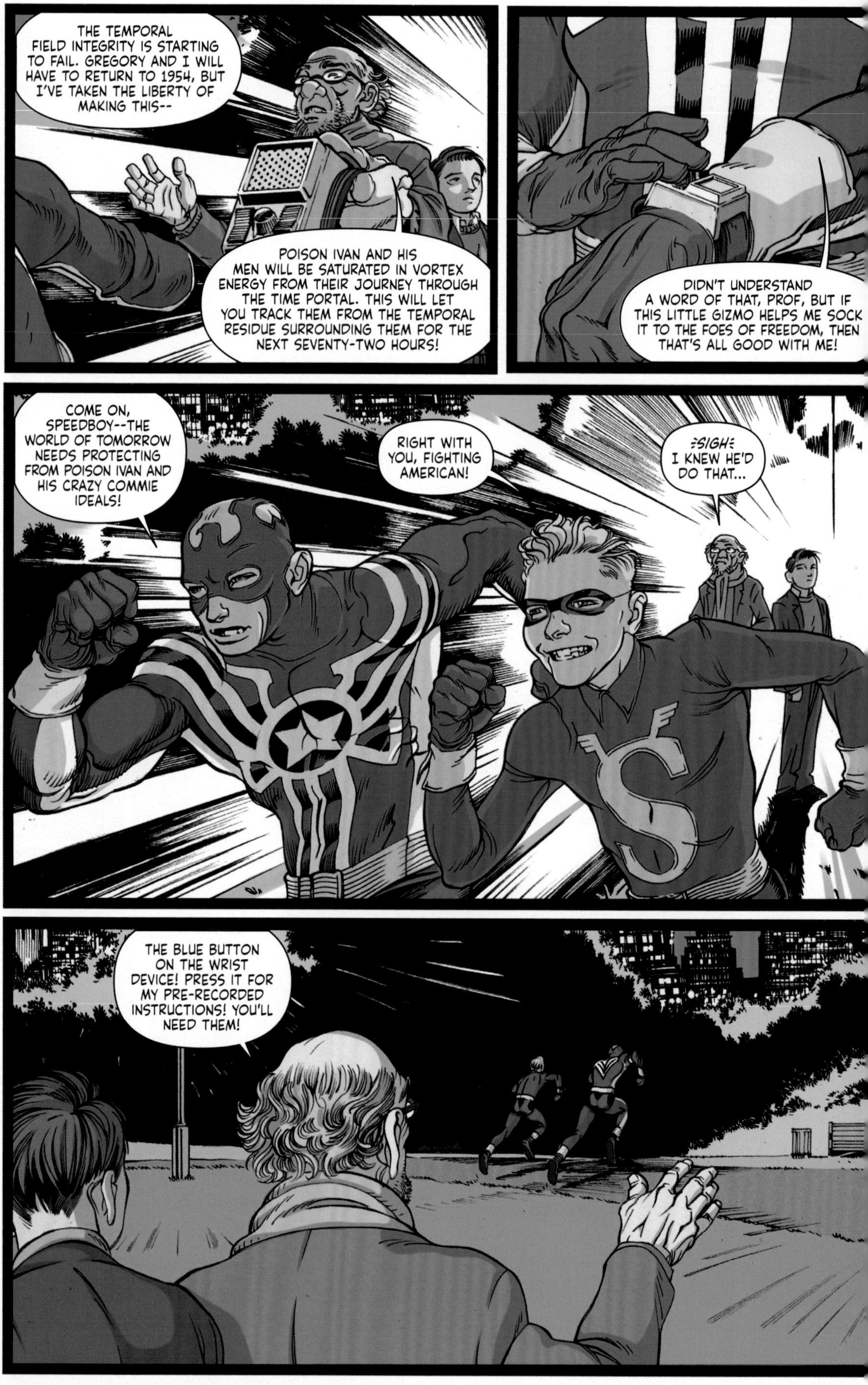
THE TEMPORAL FIELD INTEGRITY IS STARTING TO FAIL. GREGORY AND I WILL HAVE TO RETURN TO 1954, BUT I'VE TAKEN THE LIBERTY OF MAKING THIS--
POISON IVAN AND HIS MEN WILL BE SATURATED IN VORTEX ENERGY FROM THEIR JOURNEY THROUGH THE TIME PORTAL. THIS WILL LET YOU TRACK THEM FROM THE TEMPORAL RESIDUE SURROUNDING THEM FOR THE NEXT SEVENTY-TWO HOURS!
DIDN'T UNDERSTAND A WORD OF THAT, PROF, BUT IF THIS LITTLE GIZMO HELPS ME SOCK IT TO THE FOES OF FREEDOM, THEN THAT'S ALL GOOD WITH ME!
COME ON, SPEEDBOY--THE WORLD OF TOMORROW NEEDS PROTECTING FROM POISON IVAN AND HIS CRAZY COMMIE IDEALS!
RIGHT WITH YOU, FIGHTING AMERICAN!
SIGH
I KNEW HE'D DO THAT...
THE BLUE BUTTON ON THE WRIST DEVICE! PRESS IT FOR MY PRE-RECORDED INSTRUCTIONS! YOU'LL NEED THEM!

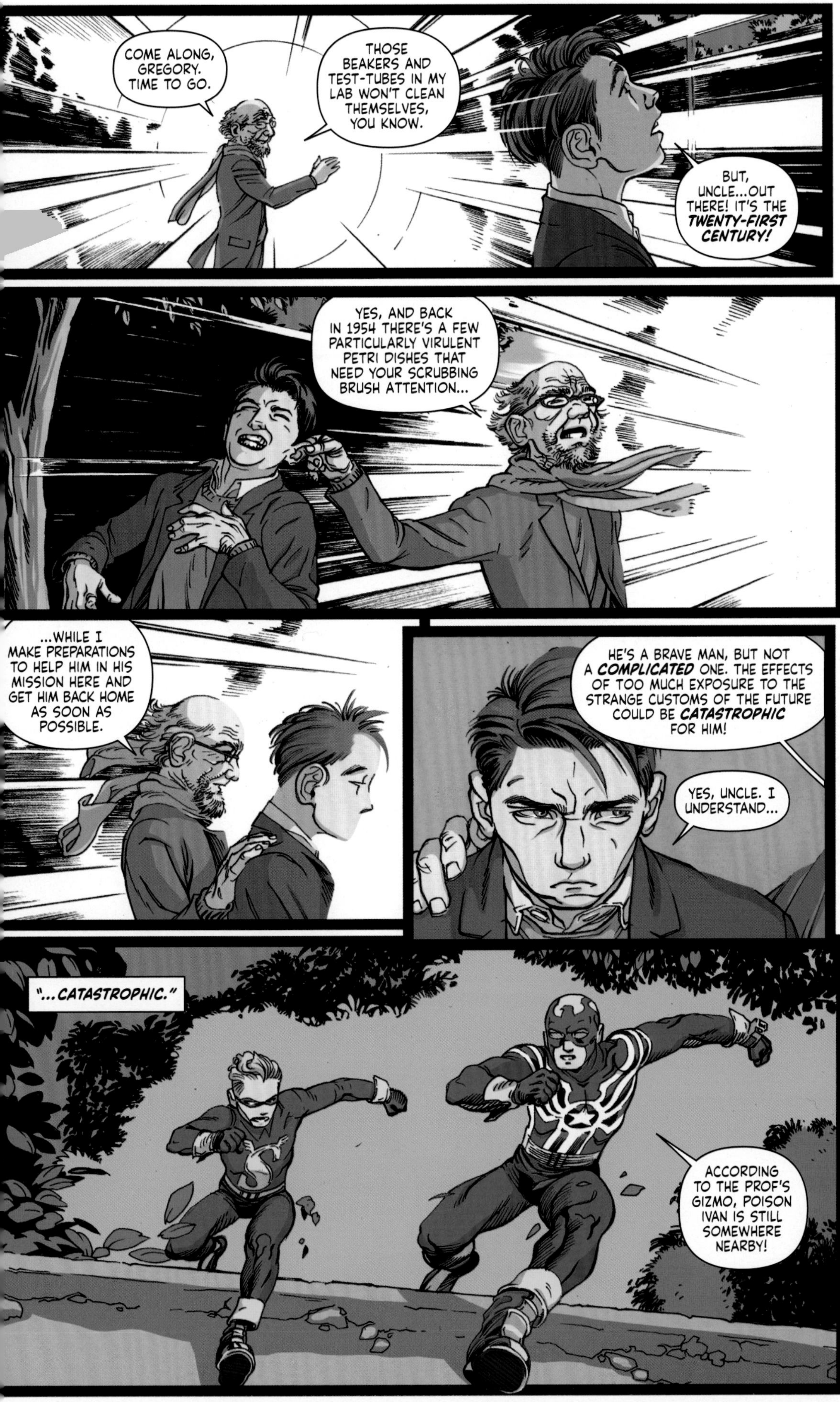
COME ALONG, GREGORY. TIME TO GO.
THOSE BEAKERS AND TEST-TUBES IN MY LAB WON'T CLEAN THEMSELVES, YOU KNOW.
BUT, UNCLE...OUT THERE! IT'S THE *TWENTY-FIRST CENTURY!*
YES, AND BACK IN 1954 THERE'S A FEW PARTICULARLY VIRULENT PETRI DISHES THAT NEED YOUR SCRUBBING BRUSH ATTENTION...
...WHILE I MAKE PREPARATIONS TO HELP HIM IN HIS MISSION HERE AND GET HIM BACK HOME AS SOON AS POSSIBLE.
HE'S A BRAVE MAN, BUT NOT A *COMPLICATED* ONE. THE EFFECTS OF TOO MUCH EXPOSURE TO THE STRANGE CUSTOMS OF THE FUTURE COULD BE *CATASTROPHIC* FOR HIM!
YES, UNCLE. I UNDERSTAND...
"...*CATASTROPHIC.*"
ACCORDING TO THE PROF'S GIZMO, POISON IVAN IS STILL SOMEWHERE NEARBY!

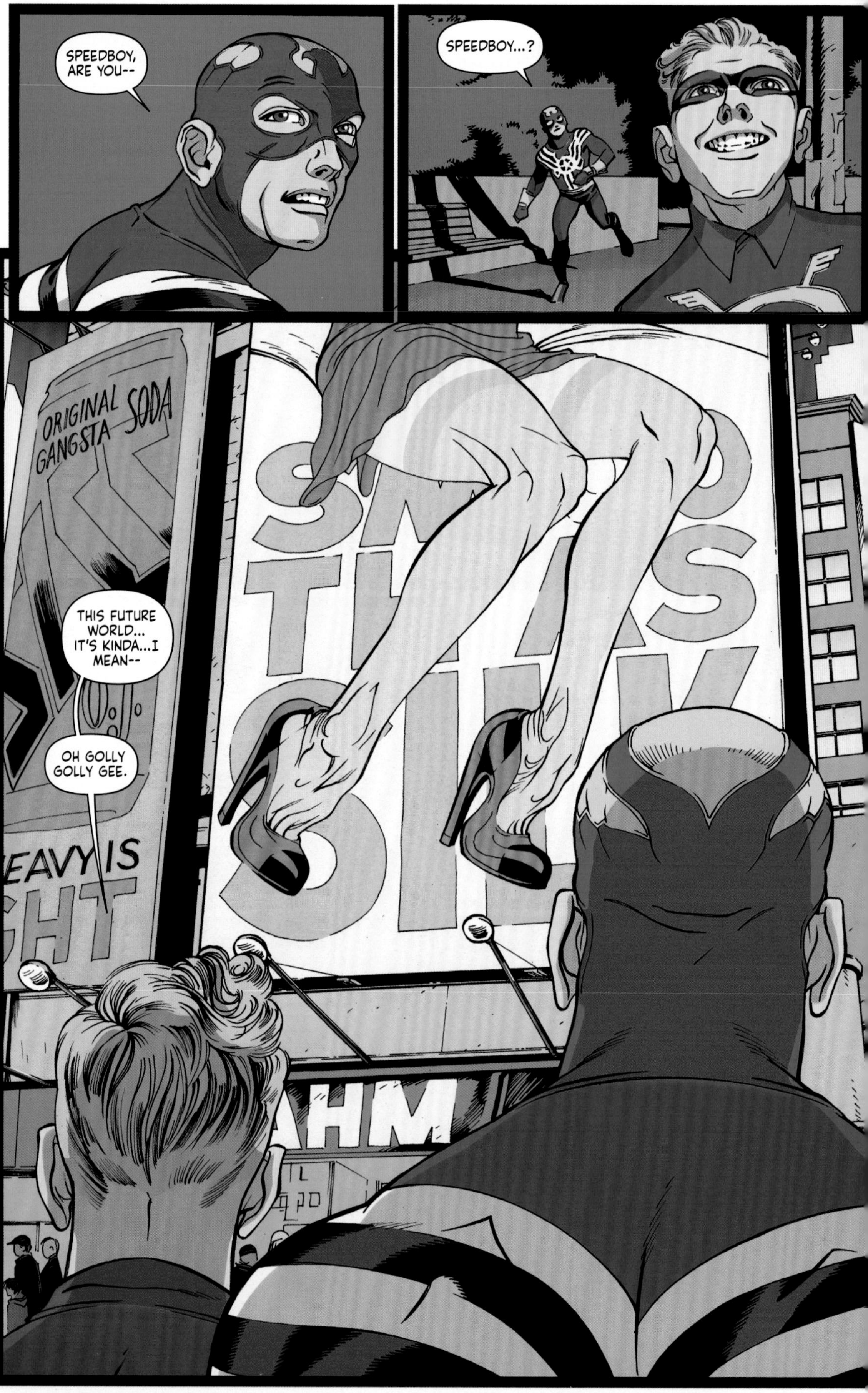
SPEEDBOY, ARE YOU--
SPEEDBOY...?
ORIGINAL GANGSTA SODA
THIS FUTURE WORLD... IT'S KINDA...I MEAN--
OH GOLLY GOLLY GEE.
EAVY IS
GHT
AHM

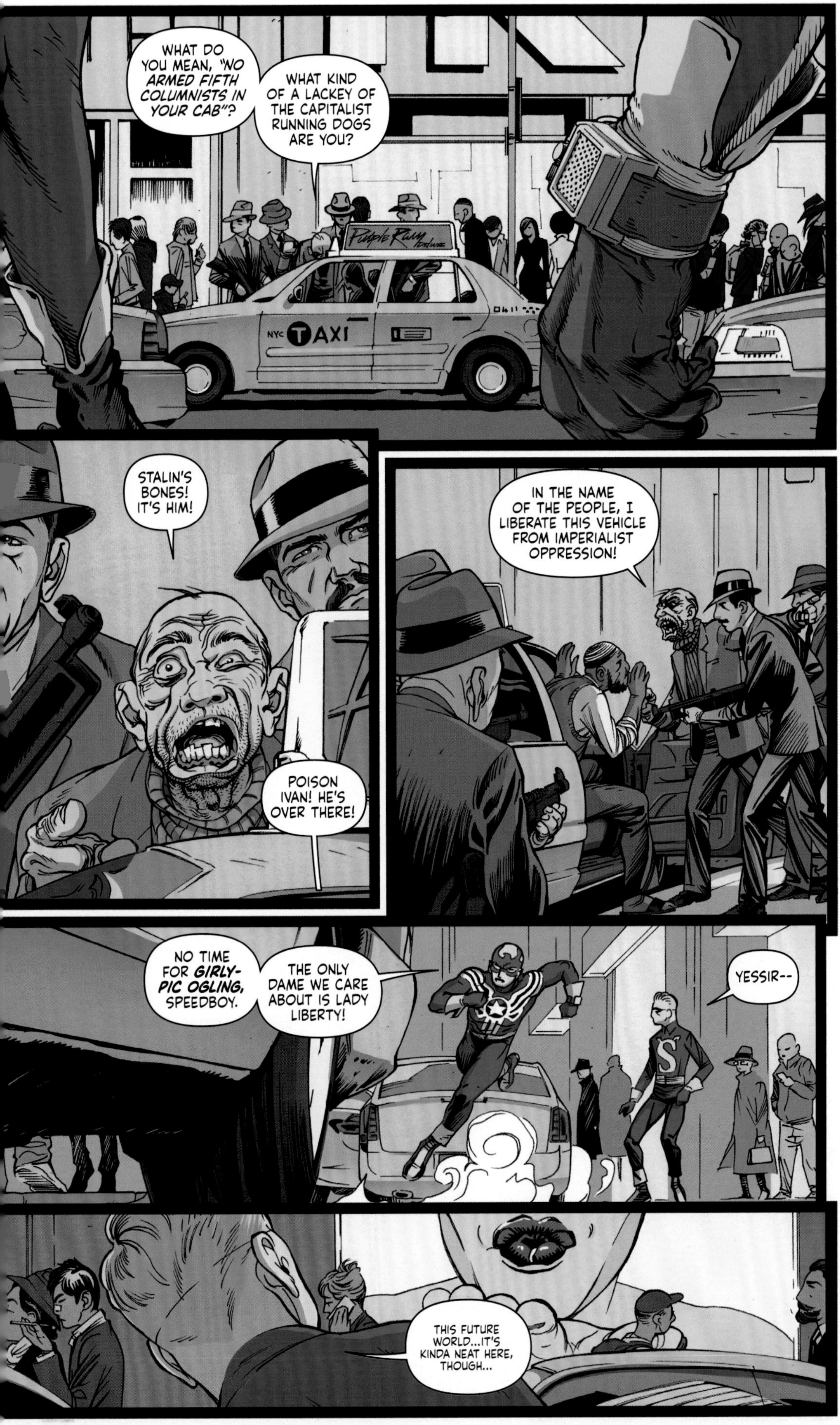
WHAT DO YOU MEAN, "NO ARMED FIFTH COLUMNISTS IN YOUR CAB"?
WHAT KIND OF A LACKEY OF THE CAPITALIST RUNNING DOGS ARE YOU?
NYC TAXI
STALIN'S BONES! IT'S HIM!
POISON IVAN! HE'S OVER THERE!
IN THE NAME OF THE PEOPLE, I LIBERATE THIS VEHICLE FROM IMPERIALIST OPPRESSION!
NO TIME FOR GIRLY-PIC OGLING, SPEEDBOY.
THE ONLY DAME WE CARE ABOUT IS LADY LIBERTY!
YESSIR--
THIS FUTURE WORLD...IT'S KINDA NEAT HERE, THOUGH...

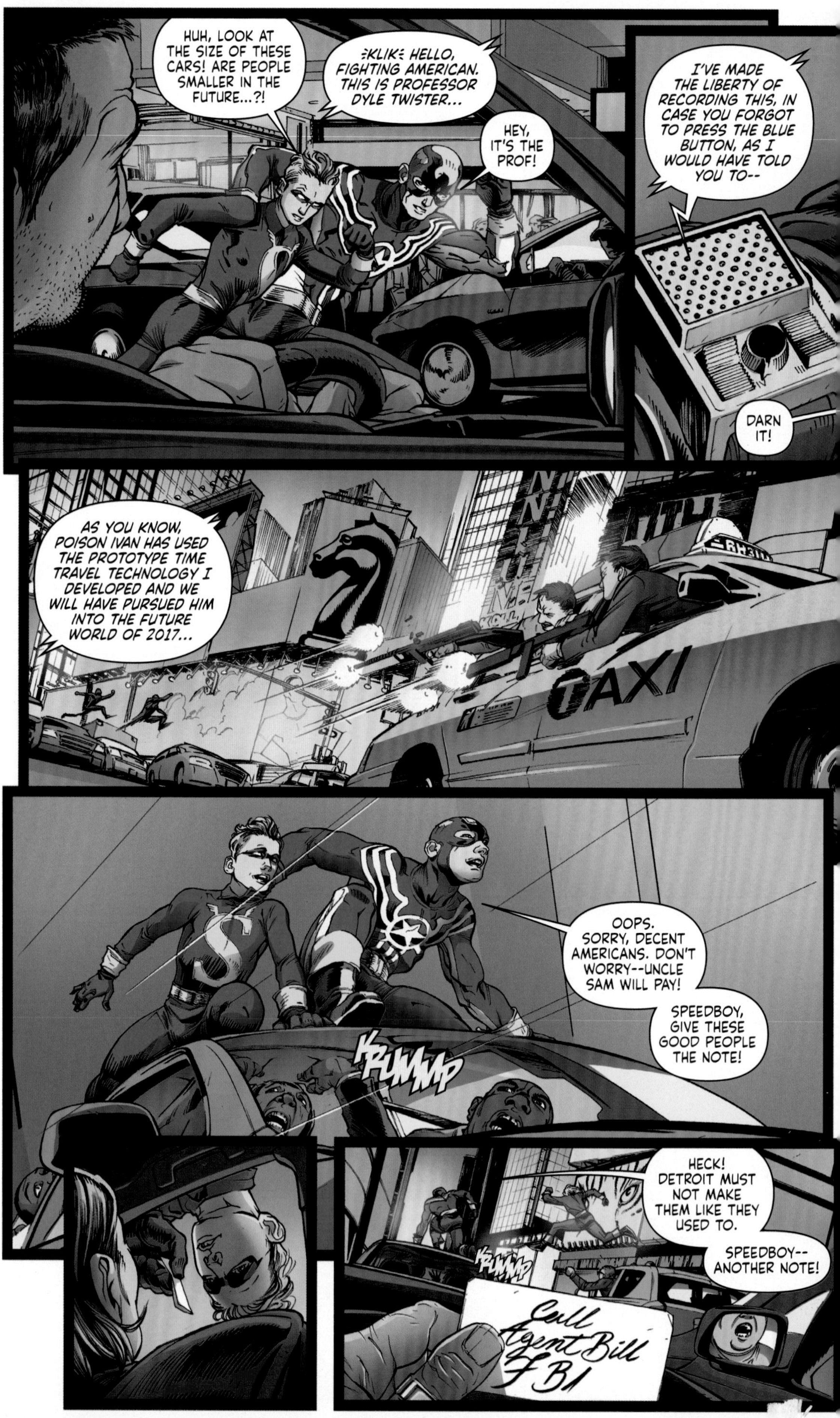
HUH, LOOK AT THE SIZE OF THESE CARS! ARE PEOPLE SMALLER IN THE FUTURE...?!
KLIK HELLO, FIGHTING AMERICAN. THIS IS PROFESSOR DYLE TWISTER...
HEY, IT'S THE PROF!
I'VE MADE THE LIBERTY OF RECORDING THIS, IN CASE YOU FORGOT TO PRESS THE BLUE BUTTON, AS I WOULD HAVE TOLD YOU TO--
DARN IT!
AS YOU KNOW, POISON IVAN HAS USED THE PROTOTYPE TIME TRAVEL TECHNOLOGY I DEVELOPED AND WE WILL HAVE PURSUED HIM INTO THE FUTURE WORLD OF 2017...
TAXI
OOPS. SORRY, DECENT AMERICANS. DON'T WORRY--UNCLE SAM WILL PAY!
SPEEDBOY, GIVE THESE GOOD PEOPLE THE NOTE!
KRUMMP
HECK! DETROIT MUST NOT MAKE THEM LIKE THEY USED TO.
SPEEDBOY-- ANOTHER NOTE!
KRUMMP
Call Agent Bill FBI

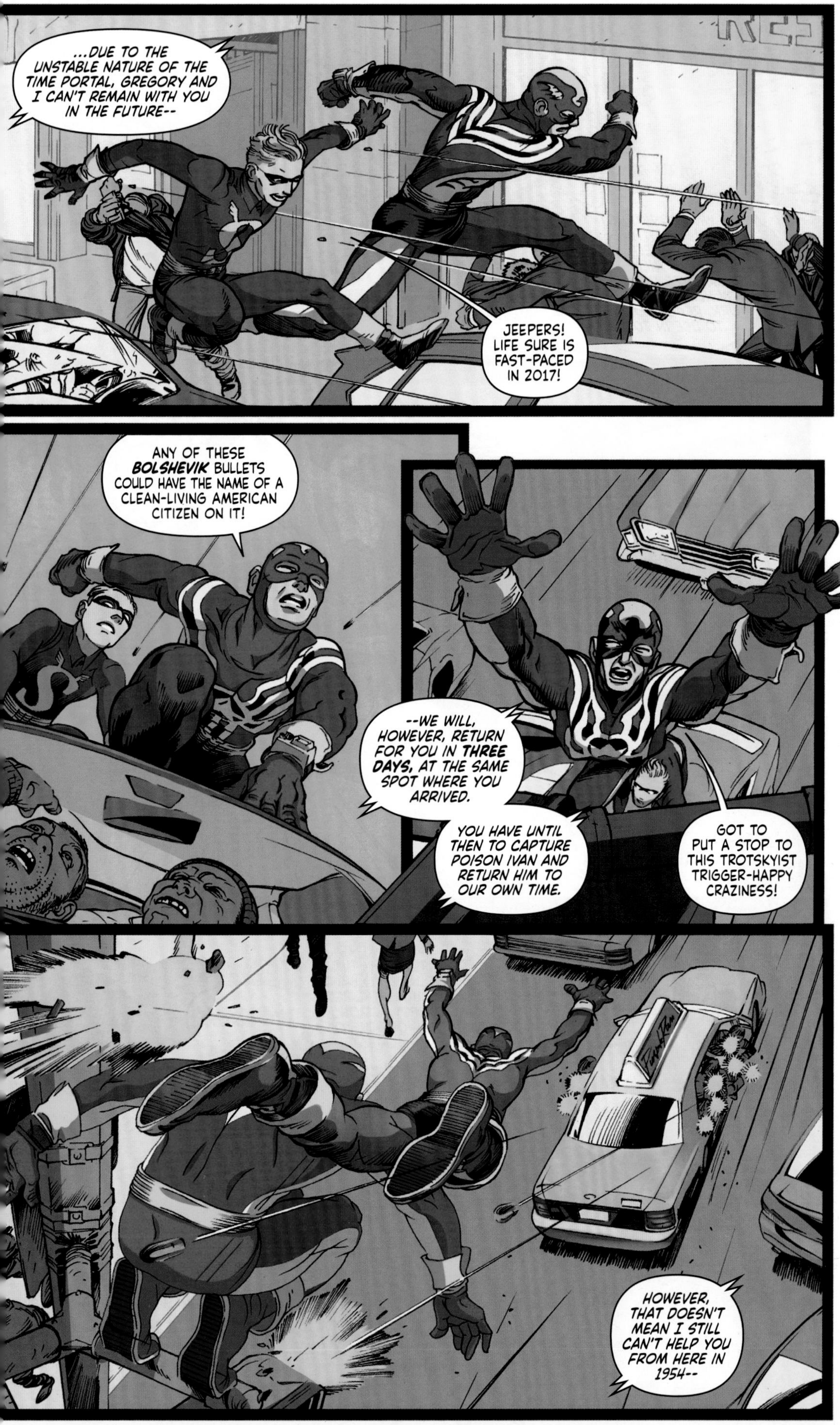
...DUE TO THE UNSTABLE NATURE OF THE TIME PORTAL, GREGORY AND I CAN'T REMAIN WITH YOU IN THE FUTURE--
JEEPERS! LIFE SURE IS FAST-PACED IN 2017!
ANY OF THESE BOLSHEVIK BULLETS COULD HAVE THE NAME OF A CLEAN-LIVING AMERICAN CITIZEN ON IT!
--WE WILL, HOWEVER, RETURN FOR YOU IN THREE DAYS, AT THE SAME SPOT WHERE YOU ARRIVED.
YOU HAVE UNTIL THEN TO CAPTURE POISON IVAN AND RETURN HIM TO OUR OWN TIME.
GOT TO PUT A STOP TO THIS TROTSKYIST TRIGGER-HAPPY CRAZINESS!
HOWEVER, THAT DOESN'T MEAN I STILL CAN'T HELP YOU FROM HERE IN 1954--

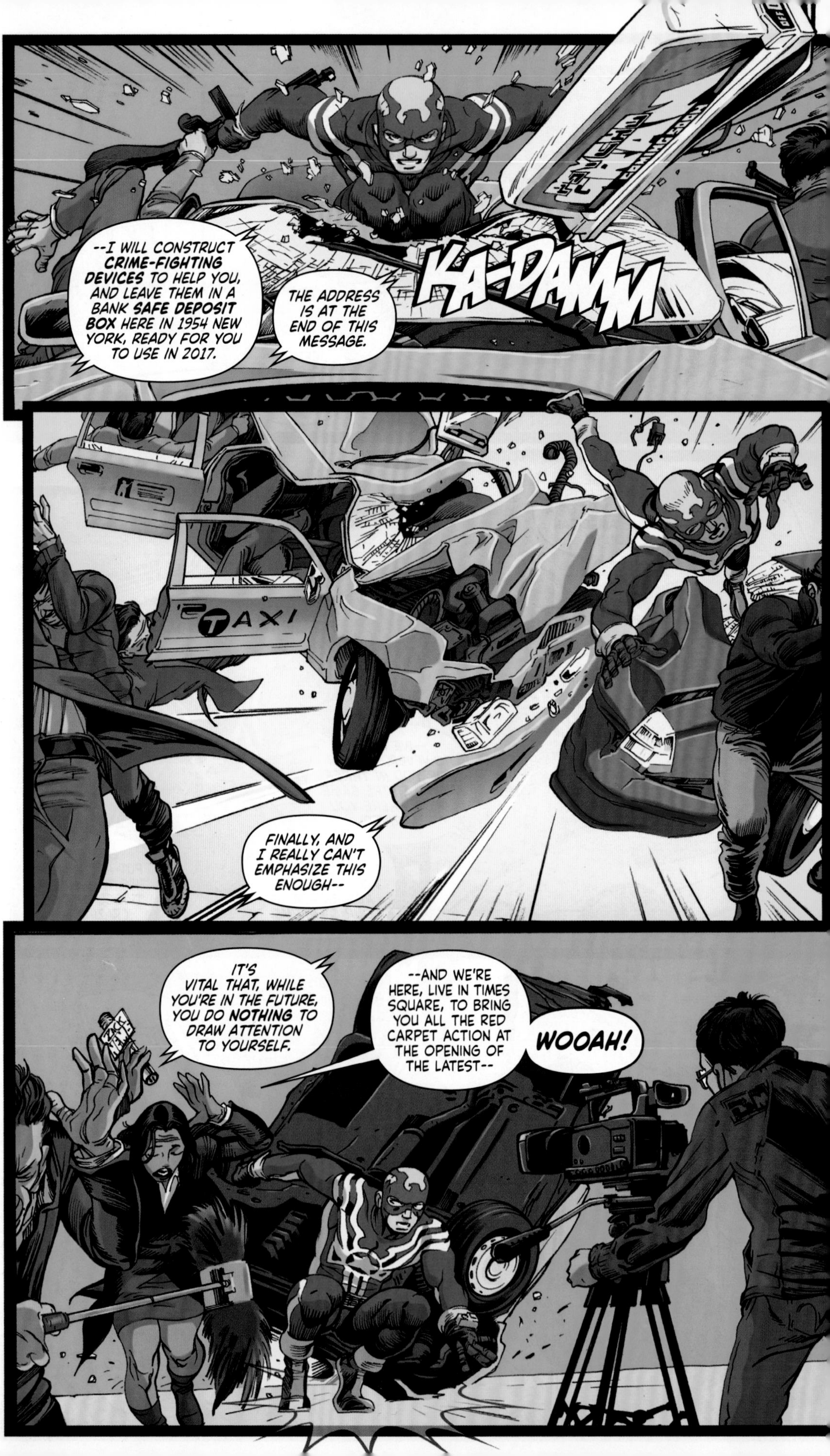
--I WILL CONSTRUCT **CRIME-FIGHTING DEVICES** TO HELP YOU, AND LEAVE THEM IN A BANK **SAFE DEPOSIT BOX** HERE IN 1954 NEW YORK, READY FOR YOU TO USE IN 2017.
THE ADDRESS IS AT THE END OF THIS MESSAGE.
KA-DAMM
TAXI
FINALLY, AND I REALLY CAN'T EMPHASIZE THIS ENOUGH--
IT'S VITAL THAT, WHILE YOU'RE IN THE FUTURE, YOU DO **NOTHING** TO DRAW ATTENTION TO YOURSELF.
--AND WE'RE HERE, LIVE IN TIMES SQUARE, TO BRING YOU ALL THE RED CARPET ACTION AT THE OPENING OF THE LATEST--
WOOAH!

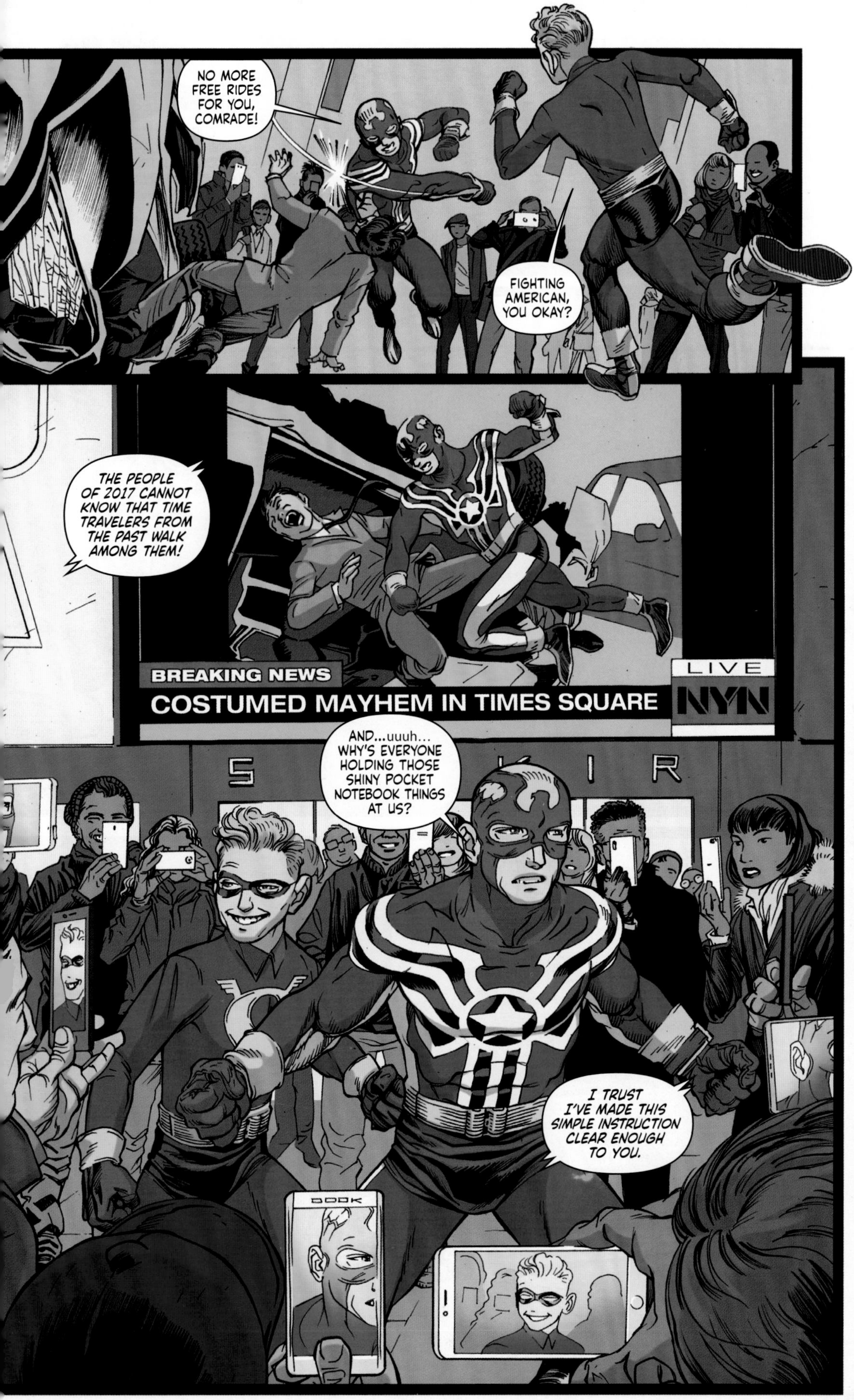
NO MORE FREE RIDES FOR YOU, COMRADE!
FIGHTING AMERICAN, YOU OKAY?
THE PEOPLE OF 2017 CANNOT KNOW THAT TIME TRAVELERS FROM THE PAST WALK AMONG THEM!
BREAKING NEWS
COSTUMED MAYHEM IN TIMES SQUARE
LIVE
NYN
AND...uuuh... WHY'S EVERYONE HOLDING THOSE SHINY POCKET NOTEBOOK THINGS AT US?
I TRUST I'VE MADE THIS SIMPLE INSTRUCTION CLEAR ENOUGH TO YOU.

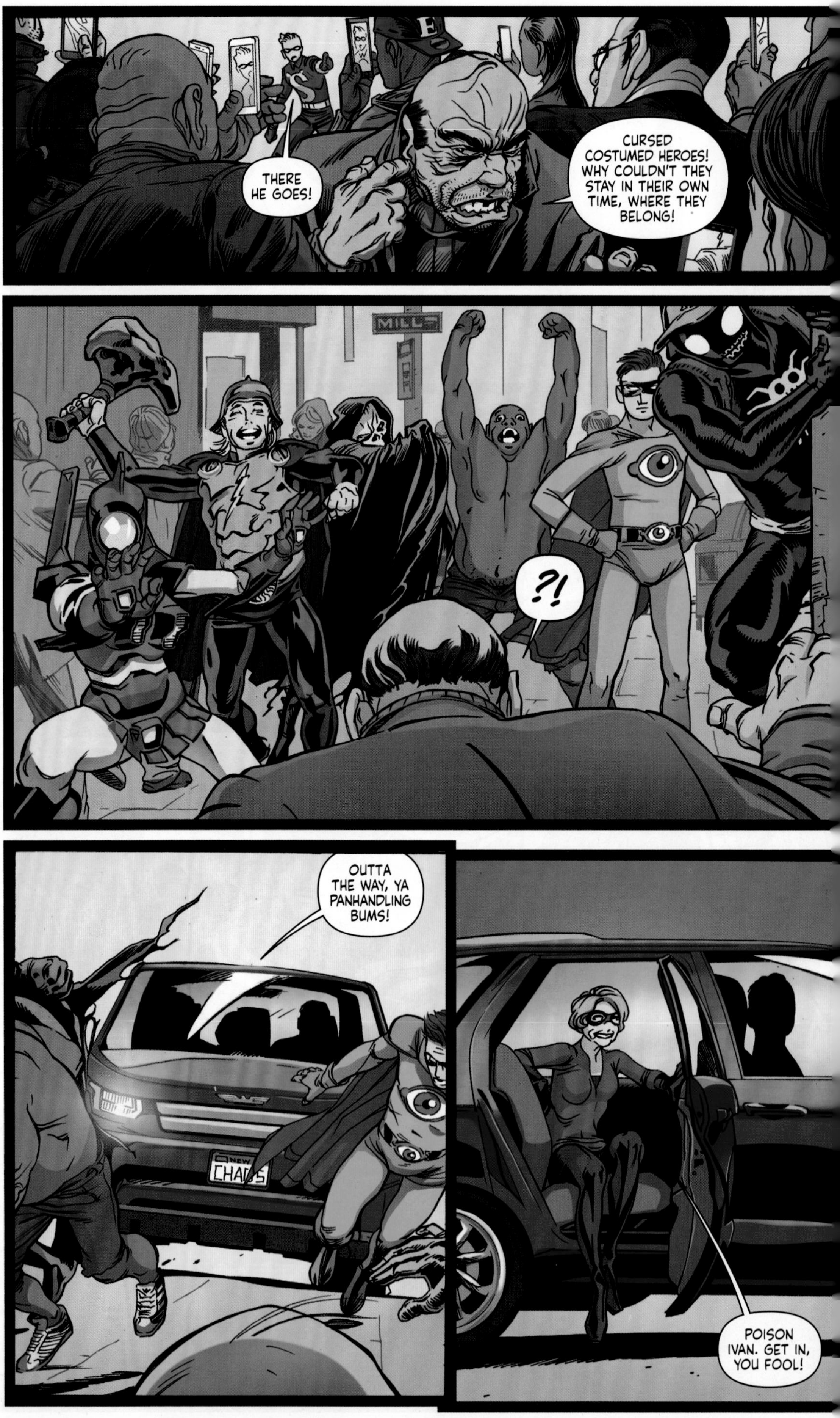
THERE HE GOES!
CURSED COSTUMED HEROES! WHY COULDN'T THEY STAY IN THEIR OWN TIME, WHERE THEY BELONG!
MILLS
?!
OUTTA THE WAY, YA PANHANDLING BUMS!
NEW CHAOS
POISON IVAN. GET IN, YOU FOOL!

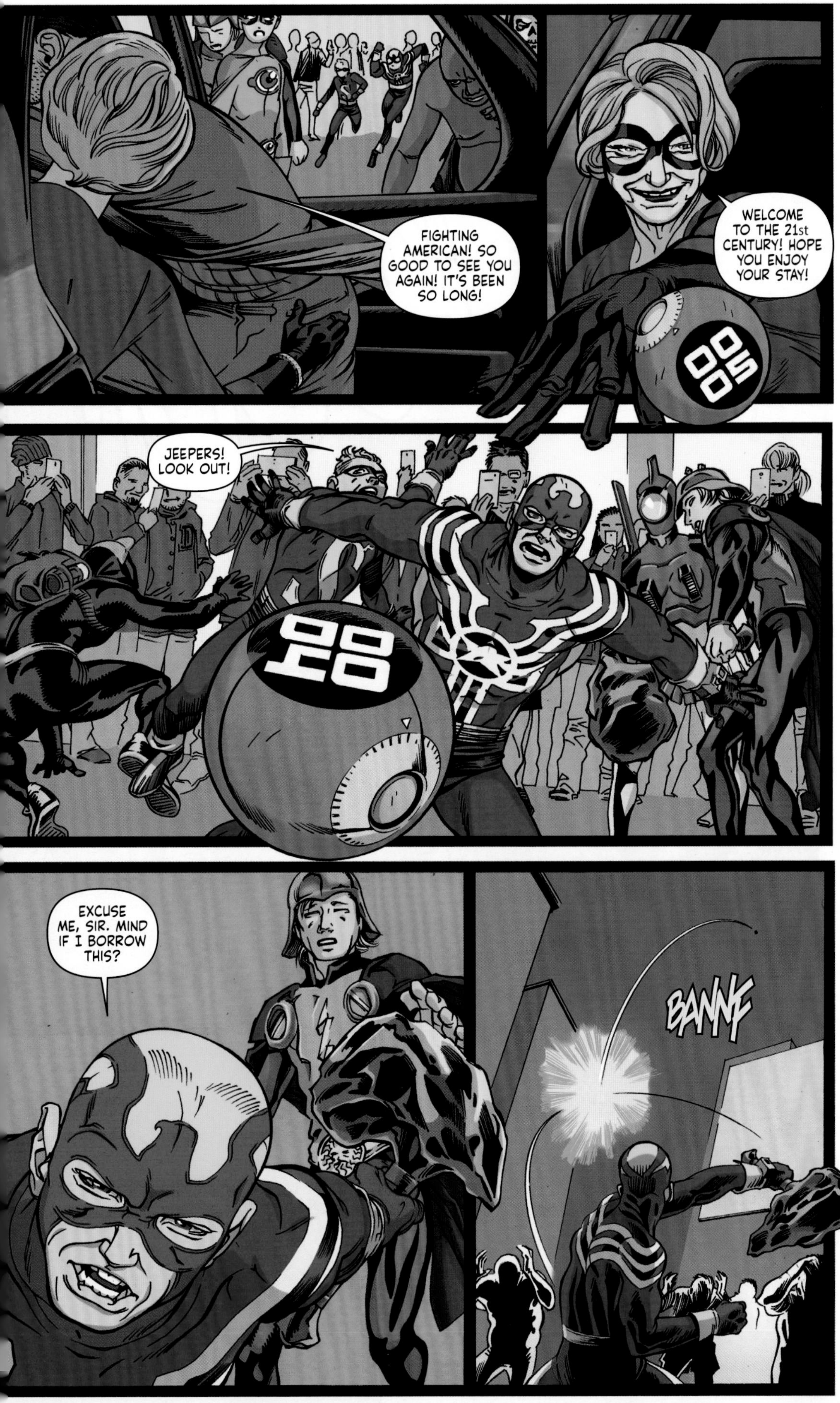
FIGHTING AMERICAN! SO GOOD TO SEE YOU AGAIN! IT'S BEEN SO LONG!
WELCOME TO THE 21st CENTURY! HOPE YOU ENJOY YOUR STAY!
JEEPERS! LOOK OUT!
EXCUSE ME, SIR. MIND IF I BORROW THIS?
BANNG

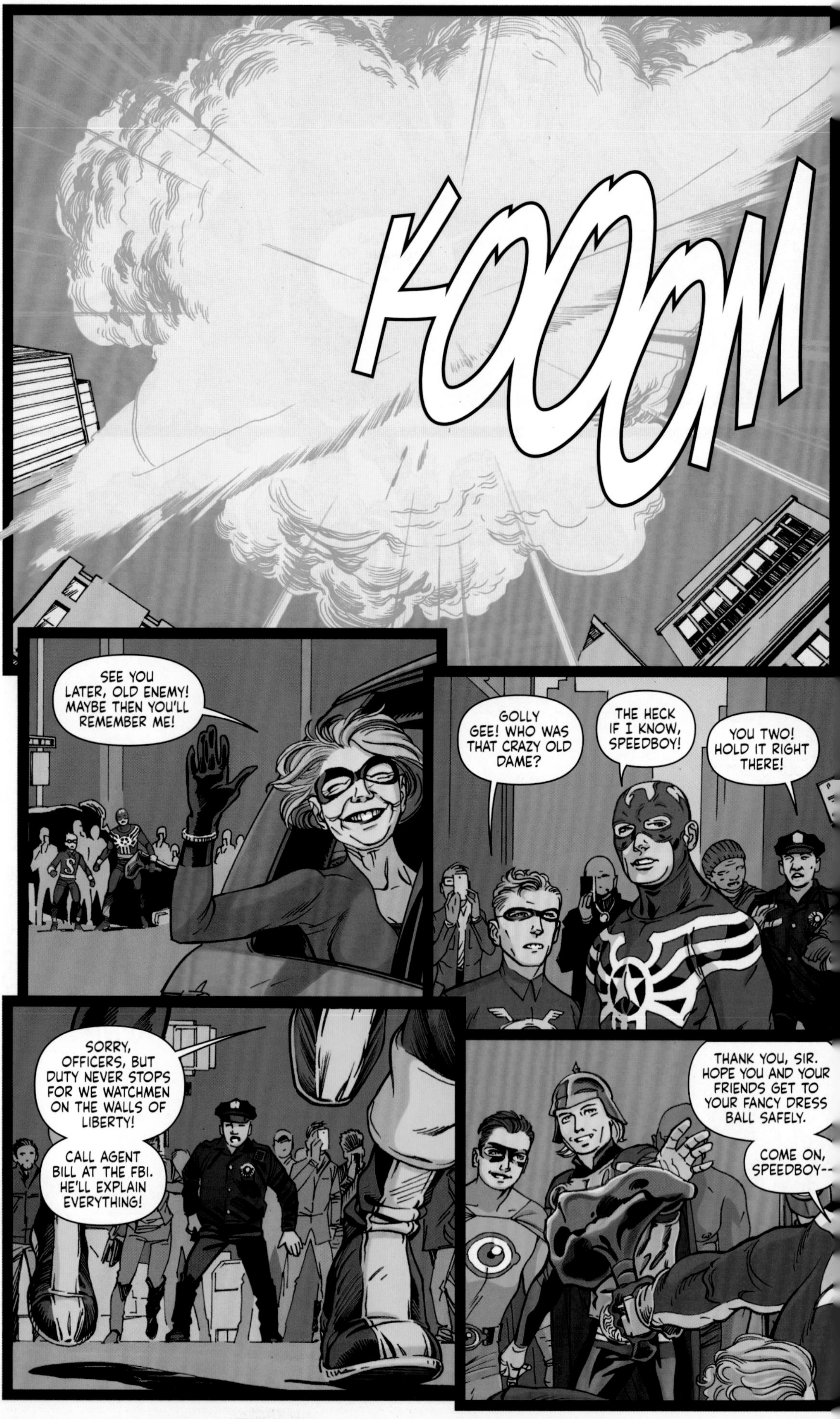
KOOOOM
SEE YOU LATER, OLD ENEMY! MAYBE THEN YOU'LL REMEMBER ME!
GOLLY GEE! WHO WAS THAT CRAZY OLD DAME?
THE HECK IF I KNOW, SPEEDBOY!
YOU TWO! HOLD IT RIGHT THERE!
SORRY, OFFICERS, BUT DUTY NEVER STOPS FOR WE WATCHMEN ON THE WALLS OF LIBERTY!
CALL AGENT BILL AT THE FBI. HE'LL EXPLAIN EVERYTHING!
THANK YOU, SIR. HOPE YOU AND YOUR FRIENDS GET TO YOUR FANCY DRESS BALL SAFELY.
COME ON, SPEEDBOY--

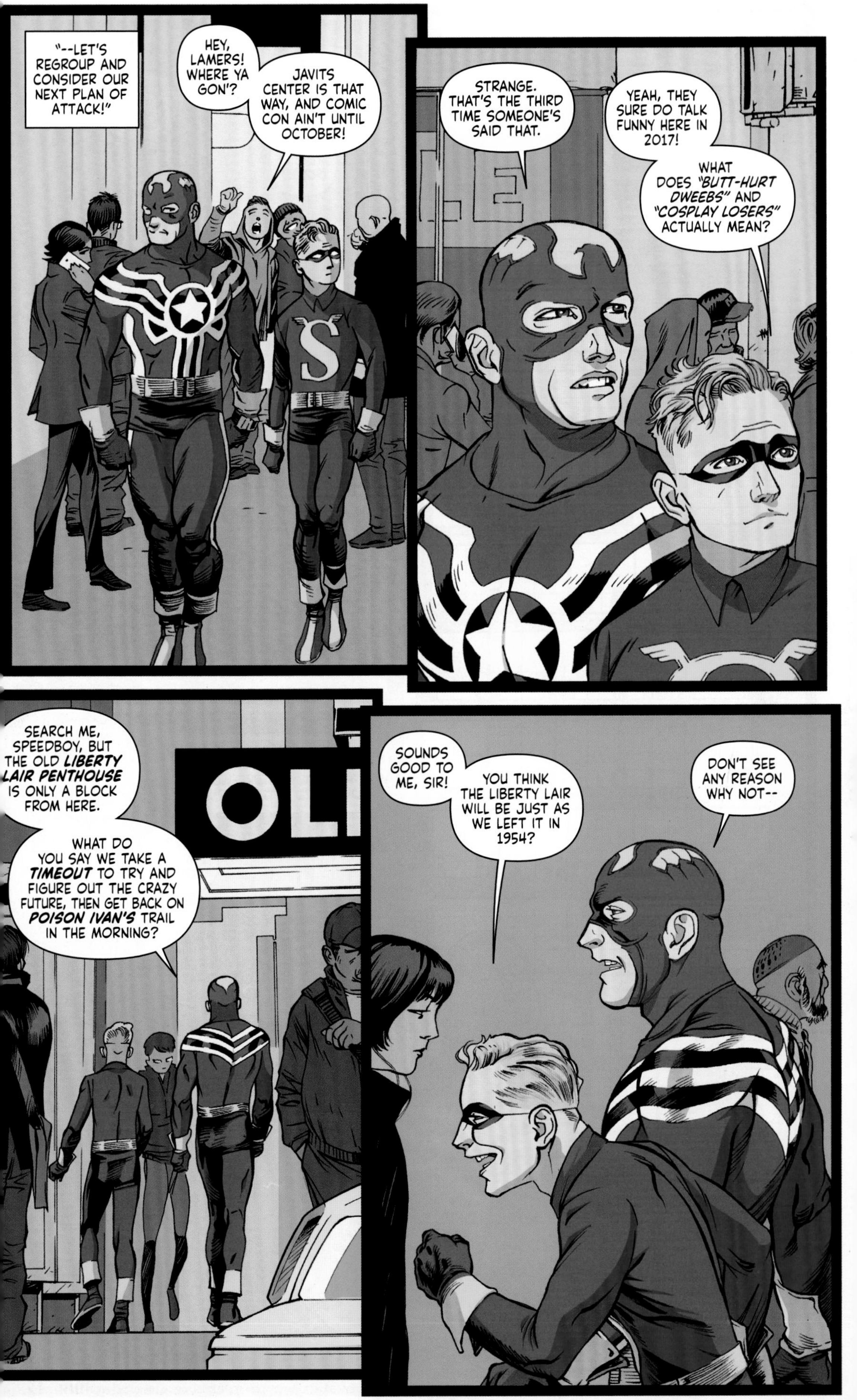
"--LET'S REGROUP AND CONSIDER OUR NEXT PLAN OF ATTACK!"
HEY, LAMERS! WHERE YA GON'?
JAVITS CENTER IS THAT WAY, AND COMIC CON AIN'T UNTIL OCTOBER!
STRANGE. THAT'S THE THIRD TIME SOMEONE'S SAID THAT.
YEAH, THEY SURE DO TALK FUNNY HERE IN 2017!
WHAT DOES *"BUTT-HURT DWEEBS"* AND *"COSPLAY LOSERS"* ACTUALLY MEAN?
SEARCH ME, SPEEDBOY, BUT THE OLD ***LIBERTY LAIR PENTHOUSE*** IS ONLY A BLOCK FROM HERE.
WHAT DO YOU SAY WE TAKE A ***TIMEOUT*** TO TRY AND FIGURE OUT THE CRAZY FUTURE, THEN GET BACK ON ***POISON IVAN'S*** TRAIL IN THE MORNING?
OLI
SOUNDS GOOD TO ME, SIR!
YOU THINK THE LIBERTY LAIR WILL BE JUST AS WE LEFT IT IN 1954?
DON'T SEE ANY REASON WHY NOT--

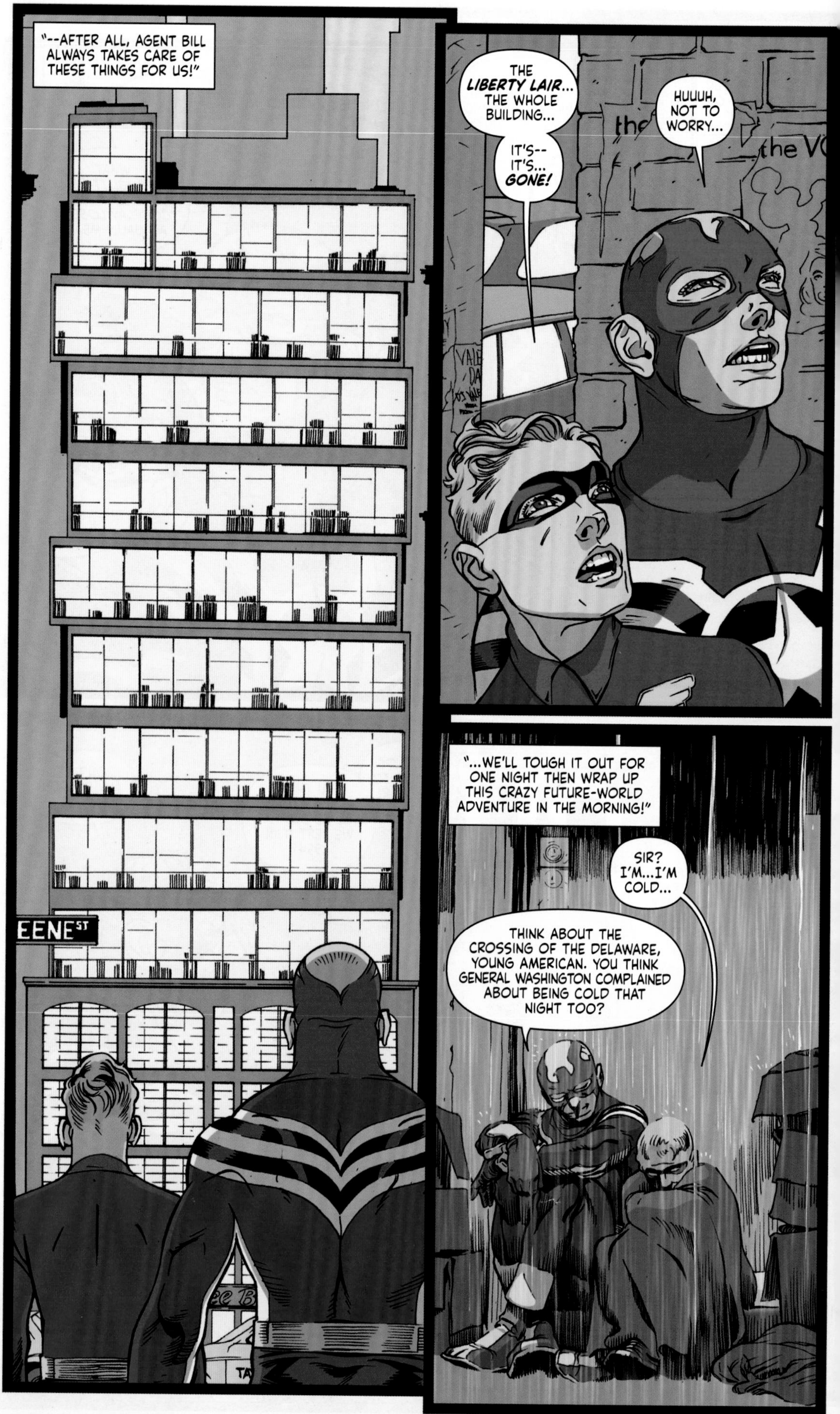
"--AFTER ALL, AGENT BILL ALWAYS TAKES CARE OF THESE THINGS FOR US!"
EENE ST
THE LIBERTY LAIR... THE WHOLE BUILDING...
IT'S-- IT'S... GONE!
HUUUH, NOT TO WORRY...
"...WE'LL TOUGH IT OUT FOR ONE NIGHT THEN WRAP UP THIS CRAZY FUTURE-WORLD ADVENTURE IN THE MORNING!"
SIR? I'M...I'M COLD...
THINK ABOUT THE CROSSING OF THE DELAWARE, YOUNG AMERICAN. YOU THINK GENERAL WASHINGTON COMPLAINED ABOUT BEING COLD THAT NIGHT TOO?

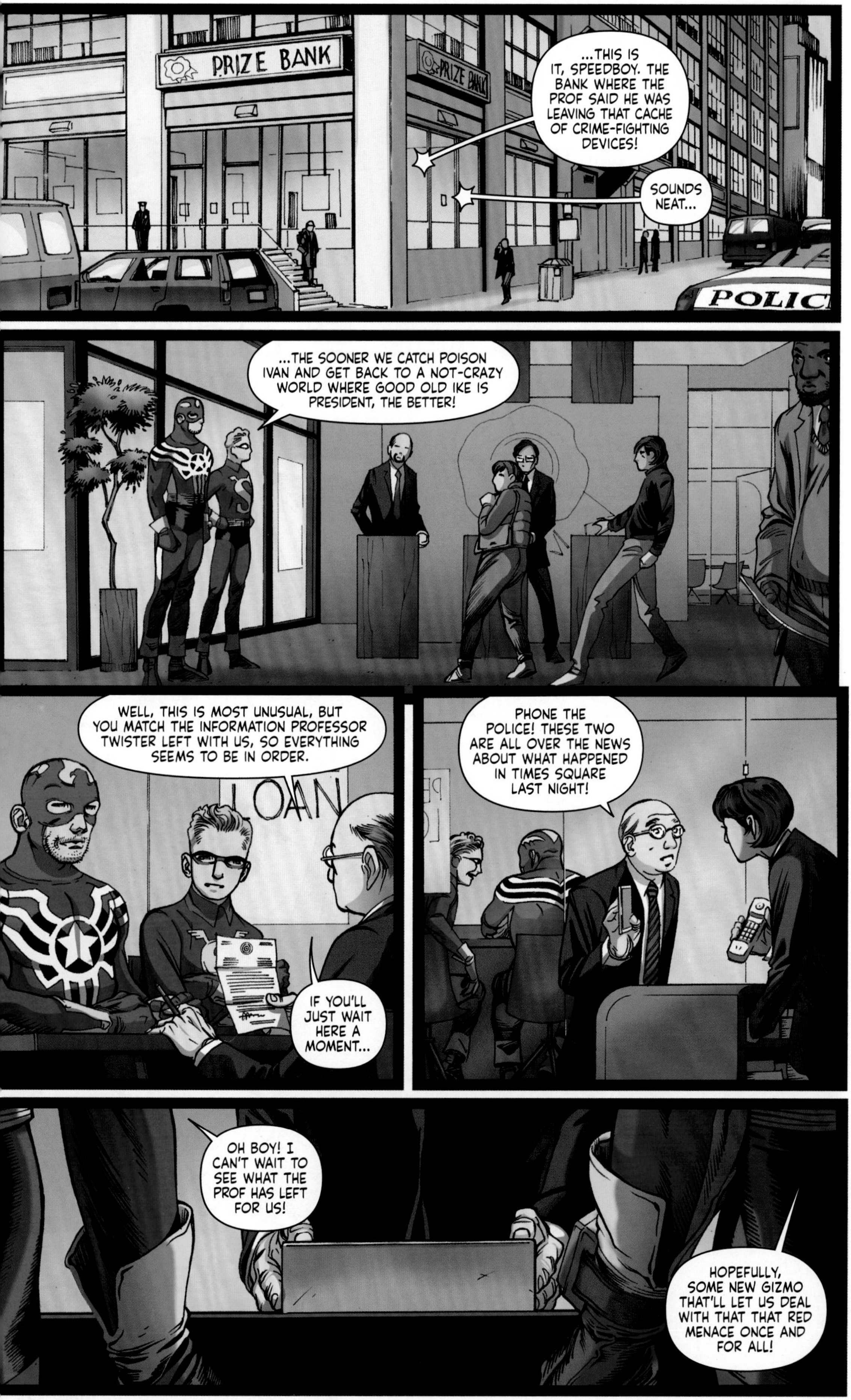

PRIZE BANK
PRIZE BANK
...THIS IS IT, SPEEDBOY. THE BANK WHERE THE PROF SAID HE WAS LEAVING THAT CACHE OF CRIME-FIGHTING DEVICES!
SOUNDS NEAT...
POLIC
...THE SOONER WE CATCH POISON IVAN AND GET BACK TO A NOT-CRAZY WORLD WHERE GOOD OLD IKE IS PRESIDENT, THE BETTER!
WELL, THIS IS MOST UNUSUAL, BUT YOU MATCH THE INFORMATION PROFESSOR TWISTER LEFT WITH US, SO EVERYTHING SEEMS TO BE IN ORDER.
LOAN
IF YOU'LL JUST WAIT HERE A MOMENT...
PHONE THE POLICE! THESE TWO ARE ALL OVER THE NEWS ABOUT WHAT HAPPENED IN TIMES SQUARE LAST NIGHT!
OH BOY! I CAN'T WAIT TO SEE WHAT THE PROF HAS LEFT FOR US!
HOPEFULLY, SOME NEW GIZMO THAT'LL LET US DEAL WITH THAT THAT RED MENACE ONCE AND FOR ALL!

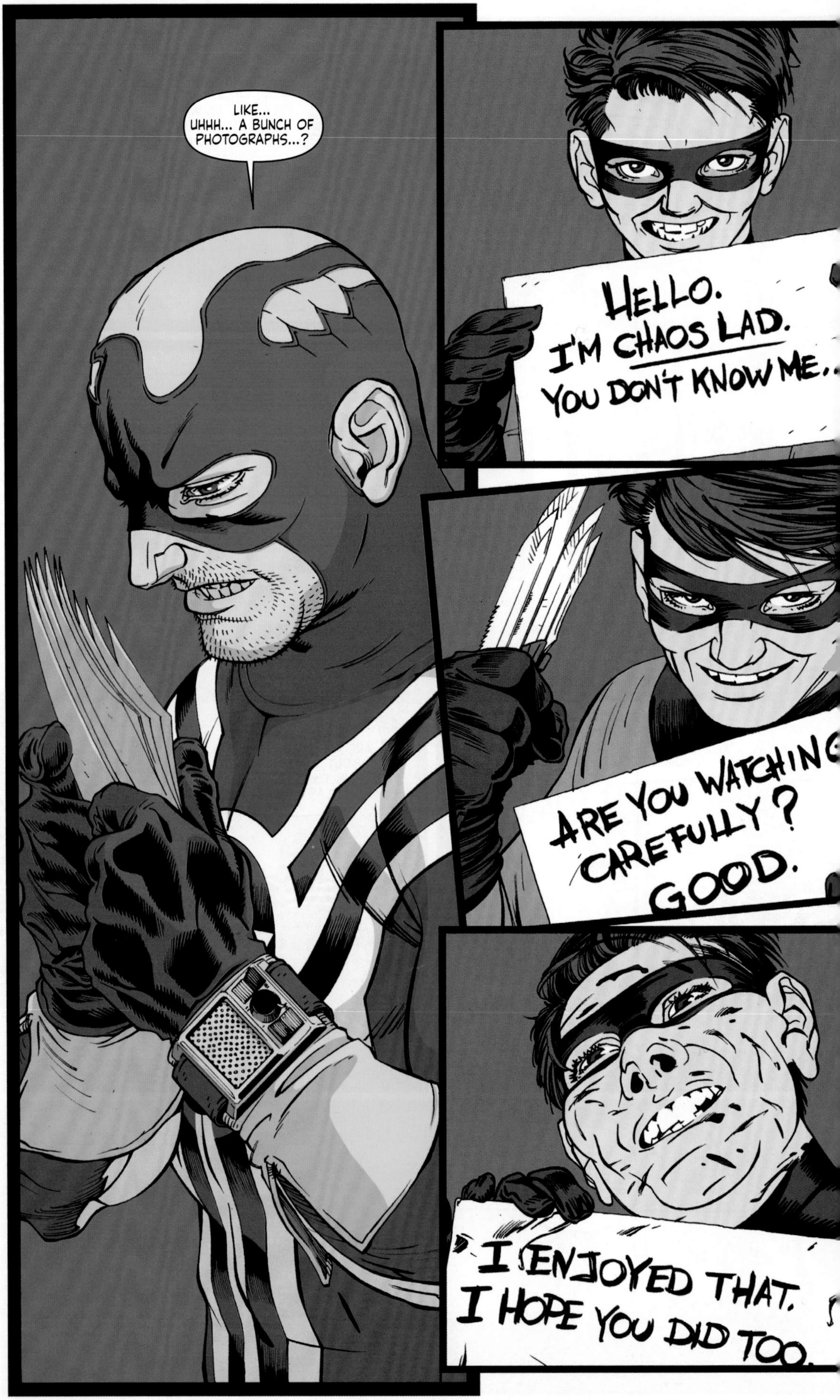

LIKE... UHHH... A BUNCH OF PHOTOGRAPHS...?
HELLO. I'M CHAOS LAD. YOU DON'T KNOW ME...
ARE YOU WATCHING CAREFULLY? GOOD.
I ENJOYED THAT. I HOPE YOU DID TOO.

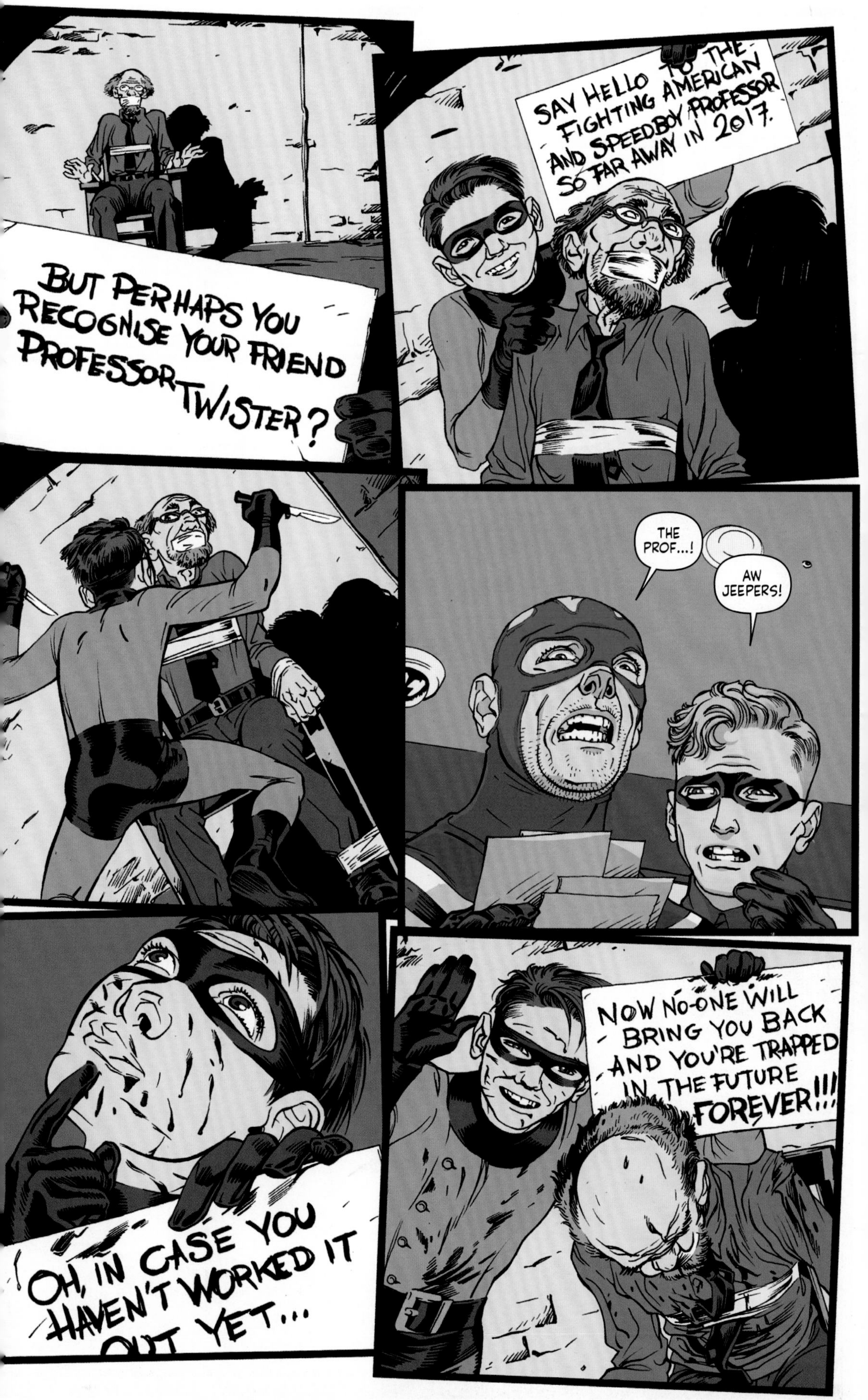
BUT PERHAPS YOU RECOGNISE YOUR FRIEND PROFESSOR TWISTER?
SAY HELLO TO THE FIGHTING AMERICAN AND SPEEDBOY PROFESSOR SO FAR AWAY IN 2017.
THE PROF...!
AW JEEPERS!
OH, IN CASE YOU HAVEN'T WORKED IT OUT YET...
NOW NO-ONE WILL BRING YOU BACK AND YOU'RE TRAPPED IN THE FUTURE FOREVER!!!

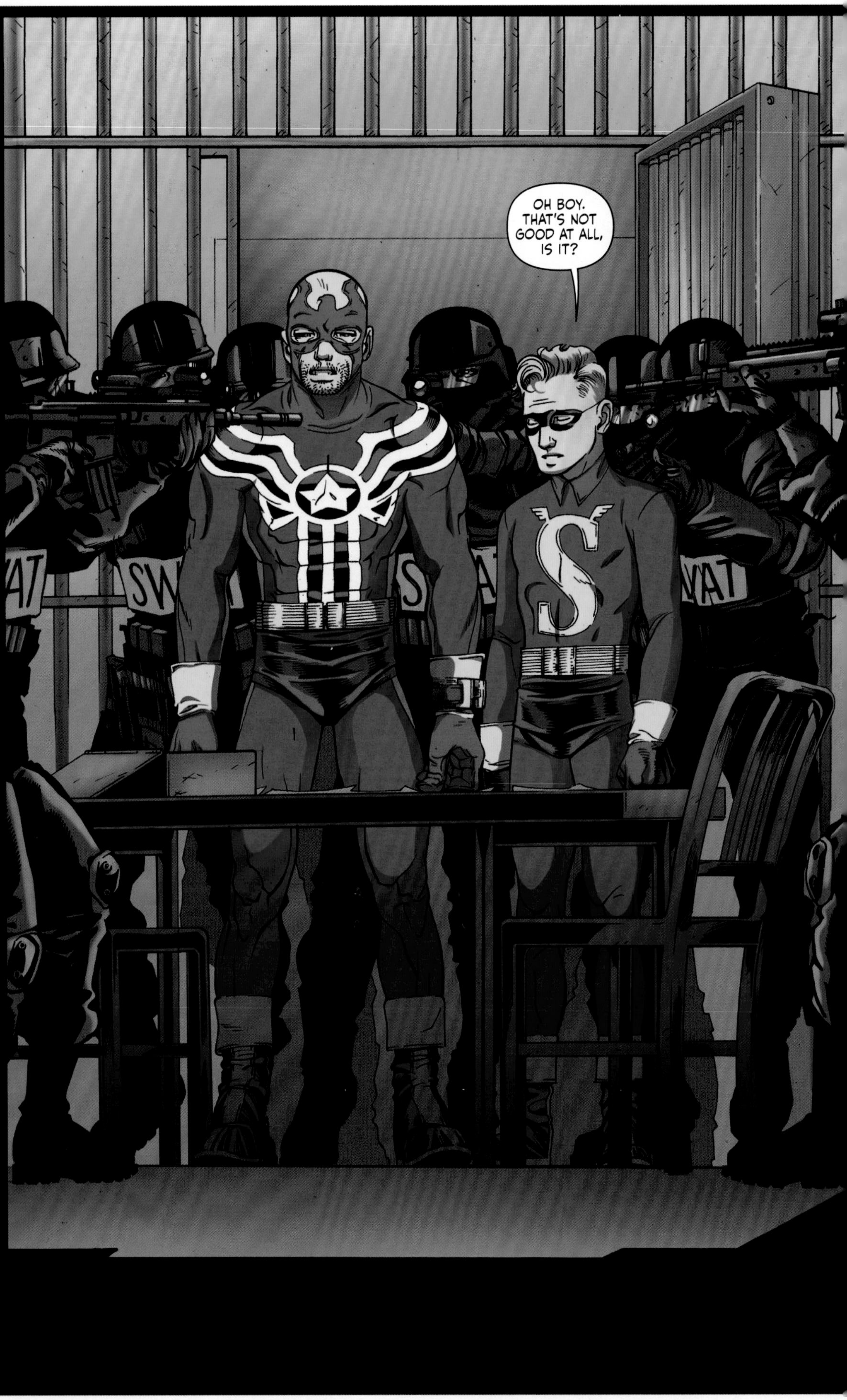
OH BOY. THAT'S NOT GOOD AT ALL, IS IT?
SWAT
SWAT

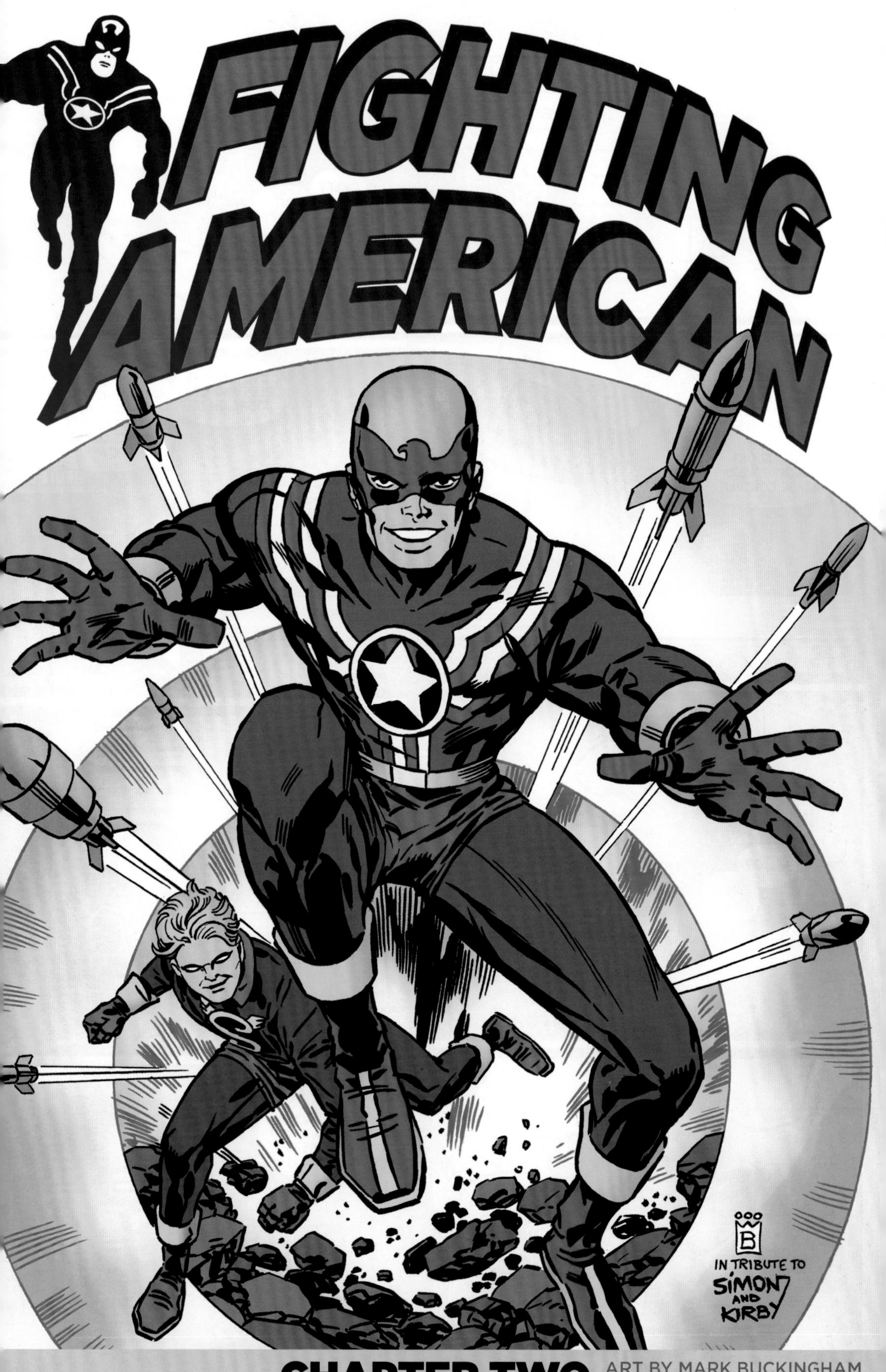
FIGHTING AMERICAN
IN TRIBUTE TO SIMON AND KIRBY

CHAPTER TWO

ART BY MARK BUCKINGHAM
COLORS BY CHRIS BLYTHE

WASHINGTON DC--

FRI JUN22 11:15A

RUTHERFORD SPEAKING.

CHIEF? I-- WAIT... WHAT?

SORRY, DID YOU JUST SAY *1954*?

NO, SIR. NO MISUNDERSTANDING. PLEASE CONTINUE.

I'LL FIND THE FILES AND GET RIGHT ON IT.

AND MAY I SAY, SIR, HOW MUCH I APPRECIATE THIS SECOND CHANCE. I WON'T LET YOU DOW--

HELLO? *UHH*, OKAY...

6
7
8
9
10
11

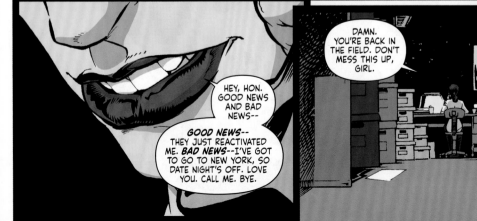

HEY, HON. GOOD NEWS AND BAD NEWS--

GOOD NEWS-- THEY JUST REACTIVATED ME. *BAD NEWS*--I'VE GOT TO GO TO NEW YORK, SO DATE NIGHT'S OFF. LOVE YOU. CALL ME. BYE.

DAMN. YOU'RE BACK IN THE FIELD. DON'T MESS THIS UP, GIRL.

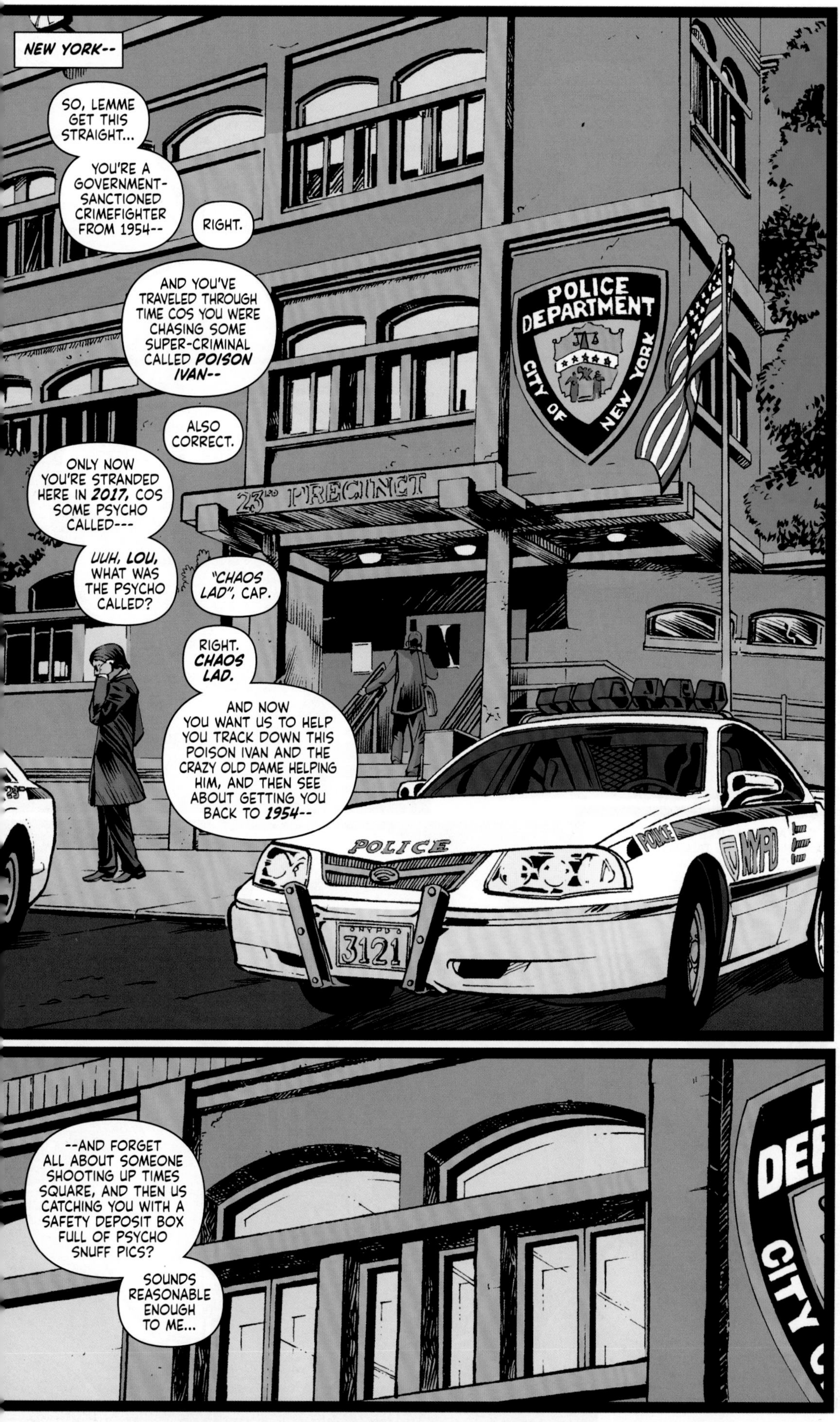

NEW YORK--
SO, LEMME GET THIS STRAIGHT...
YOU'RE A GOVERNMENT-SANCTIONED CRIMEFIGHTER FROM 1954--
RIGHT.
AND YOU'VE TRAVELED THROUGH TIME COS YOU WERE CHASING SOME SUPER-CRIMINAL CALLED POISON IVAN--
ALSO CORRECT.
ONLY NOW YOU'RE STRANDED HERE IN 2017, COS SOME PSYCHO CALLED---
UUH, LOU, WHAT WAS THE PSYCHO CALLED?
"CHAOS LAD", CAP.
RIGHT. CHAOS LAD.
AND NOW YOU WANT US TO HELP YOU TRACK DOWN THIS POISON IVAN AND THE CRAZY OLD DAME HELPING HIM, AND THEN SEE ABOUT GETTING YOU BACK TO 1954--
POLICE DEPARTMENT
CITY OF NEW YORK
23RD PRECINCT
POLICE
NYPD
3121
--AND FORGET ALL ABOUT SOMEONE SHOOTING UP TIMES SQUARE, AND THEN US CATCHING YOU WITH A SAFETY DEPOSIT BOX FULL OF PSYCHO SNUFF PICS?
SOUNDS REASONABLE ENOUGH TO ME...

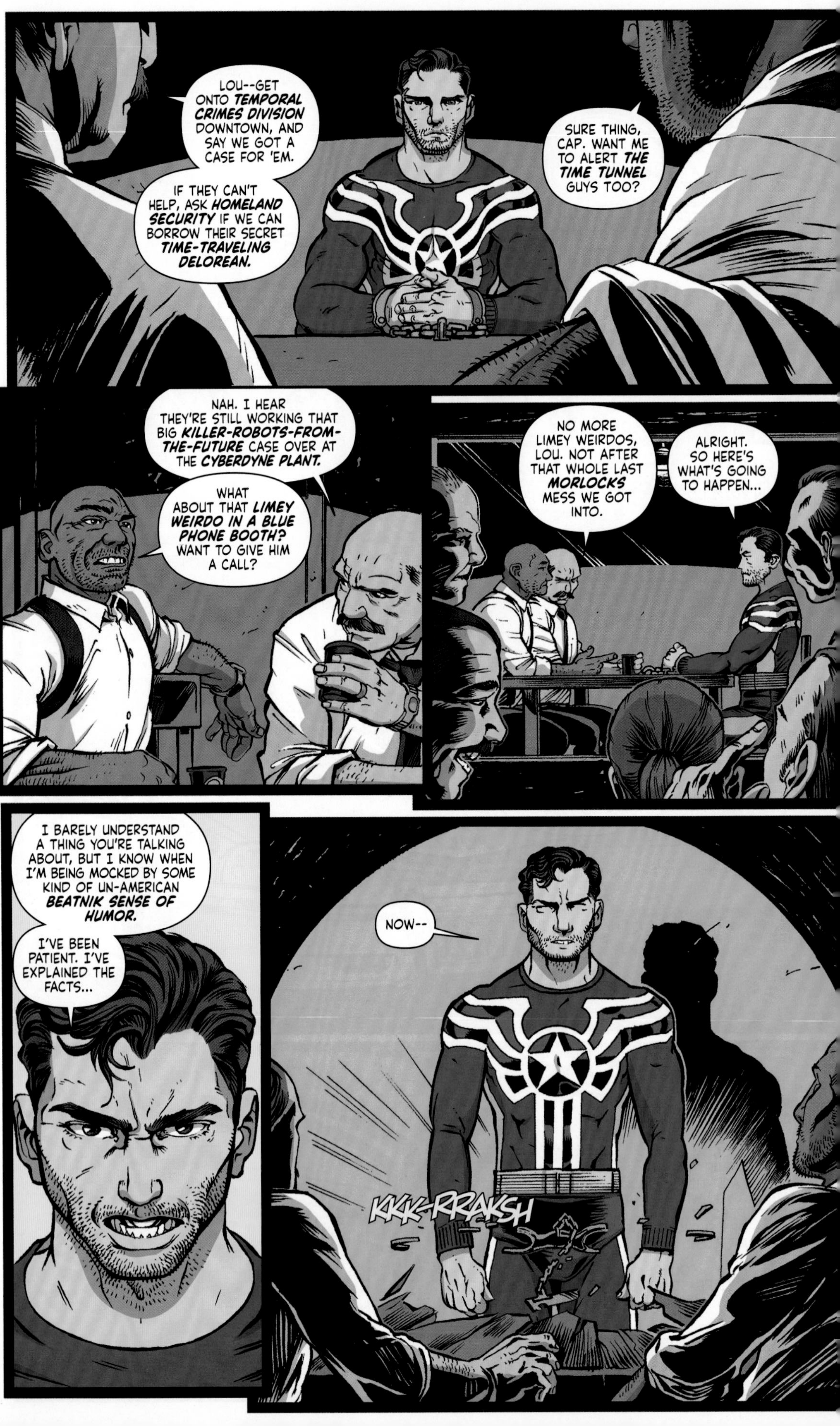
LOU--GET ONTO TEMPORAL CRIMES DIVISION DOWNTOWN, AND SAY WE GOT A CASE FOR 'EM.
IF THEY CAN'T HELP, ASK HOMELAND SECURITY IF WE CAN BORROW THEIR SECRET TIME-TRAVELING DELOREAN.
SURE THING, CAP. WANT ME TO ALERT THE TIME TUNNEL GUYS TOO?
NAH. I HEAR THEY'RE STILL WORKING THAT BIG KILLER-ROBOTS-FROM-THE-FUTURE CASE OVER AT THE CYBERDYNE PLANT.
WHAT ABOUT THAT LIMEY WEIRDO IN A BLUE PHONE BOOTH? WANT TO GIVE HIM A CALL?
NO MORE LIMEY WEIRDOS, LOU. NOT AFTER THAT WHOLE LAST MORLOCKS MESS WE GOT INTO.
ALRIGHT. SO HERE'S WHAT'S GOING TO HAPPEN...
I BARELY UNDERSTAND A THING YOU'RE TALKING ABOUT, BUT I KNOW WHEN I'M BEING MOCKED BY SOME KIND OF UN-AMERICAN BEATNIK SENSE OF HUMOR.
I'VE BEEN PATIENT. I'VE EXPLAINED THE FACTS...
NOW--
KKK-RRAKSH

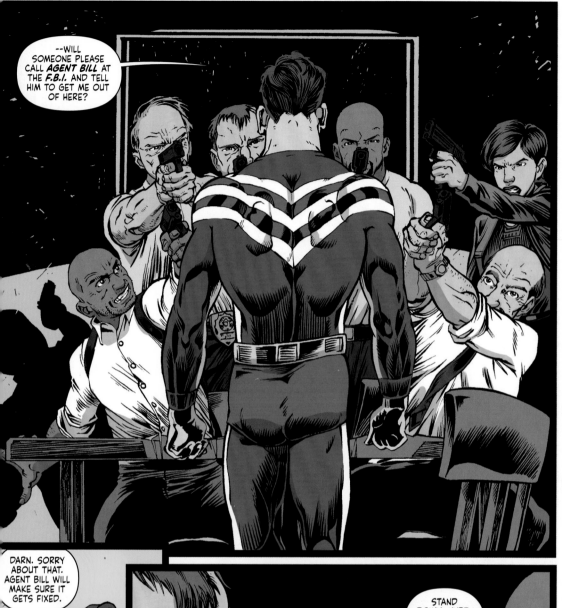

--WILL SOMEONE PLEASE CALL *AGENT BILL* AT THE *F.B.I.* AND TELL HIM TO GET ME OUT OF HERE?

DARN. SORRY ABOUT THAT. AGENT BILL WILL MAKE SURE IT GETS FIXED.

STAND DOWN, NYPD. *FART BARF* AND *ITCH* WILL TAKE IT FROM HERE.

DEPARTMENT OF INVESTIGATIO
FBI
SPECIAL AGENT

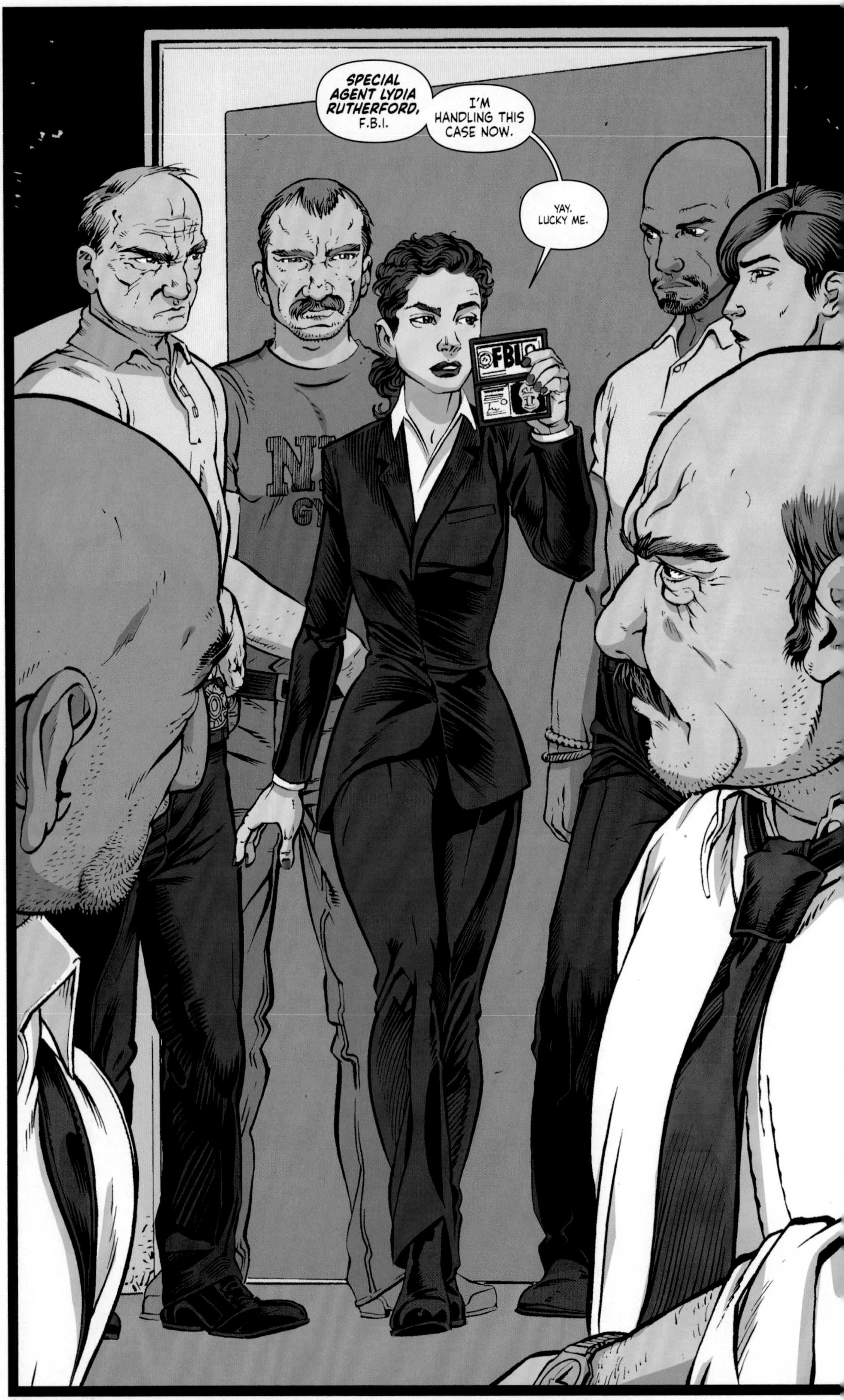
SPECIAL AGENT LYDIA RUTHERFORD, F.B.I.
I'M HANDLING THIS CASE NOW.
YAY. LUCKY ME.

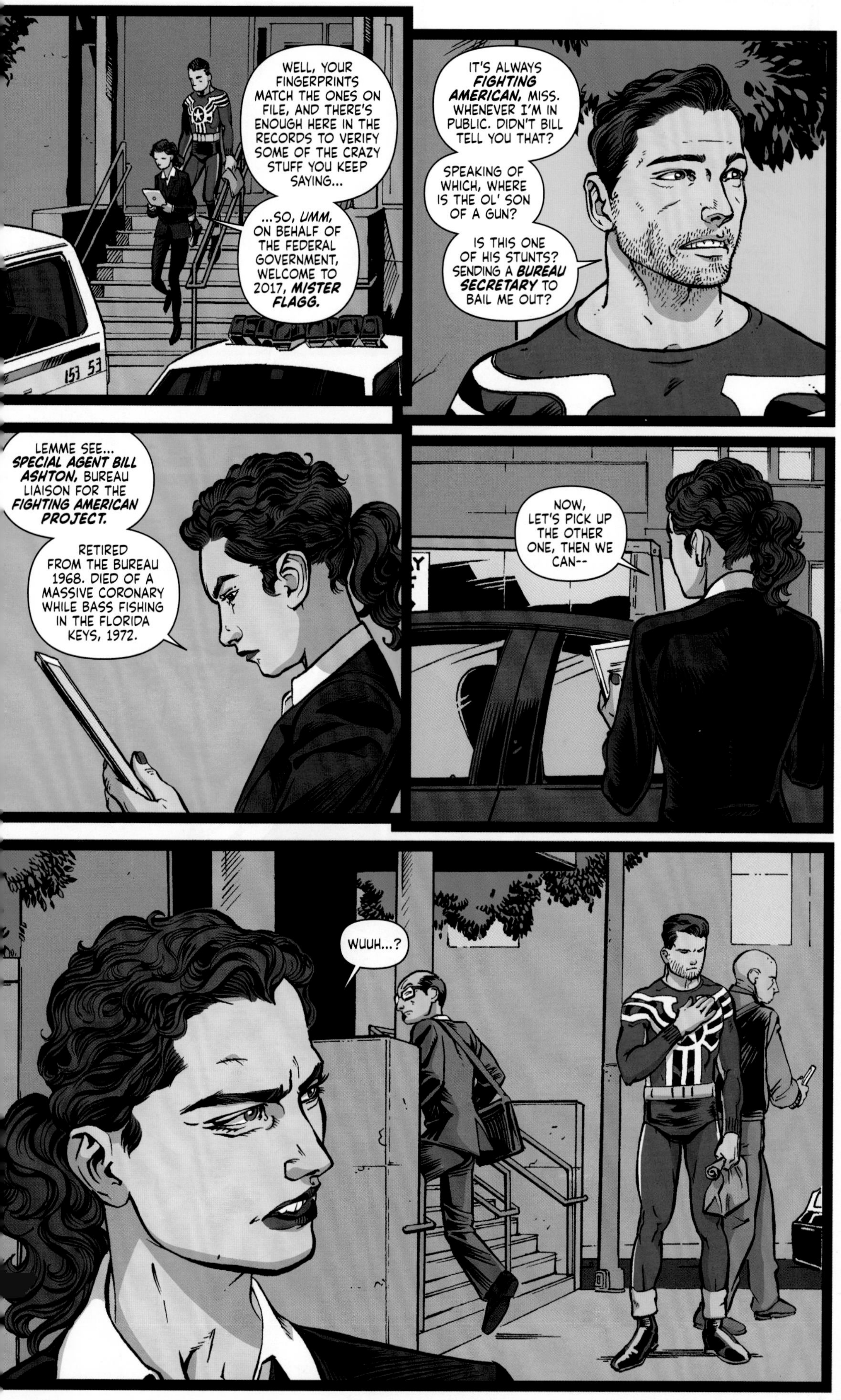
WELL, YOUR FINGERPRINTS MATCH THE ONES ON FILE, AND THERE'S ENOUGH HERE IN THE RECORDS TO VERIFY SOME OF THE CRAZY STUFF YOU KEEP SAYING...
...SO, *UMM*, ON BEHALF OF THE FEDERAL GOVERNMENT, WELCOME TO 2017, **MISTER FLAGG.**
IT'S ALWAYS **FIGHTING AMERICAN,** MISS. WHENEVER I'M IN PUBLIC. DIDN'T BILL TELL YOU THAT?
SPEAKING OF WHICH, WHERE IS THE OL' SON OF A GUN?
IS THIS ONE OF HIS STUNTS? SENDING A **BUREAU SECRETARY** TO BAIL ME OUT?
LEMME SEE... **SPECIAL AGENT BILL ASHTON,** BUREAU LIAISON FOR THE **FIGHTING AMERICAN PROJECT.**
RETIRED FROM THE BUREAU 1968. DIED OF A MASSIVE CORONARY WHILE BASS FISHING IN THE FLORIDA KEYS, 1972.
NOW, LET'S PICK UP THE OTHER ONE, THEN WE CAN--
WUUH...?

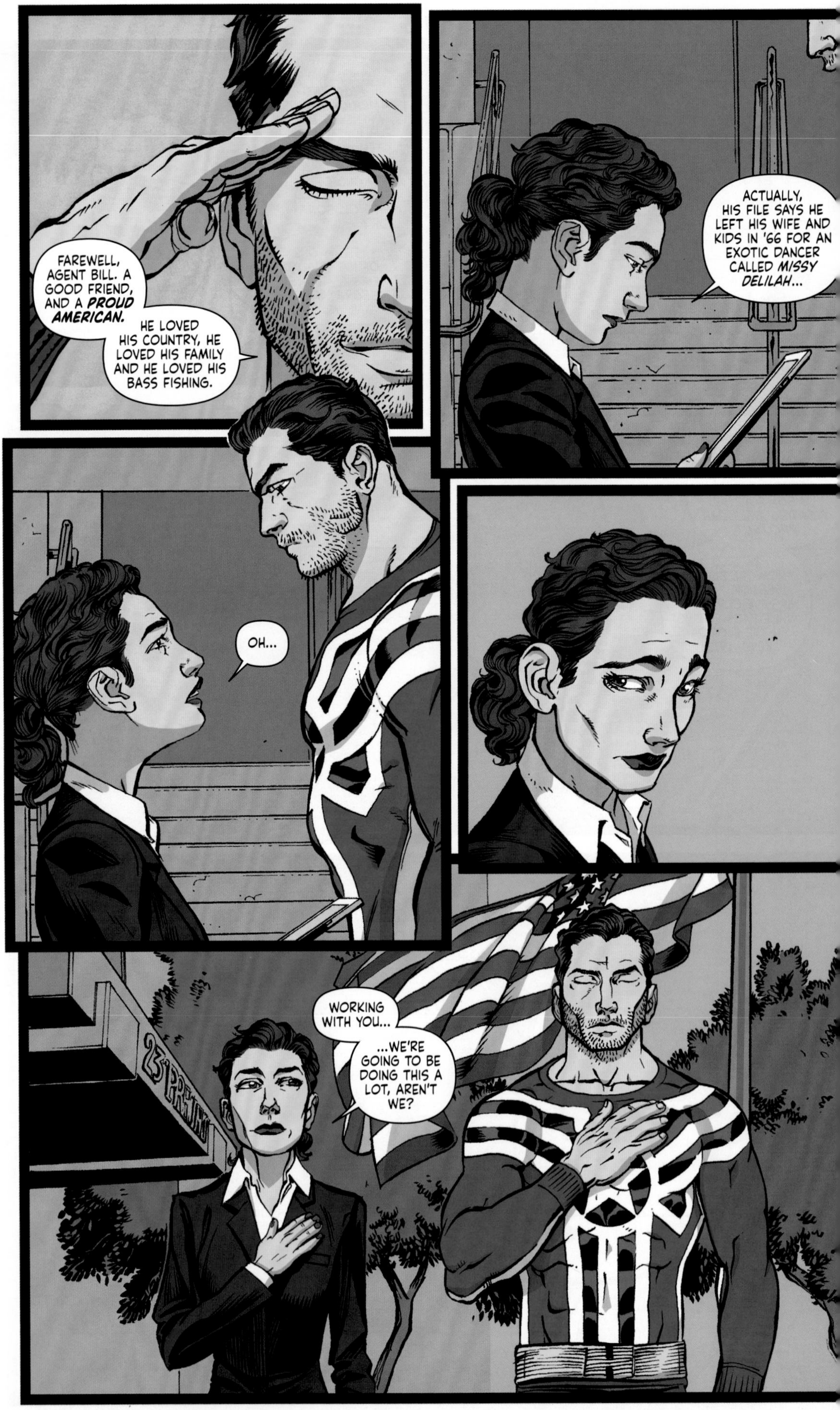
FAREWELL, AGENT BILL. A GOOD FRIEND, AND A ***PROUD AMERICAN.***
HE LOVED HIS COUNTRY, HE LOVED HIS FAMILY AND HE LOVED HIS BASS FISHING.
ACTUALLY, HIS FILE SAYS HE LEFT HIS WIFE AND KIDS IN '66 FOR AN EXOTIC DANCER CALLED *MISSY DELILAH*...
OH...
WORKING WITH YOU...
...WE'RE GOING TO BE DOING THIS A LOT, AREN'T WE?

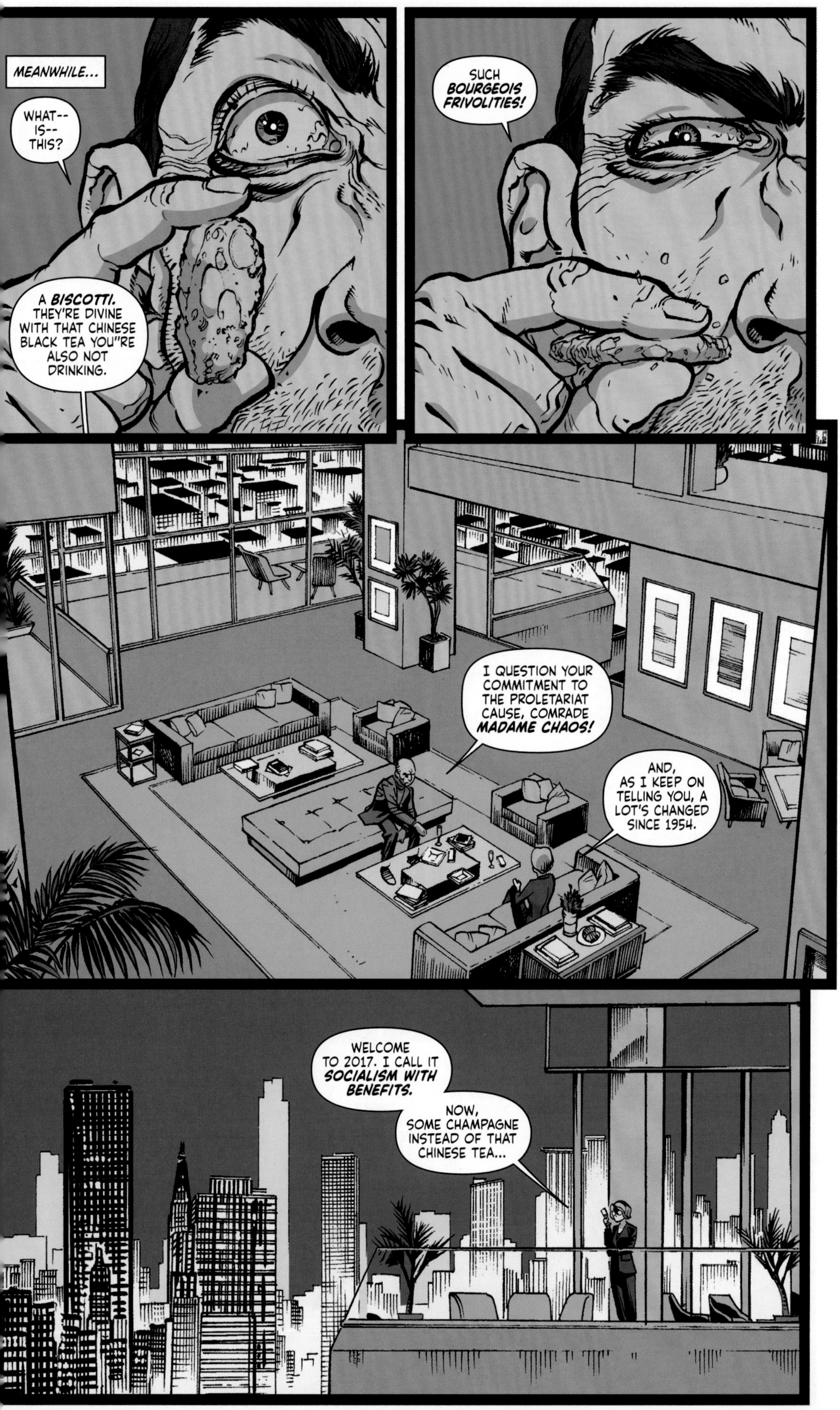
MEANWHILE...
WHAT-- IS-- THIS?
A BISCOTTI. THEY'RE DIVINE WITH THAT CHINESE BLACK TEA YOU''RE ALSO NOT DRINKING.
SUCH BOURGEOIS FRIVOLITIES!
I QUESTION YOUR COMMITMENT TO THE PROLETARIAT CAUSE, COMRADE MADAME CHAOS!
AND, AS I KEEP ON TELLING YOU, A LOT'S CHANGED SINCE 1954.
WELCOME TO 2017. I CALL IT SOCIALISM WITH BENEFITS.
NOW, SOME CHAMPAGNE INSTEAD OF THAT CHINESE TEA...

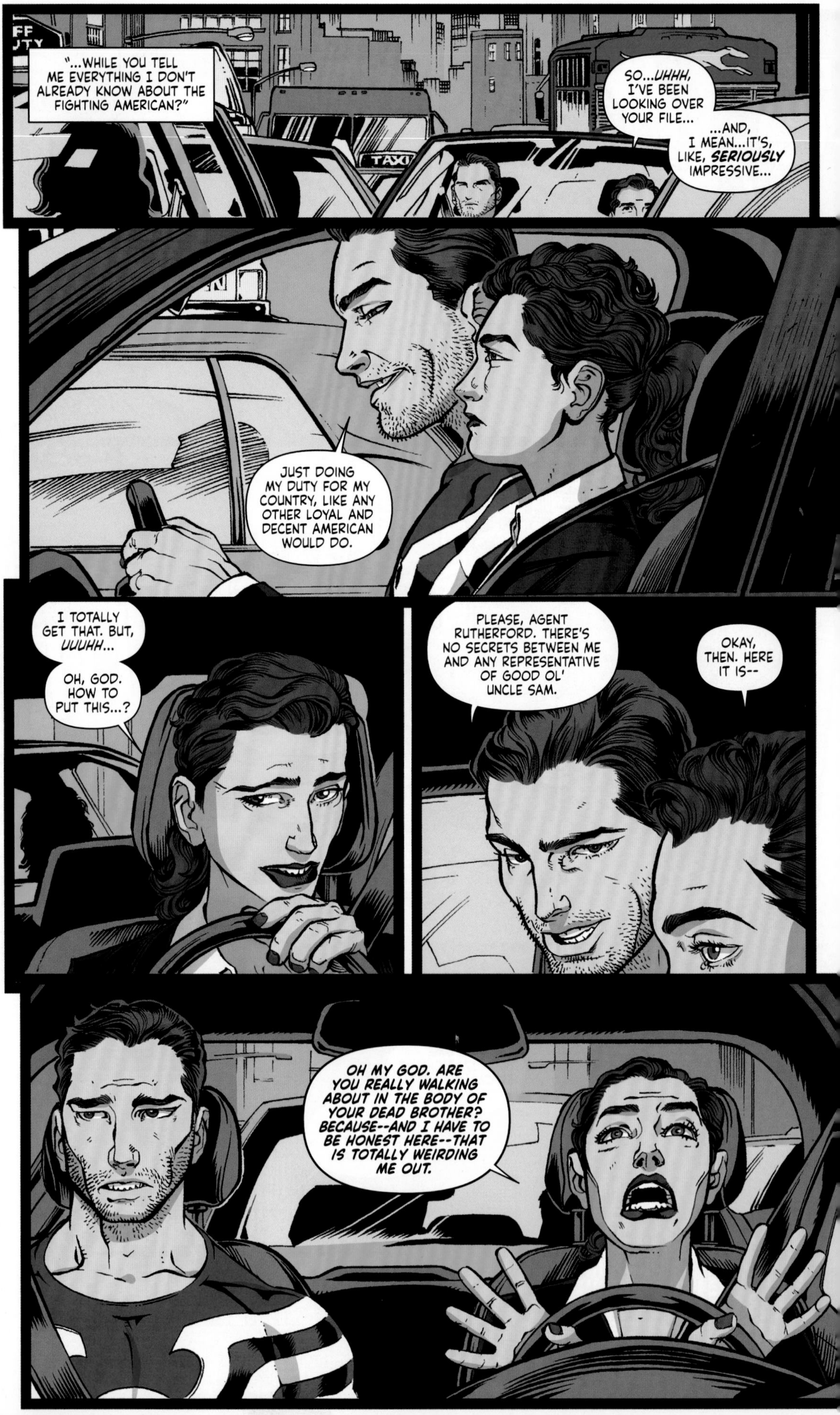

FF
UTY
"...WHILE YOU TELL ME EVERYTHING I DON'T ALREADY KNOW ABOUT THE FIGHTING AMERICAN?"
TAXI
SO...*UHHH,* I'VE BEEN LOOKING OVER YOUR FILE...
...AND, I MEAN...IT'S, LIKE, ***SERIOUSLY*** IMPRESSIVE...
JUST DOING MY DUTY FOR MY COUNTRY, LIKE ANY OTHER LOYAL AND DECENT AMERICAN WOULD DO.
I TOTALLY GET THAT. BUT, *UUUHH*...
OH, GOD. HOW TO PUT THIS...?
PLEASE, AGENT RUTHERFORD. THERE'S NO SECRETS BETWEEN ME AND ANY REPRESENTATIVE OF GOOD OL' UNCLE SAM.
OKAY, THEN. HERE IT IS--
OH MY GOD. ARE YOU REALLY WALKING ABOUT IN THE BODY OF YOUR DEAD BROTHER? BECAUSE--AND I HAVE TO BE HONEST HERE--THAT IS TOTALLY WEIRDING ME OUT.

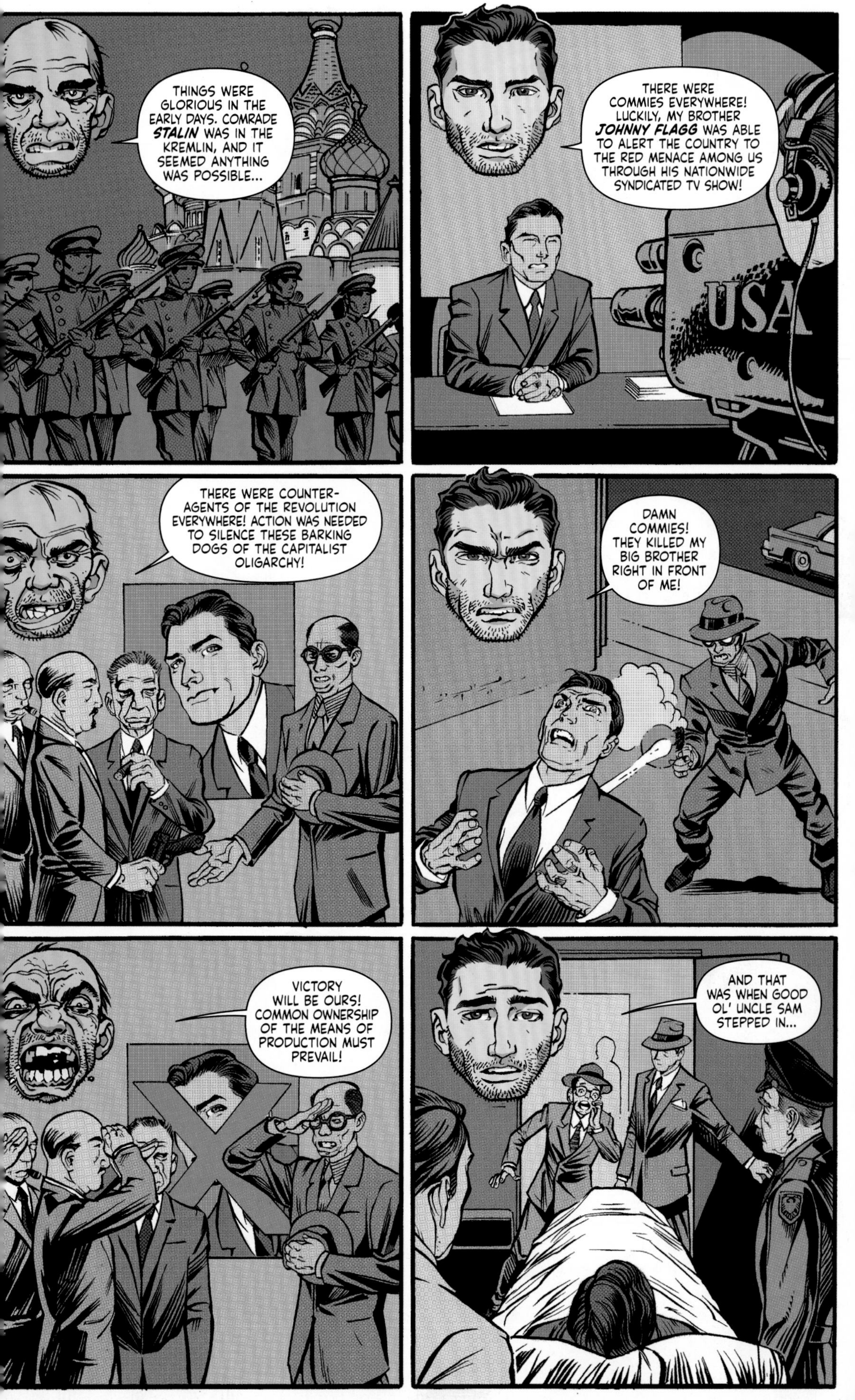

THINGS WERE GLORIOUS IN THE EARLY DAYS. COMRADE STALIN WAS IN THE KREMLIN, AND IT SEEMED ANYTHING WAS POSSIBLE...
THERE WERE COMMIES EVERYWHERE! LUCKILY, MY BROTHER JOHNNY FLAGG WAS ABLE TO ALERT THE COUNTRY TO THE RED MENACE AMONG US THROUGH HIS NATIONWIDE SYNDICATED TV SHOW!
USA
THERE WERE COUNTER-AGENTS OF THE REVOLUTION EVERYWHERE! ACTION WAS NEEDED TO SILENCE THESE BARKING DOGS OF THE CAPITALIST OLIGARCHY!
DAMN COMMIES! THEY KILLED MY BIG BROTHER RIGHT IN FRONT OF ME!
VICTORY WILL BE OURS! COMMON OWNERSHIP OF THE MEANS OF PRODUCTION MUST PREVAIL!
AND THAT WAS WHEN GOOD OL' UNCLE SAM STEPPED IN...

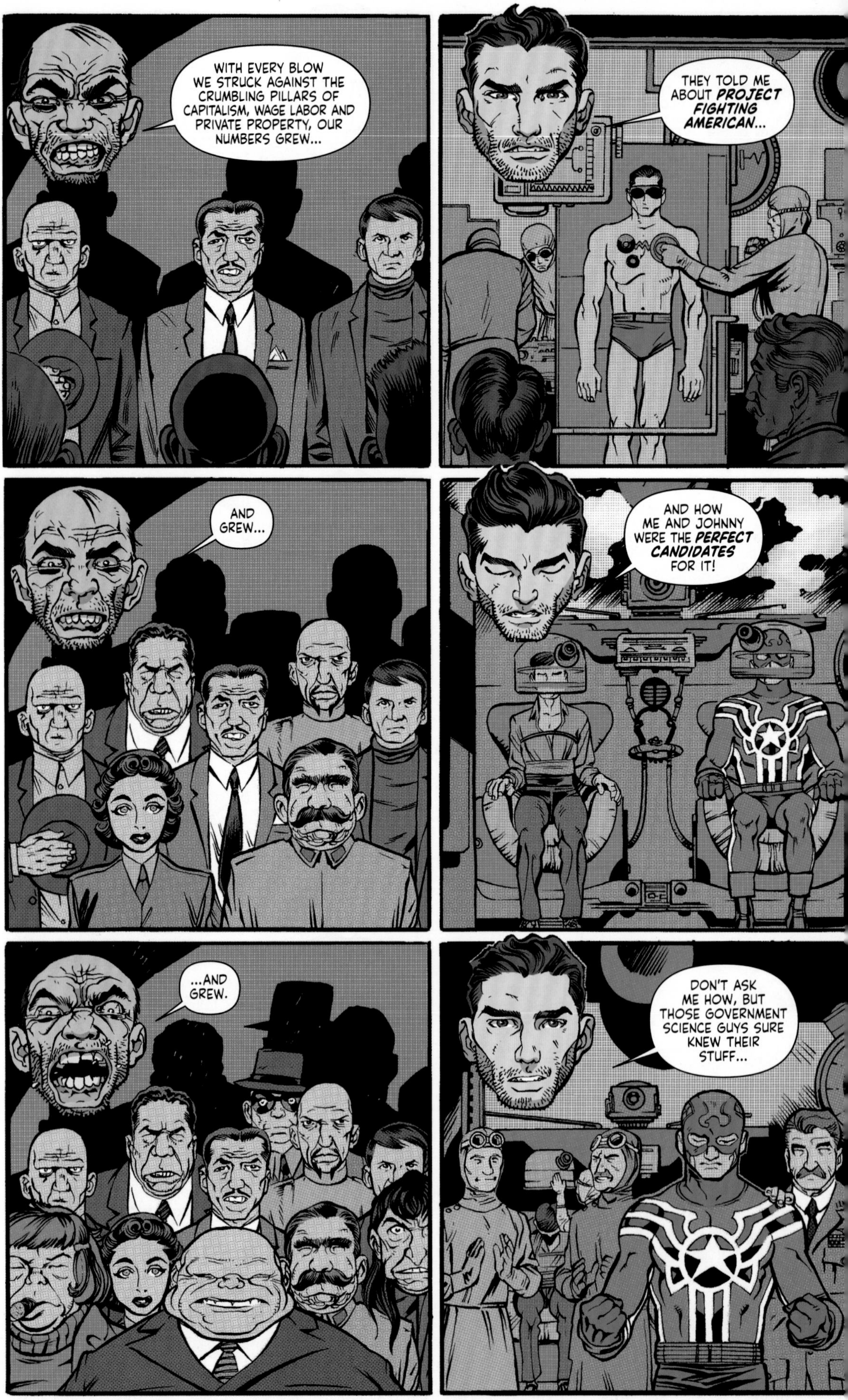
WITH EVERY BLOW WE STRUCK AGAINST THE CRUMBLING PILLARS OF CAPITALISM, WAGE LABOR AND PRIVATE PROPERTY, OUR NUMBERS GREW...
THEY TOLD ME ABOUT PROJECT FIGHTING AMERICAN...
AND GREW...
AND HOW ME AND JOHNNY WERE THE PERFECT CANDIDATES FOR IT!
...AND GREW.
DON'T ASK ME HOW, BUT THOSE GOVERNMENT SCIENCE GUYS SURE KNEW THEIR STUFF...

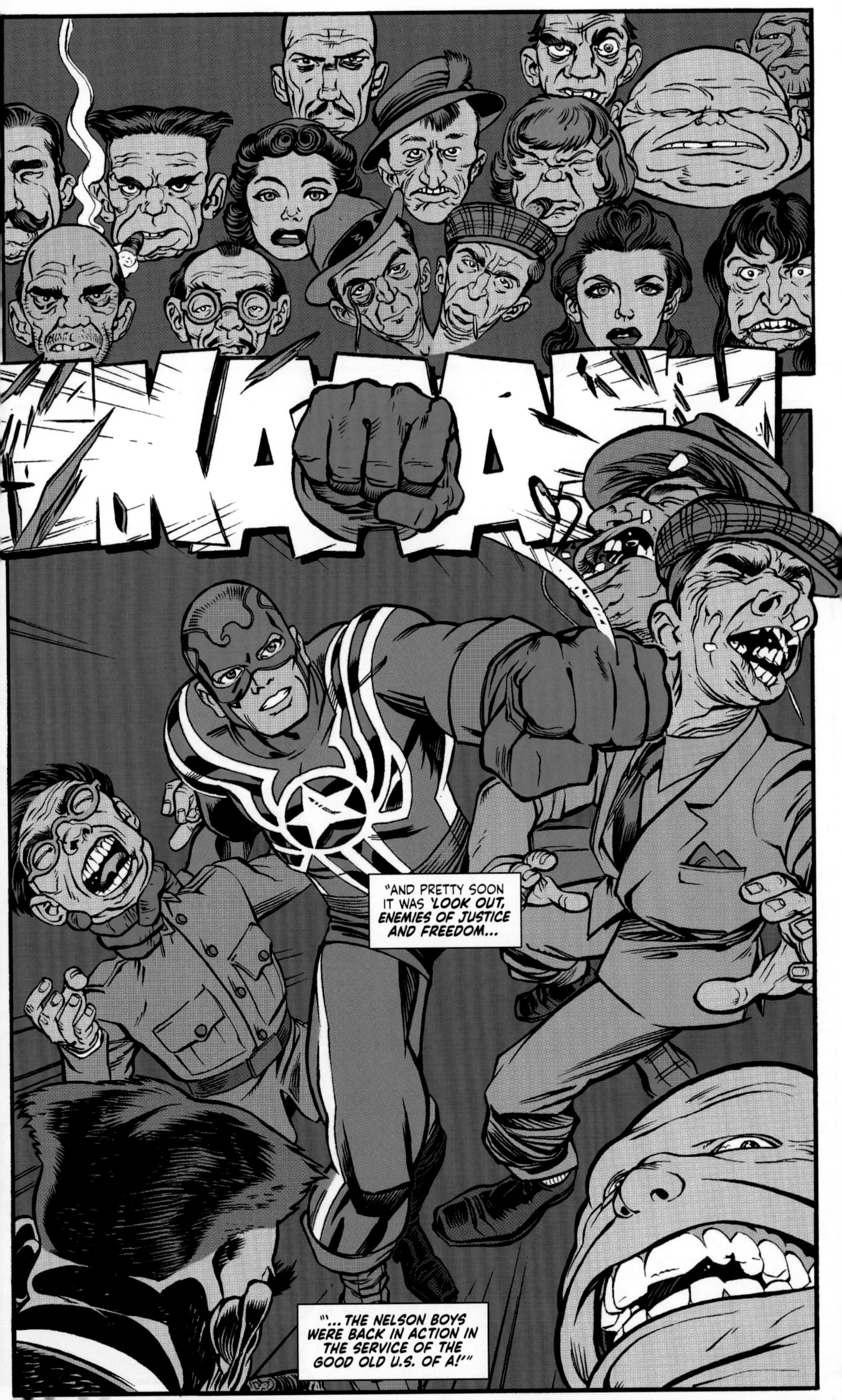
"AND PRETTY SOON IT WAS 'LOOK OUT, ENEMIES OF JUSTICE AND FREEDOM...
"'...THE NELSON BOYS WERE BACK IN ACTION IN THE SERVICE OF THE GOOD OLD U.S. OF A!'"

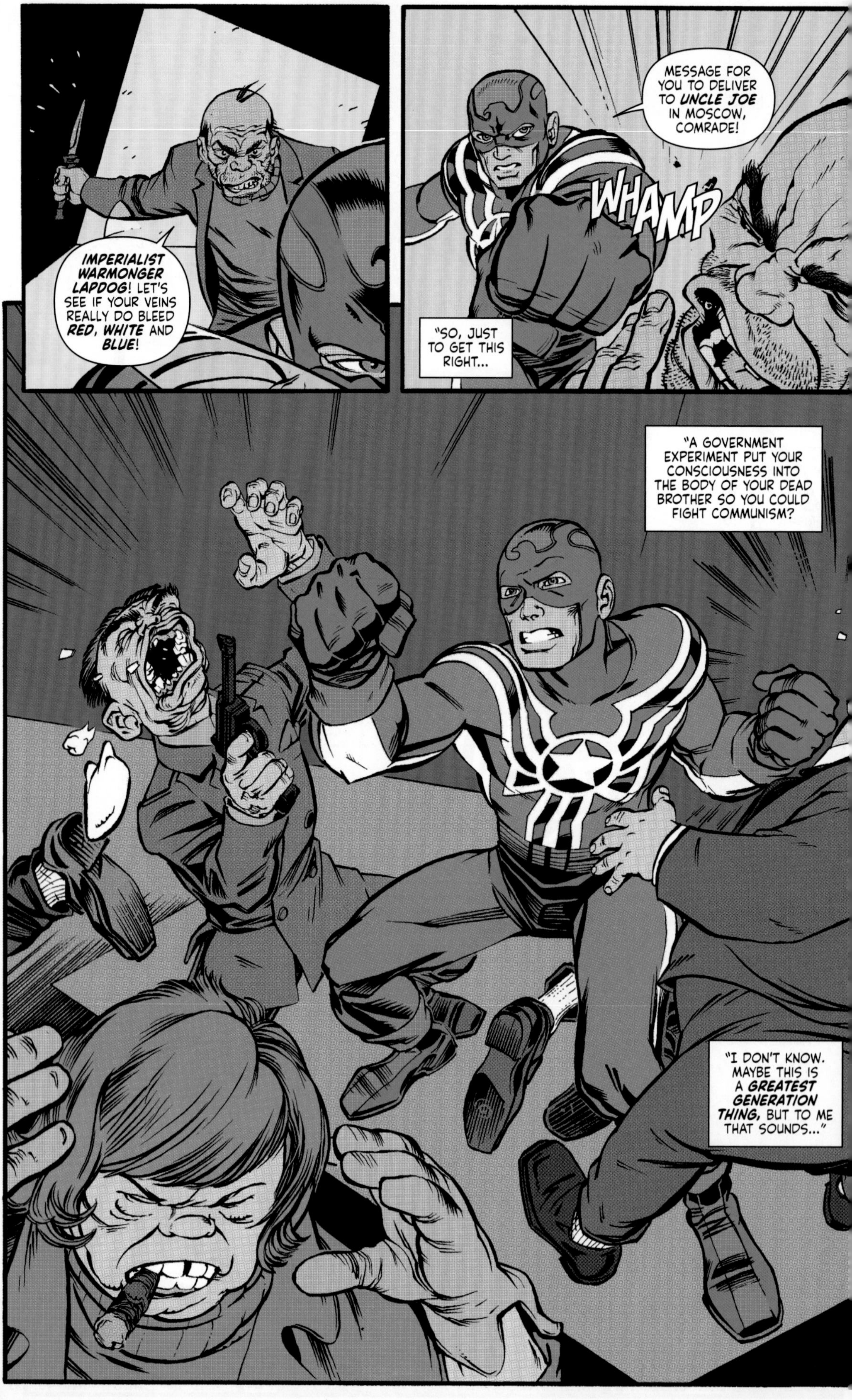
IMPERIALIST WARMONGER LAPDOG! LET'S SEE IF YOUR VEINS REALLY DO BLEED RED, WHITE AND BLUE!
MESSAGE FOR YOU TO DELIVER TO UNCLE JOE IN MOSCOW, COMRADE!
WHAMP
"SO, JUST TO GET THIS RIGHT...
"A GOVERNMENT EXPERIMENT PUT YOUR CONSCIOUSNESS INTO THE BODY OF YOUR DEAD BROTHER SO YOU COULD FIGHT COMMUNISM?
"I DON'T KNOW. MAYBE THIS IS A GREATEST GENERATION THING, BUT TO ME THAT SOUNDS..."

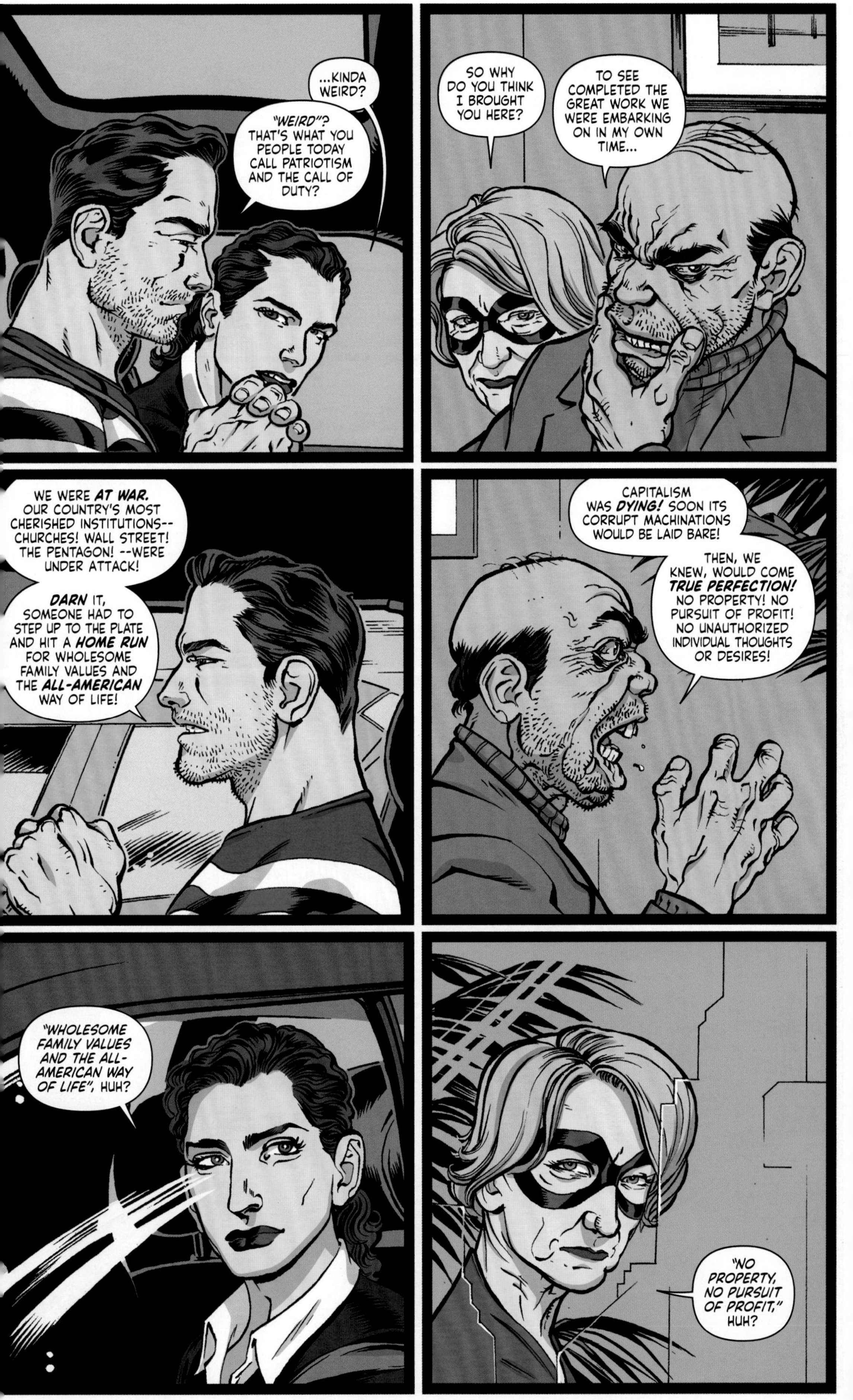

...KINDA WEIRD?
"WEIRD"? THAT'S WHAT YOU PEOPLE TODAY CALL PATRIOTISM AND THE CALL OF DUTY?
SO WHY DO YOU THINK I BROUGHT YOU HERE?
TO SEE COMPLETED THE GREAT WORK WE WERE EMBARKING ON IN MY OWN TIME...
WE WERE AT WAR. OUR COUNTRY'S MOST CHERISHED INSTITUTIONS-- CHURCHES! WALL STREET! THE PENTAGON! --WERE UNDER ATTACK!
DARN IT, SOMEONE HAD TO STEP UP TO THE PLATE AND HIT A HOME RUN FOR WHOLESOME FAMILY VALUES AND THE ALL-AMERICAN WAY OF LIFE!
CAPITALISM WAS DYING! SOON ITS CORRUPT MACHINATIONS WOULD BE LAID BARE!
THEN, WE KNEW, WOULD COME TRUE PERFECTION! NO PROPERTY! NO PURSUIT OF PROFIT! NO UNAUTHORIZED INDIVIDUAL THOUGHTS OR DESIRES!
"WHOLESOME FAMILY VALUES AND THE ALL-AMERICAN WAY OF LIFE", HUH?
"NO PROPERTY, NO PURSUIT OF PROFIT," HUH?

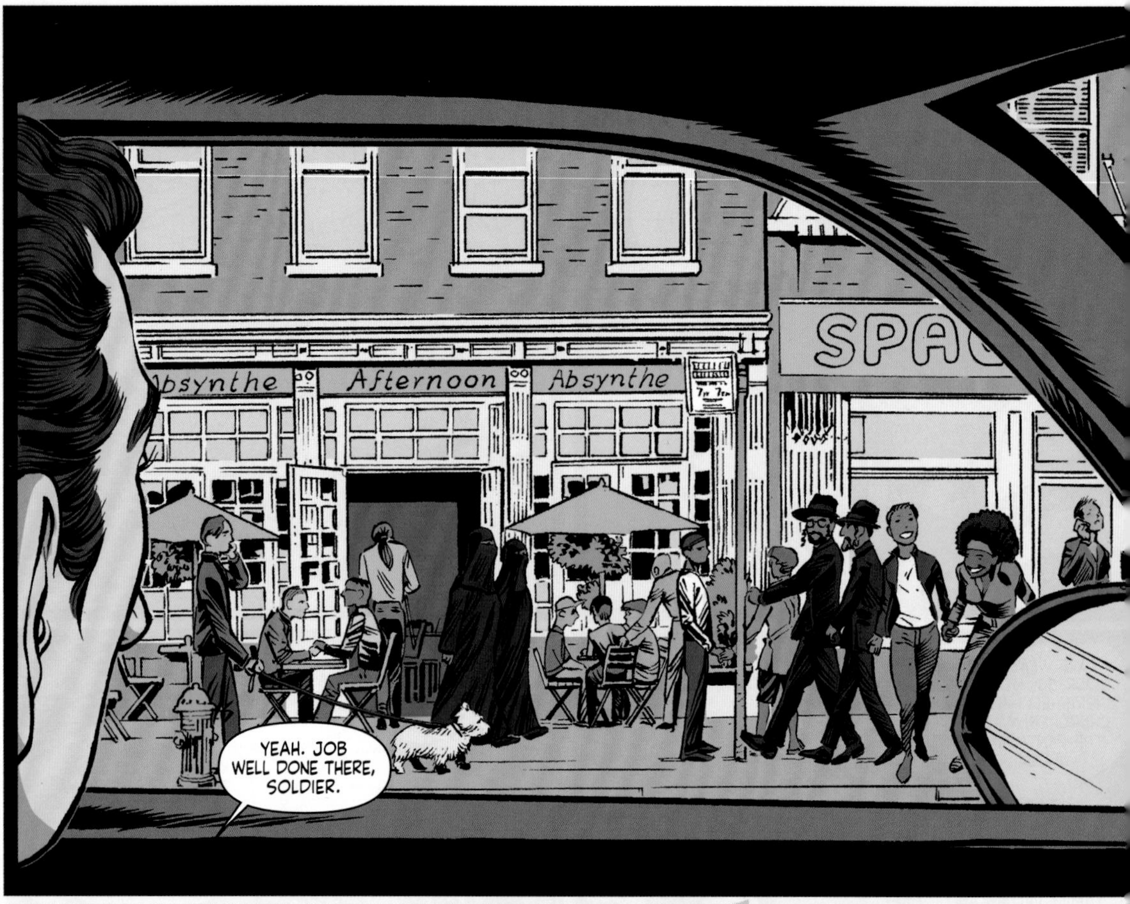
Absynthe
Afternoon
Absynthe
SPAC
YEAH. JOB WELL DONE THERE, SOLDIER.

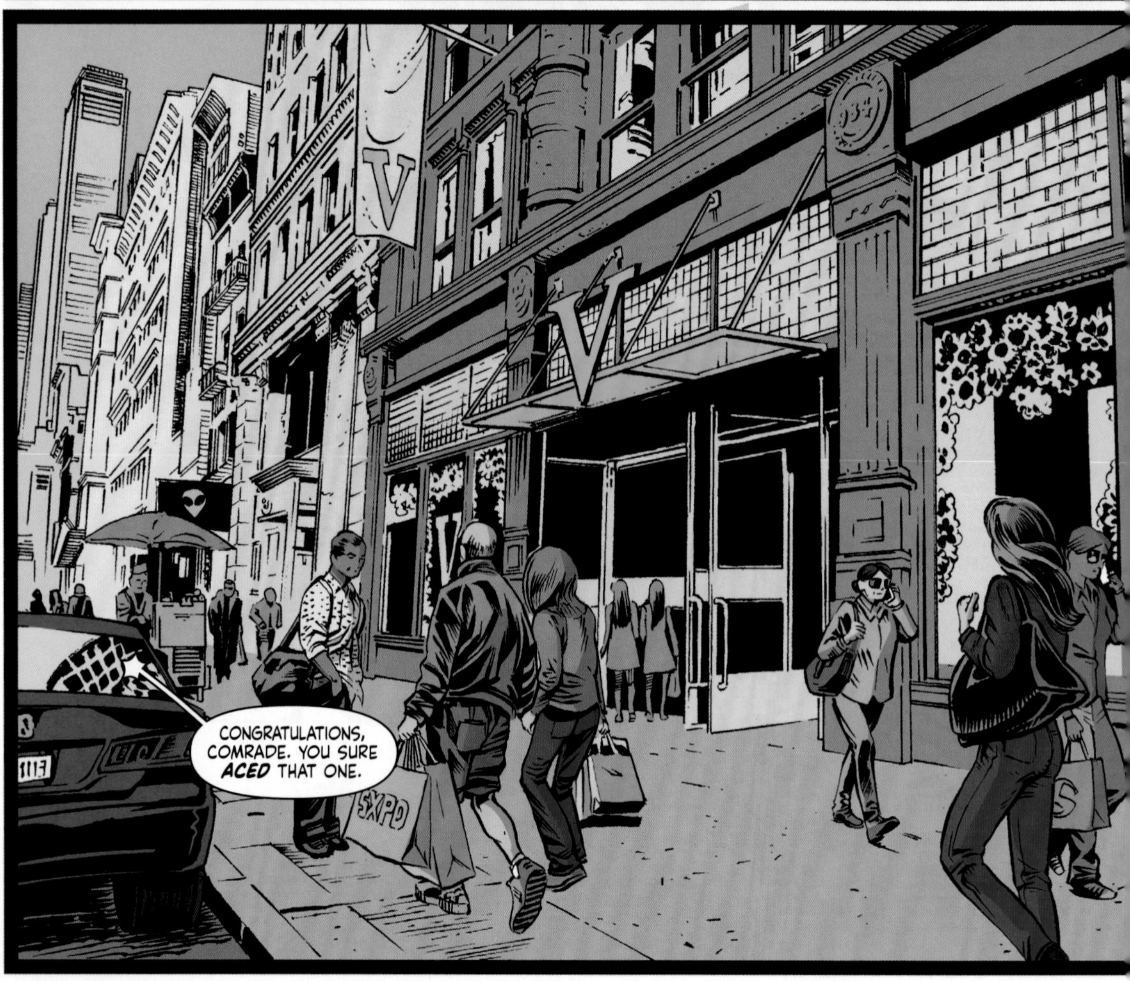
V
V
EXPO
CONGRATULATIONS, COMRADE. YOU SURE ***ACED*** THAT ONE.

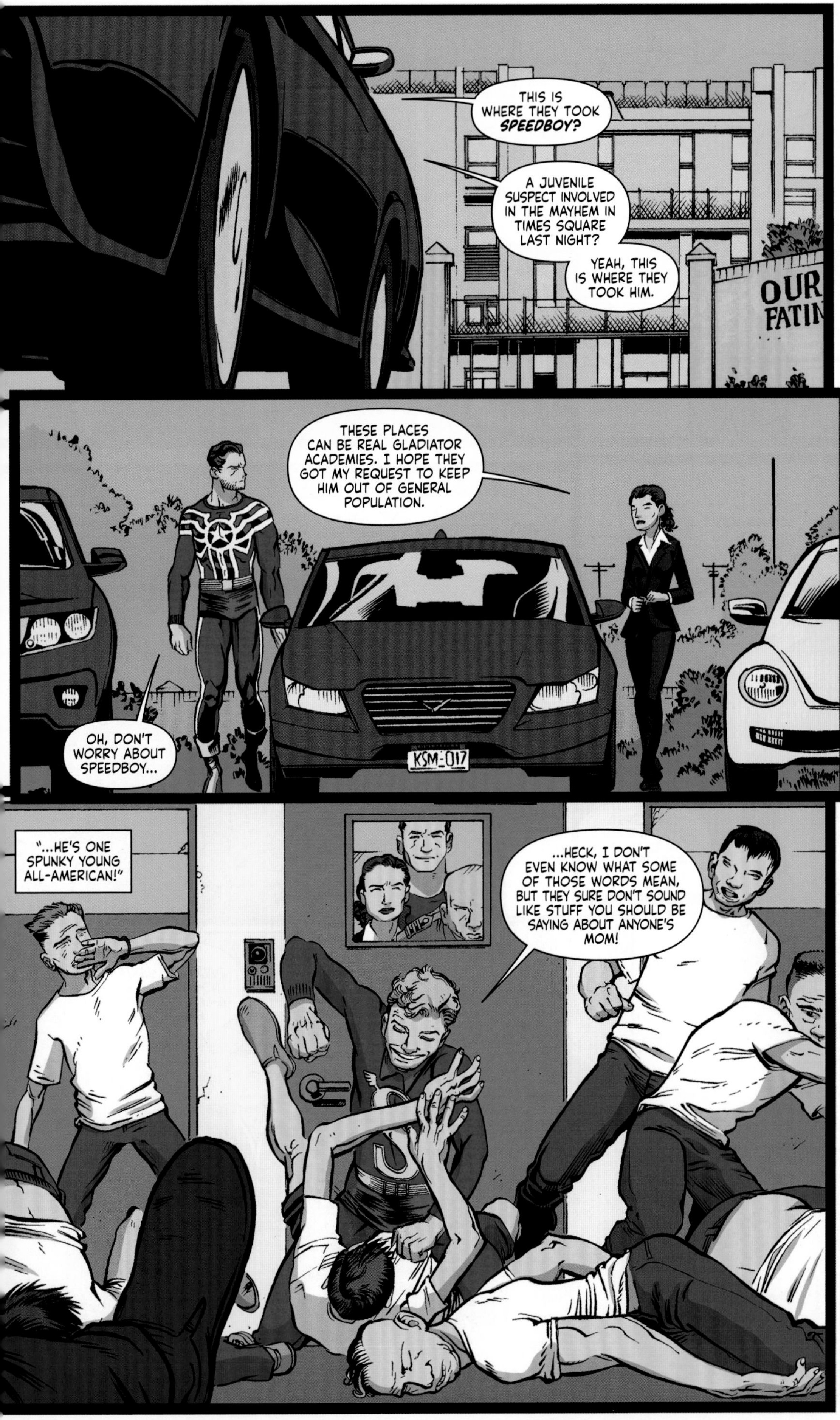
THIS IS WHERE THEY TOOK SPEEDBOY?
A JUVENILE SUSPECT INVOLVED IN THE MAYHEM IN TIMES SQUARE LAST NIGHT?
YEAH, THIS IS WHERE THEY TOOK HIM.
THESE PLACES CAN BE REAL GLADIATOR ACADEMIES. I HOPE THEY GOT MY REQUEST TO KEEP HIM OUT OF GENERAL POPULATION.
OH, DON'T WORRY ABOUT SPEEDBOY...
KSM-017
"...HE'S ONE SPUNKY YOUNG ALL-AMERICAN!"
...HECK, I DON'T EVEN KNOW WHAT SOME OF THOSE WORDS MEAN, BUT THEY SURE DON'T SOUND LIKE STUFF YOU SHOULD BE SAYING ABOUT ANYONE'S MOM!

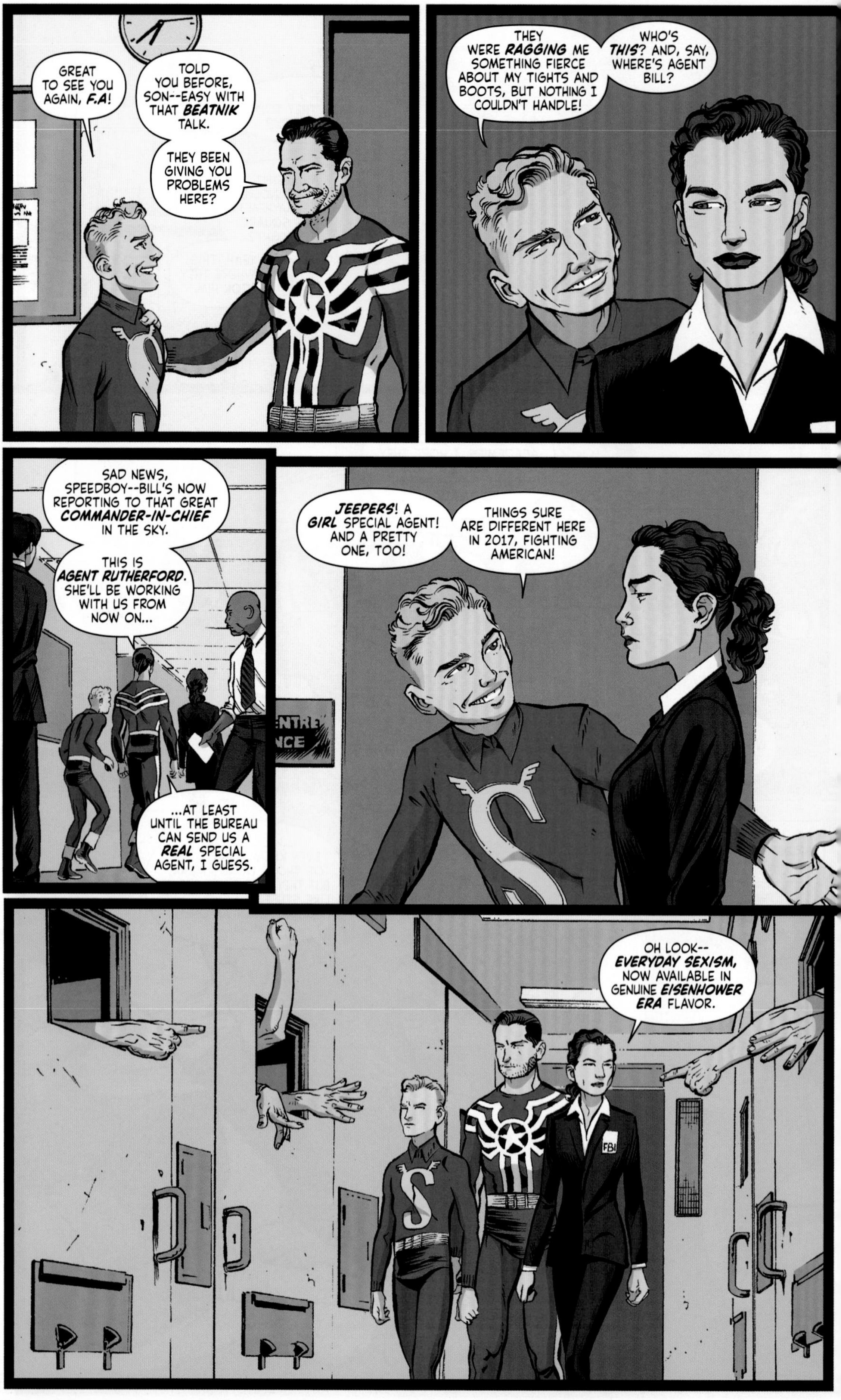

GREAT TO SEE YOU AGAIN, F.A!
TOLD YOU BEFORE, SON--EASY WITH THAT BEATNIK TALK.
THEY BEEN GIVING YOU PROBLEMS HERE?
THEY WERE RAGGING ME SOMETHING FIERCE ABOUT MY TIGHTS AND BOOTS, BUT NOTHING I COULDN'T HANDLE!
WHO'S THIS? AND, SAY, WHERE'S AGENT BILL?
SAD NEWS, SPEEDBOY--BILL'S NOW REPORTING TO THAT GREAT COMMANDER-IN-CHIEF IN THE SKY.
THIS IS AGENT RUTHERFORD. SHE'LL BE WORKING WITH US FROM NOW ON...
...AT LEAST UNTIL THE BUREAU CAN SEND US A REAL SPECIAL AGENT, I GUESS.
JEEPERS! A GIRL SPECIAL AGENT! AND A PRETTY ONE, TOO!
THINGS SURE ARE DIFFERENT HERE IN 2017, FIGHTING AMERICAN!
OH LOOK-- EVERYDAY SEXISM, NOW AVAILABLE IN GENUINE EISENHOWER ERA FLAVOR.
FBI

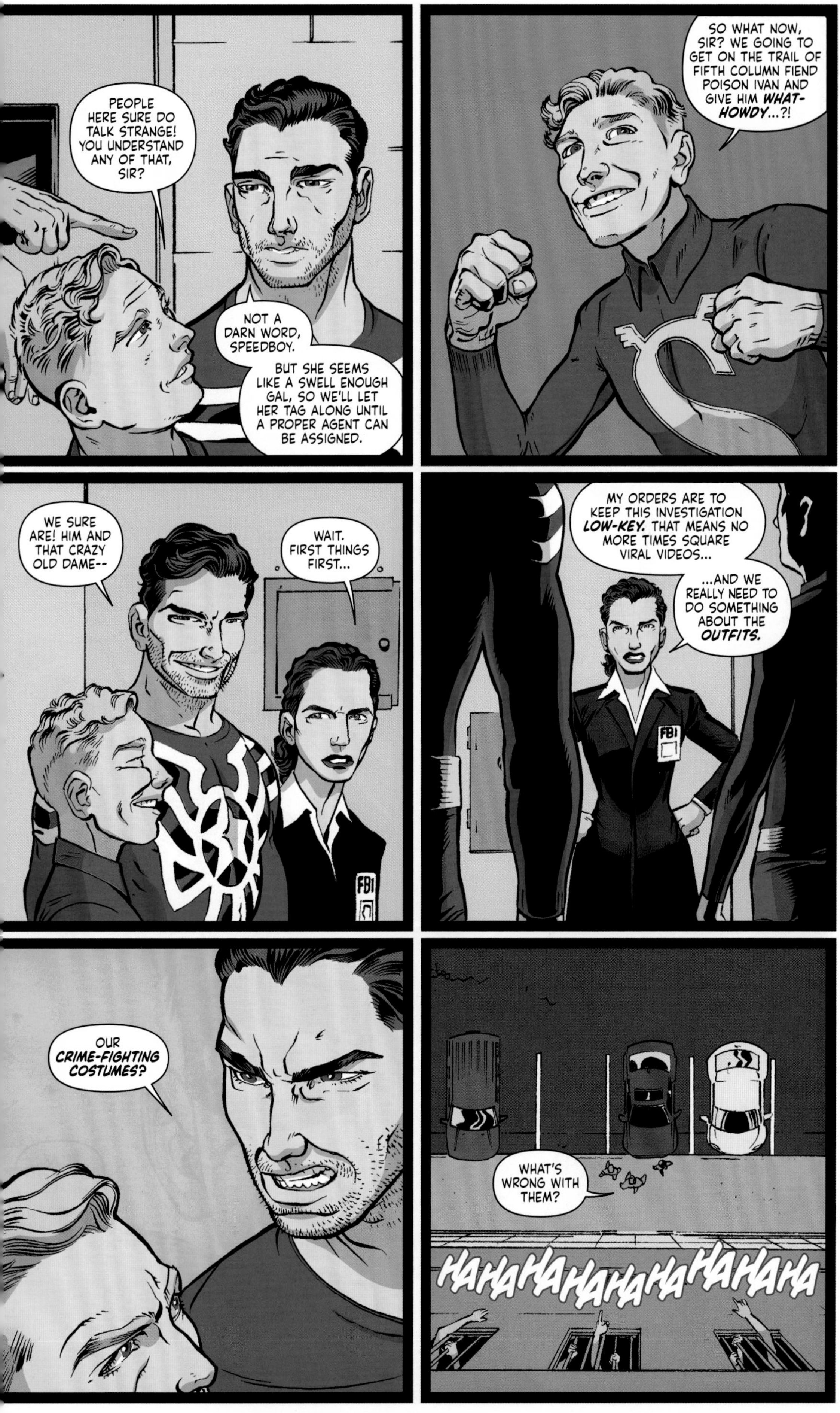

PEOPLE HERE SURE DO TALK STRANGE! YOU UNDERSTAND ANY OF THAT, SIR?
NOT A DARN WORD, SPEEDBOY.
BUT SHE SEEMS LIKE A SWELL ENOUGH GAL, SO WE'LL LET HER TAG ALONG UNTIL A PROPER AGENT CAN BE ASSIGNED.
SO WHAT NOW, SIR? WE GOING TO GET ON THE TRAIL OF FIFTH COLUMN FIEND POISON IVAN AND GIVE HIM WHAT-HOWDY...?!
WE SURE ARE! HIM AND THAT CRAZY OLD DAME--
WAIT. FIRST THINGS FIRST...
FBI
MY ORDERS ARE TO KEEP THIS INVESTIGATION LOW-KEY. THAT MEANS NO MORE TIMES SQUARE VIRAL VIDEOS...
...AND WE REALLY NEED TO DO SOMETHING ABOUT THE OUTFITS.
FBI
OUR CRIME-FIGHTING COSTUMES?
WHAT'S WRONG WITH THEM?
HAHAHAHAHAHAHAHAHAHAHA

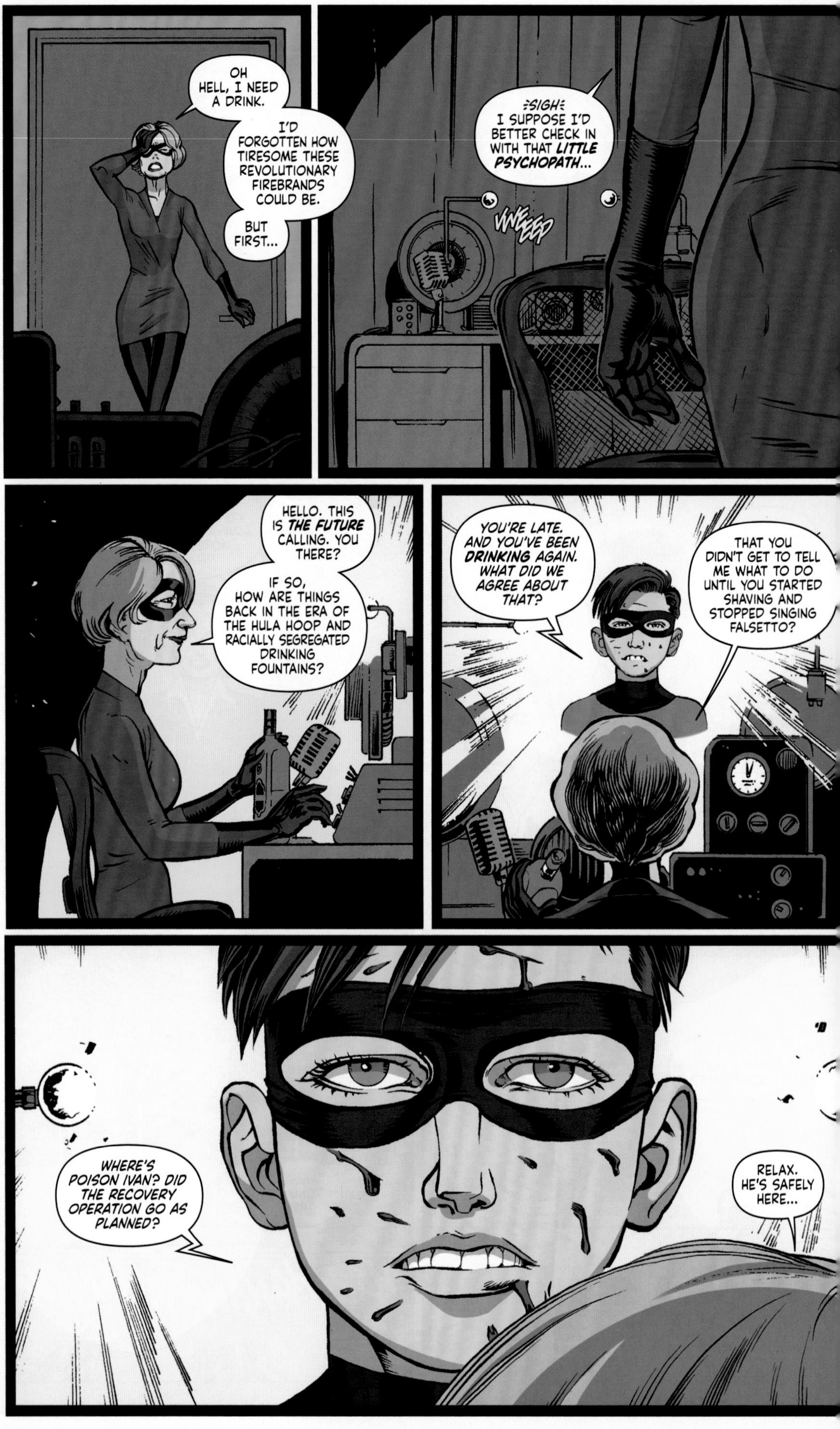
OH HELL, I NEED A DRINK.
I'D FORGOTTEN HOW TIRESOME THESE REVOLUTIONARY FIREBRANDS COULD BE.
BUT FIRST...
SIGH
I SUPPOSE I'D BETTER CHECK IN WITH THAT LITTLE PSYCHOPATH...
VWEEEP
HELLO. THIS IS THE FUTURE CALLING. YOU THERE?
IF SO, HOW ARE THINGS BACK IN THE ERA OF THE HULA HOOP AND RACIALLY SEGREGATED DRINKING FOUNTAINS?
YOU'RE LATE. AND YOU'VE BEEN DRINKING AGAIN. WHAT DID WE AGREE ABOUT THAT?
THAT YOU DIDN'T GET TO TELL ME WHAT TO DO UNTIL YOU STARTED SHAVING AND STOPPED SINGING FALSETTO?
WHERE'S POISON IVAN? DID THE RECOVERY OPERATION GO AS PLANNED?
RELAX. HE'S SAFELY HERE...

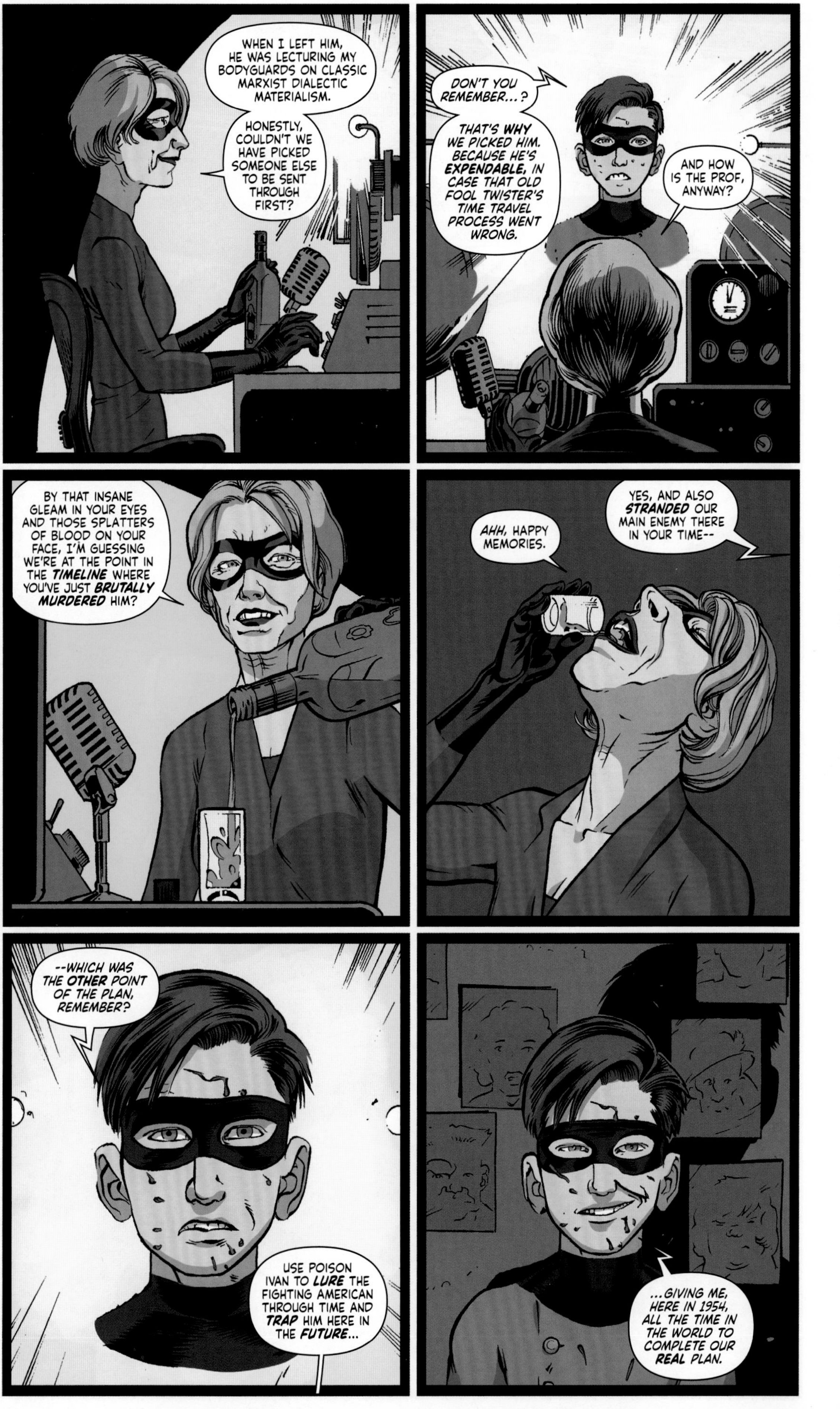

WHEN I LEFT HIM, HE WAS LECTURING MY BODYGUARDS ON CLASSIC MARXIST DIALECTIC MATERIALISM.
HONESTLY, COULDN'T WE HAVE PICKED SOMEONE ELSE TO BE SENT THROUGH FIRST?
DON'T YOU REMEMBER...?
THAT'S WHY WE PICKED HIM. BECAUSE HE'S EXPENDABLE, IN CASE THAT OLD FOOL TWISTER'S TIME TRAVEL PROCESS WENT WRONG.
AND HOW IS THE PROF, ANYWAY?
BY THAT INSANE GLEAM IN YOUR EYES AND THOSE SPLATTERS OF BLOOD ON YOUR FACE, I'M GUESSING WE'RE AT THE POINT IN THE TIMELINE WHERE YOU'VE JUST BRUTALLY MURDERED HIM?
YES, AND ALSO STRANDED OUR MAIN ENEMY THERE IN YOUR TIME--
AHH, HAPPY MEMORIES.
--WHICH WAS THE OTHER POINT OF THE PLAN, REMEMBER?
USE POISON IVAN TO LURE THE FIGHTING AMERICAN THROUGH TIME AND TRAP HIM HERE IN THE FUTURE...
...GIVING ME, HERE IN 1954, ALL THE TIME IN THE WORLD TO COMPLETE OUR REAL PLAN.

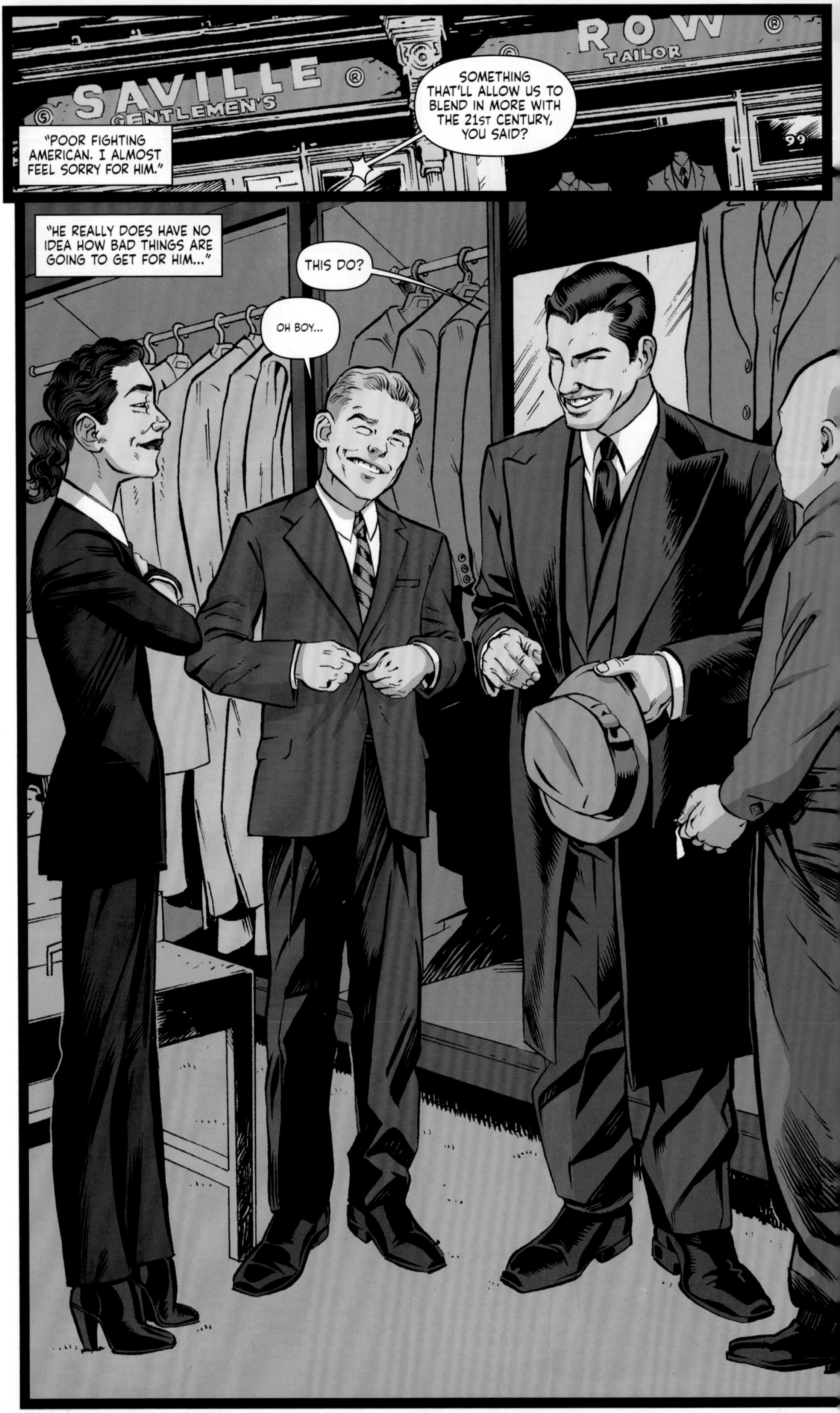

SAVILLE GENTLEMEN'S
ROW TAILOR
"POOR FIGHTING AMERICAN. I ALMOST FEEL SORRY FOR HIM."
SOMETHING THAT'LL ALLOW US TO BLEND IN MORE WITH THE 21ST CENTURY, YOU SAID?
"HE REALLY DOES HAVE NO IDEA HOW BAD THINGS ARE GOING TO GET FOR HIM..."
THIS DO?
OH BOY...

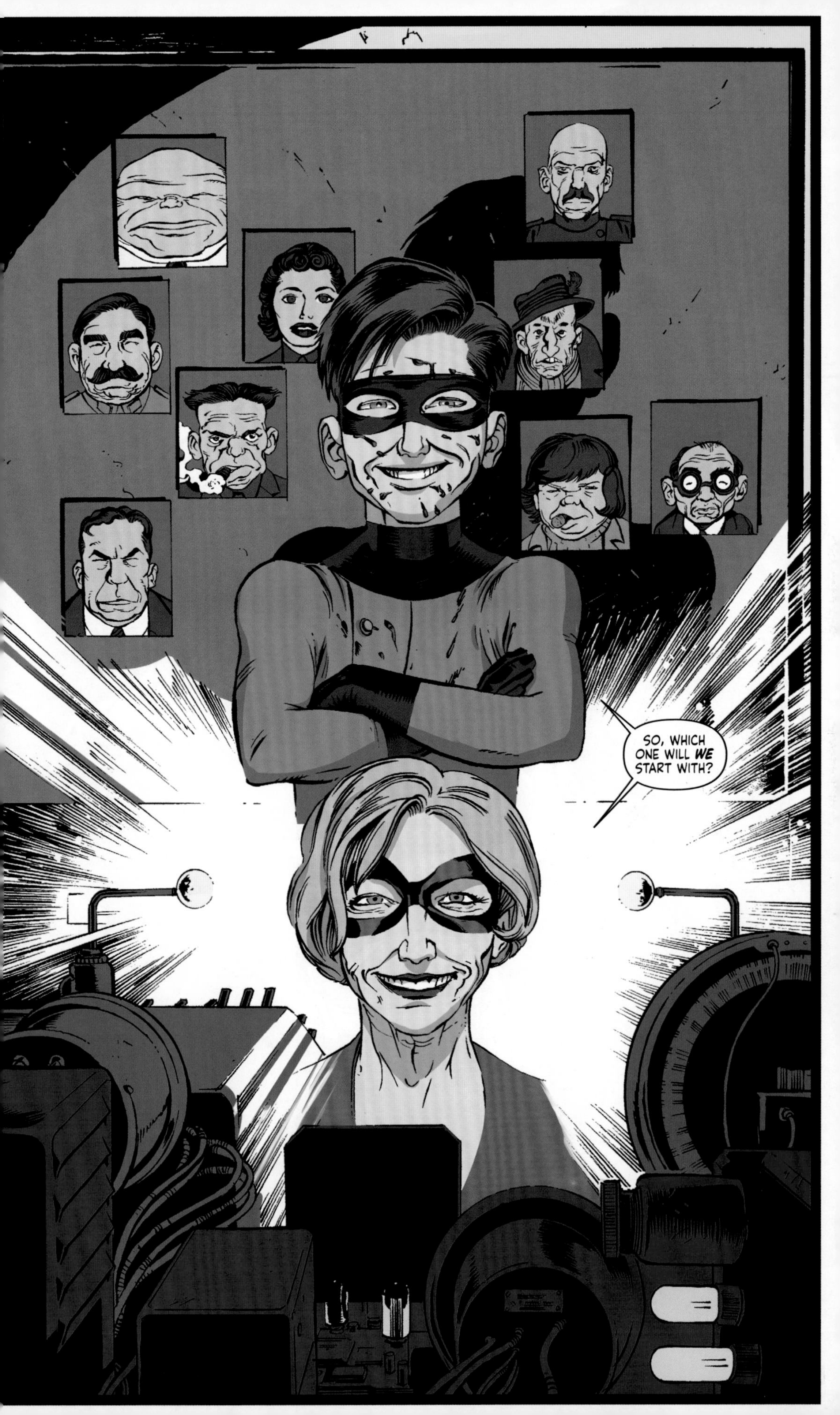
SO, WHICH ONE WILL *WE* START WITH?

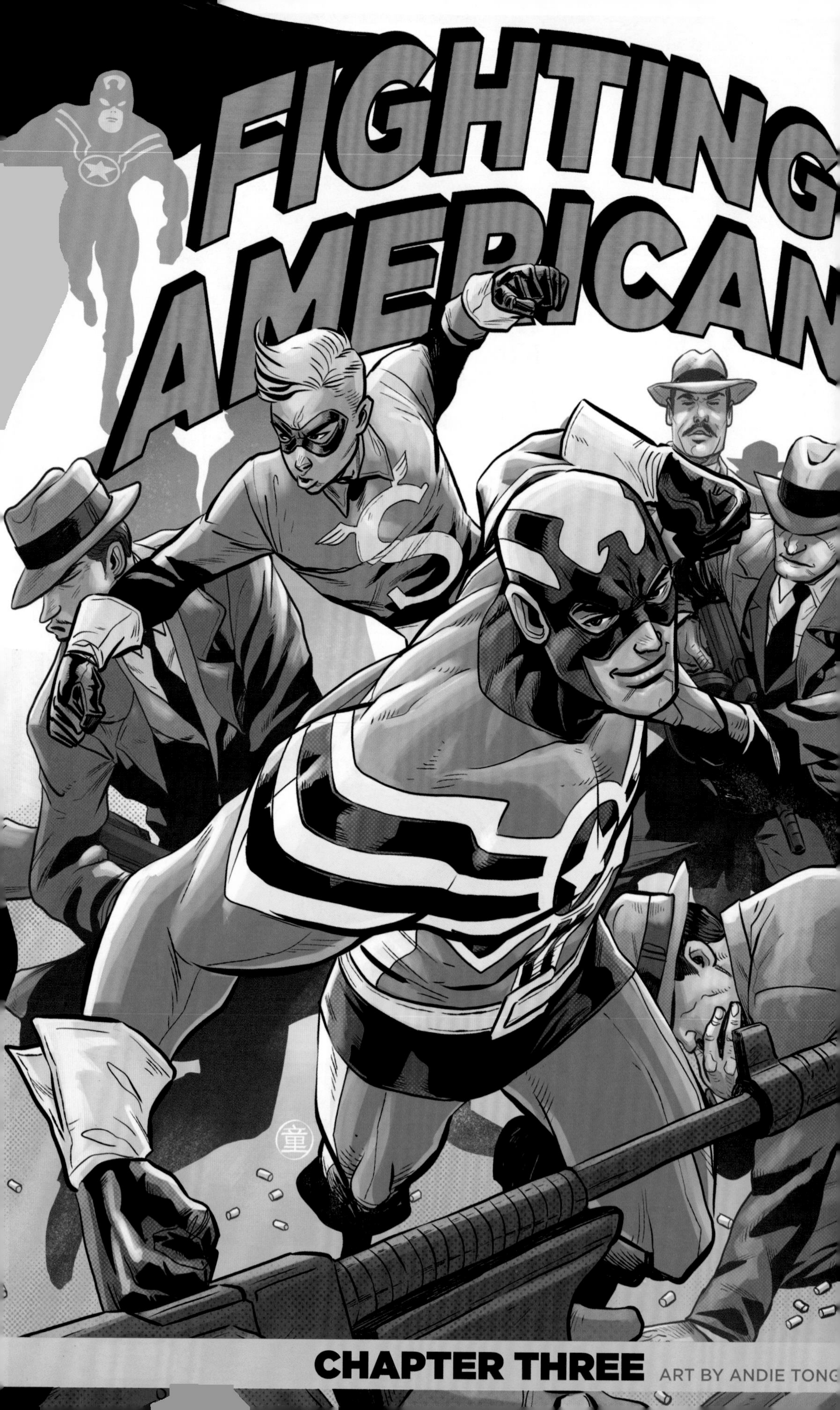
FIGHTING AMERICAN
CHAPTER THREE
ART BY ANDIE TONG

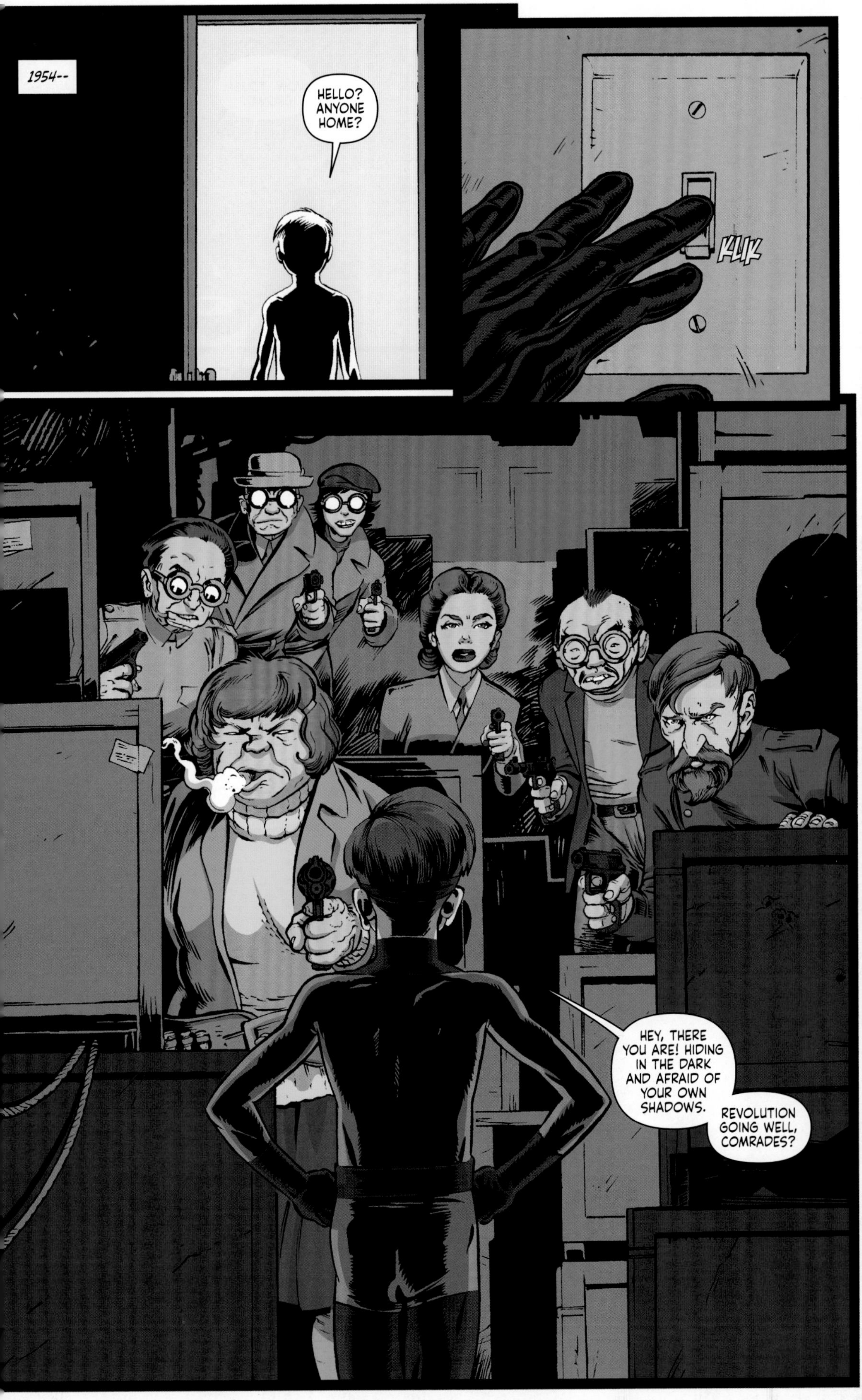
1954--
HELLO? ANYONE HOME?
KLIK
HEY, THERE YOU ARE! HIDING IN THE DARK AND AFRAID OF YOUR OWN SHADOWS.
REVOLUTION GOING WELL, COMRADES?

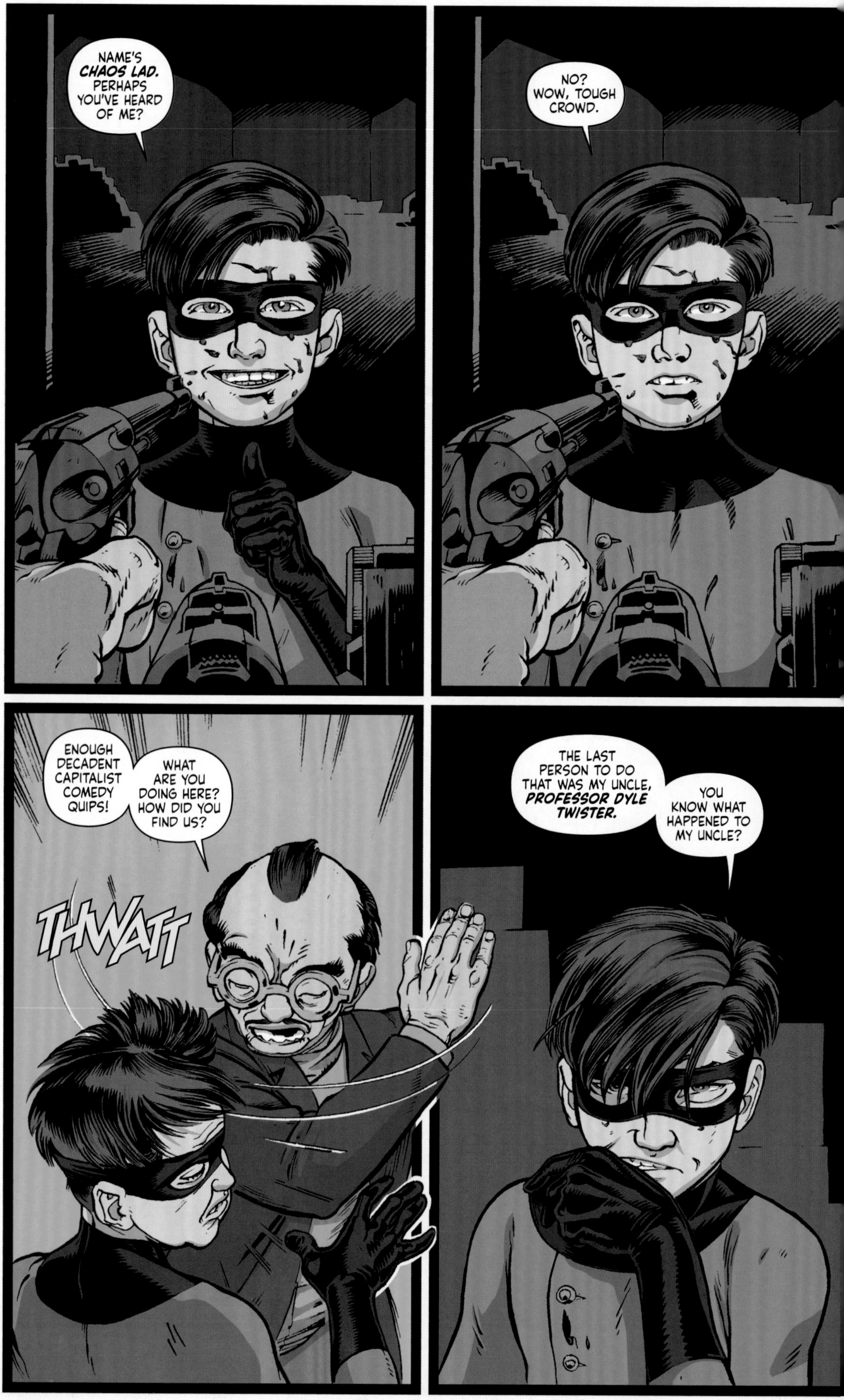
NAME'S CHAOS LAD. PERHAPS YOU'VE HEARD OF ME?
NO? WOW, TOUGH CROWD.
ENOUGH DECADENT CAPITALIST COMEDY QUIPS!
WHAT ARE YOU DOING HERE? HOW DID YOU FIND US?
THWATT
THE LAST PERSON TO DO THAT WAS MY UNCLE, PROFESSOR DYLE TWISTER.
YOU KNOW WHAT HAPPENED TO MY UNCLE?

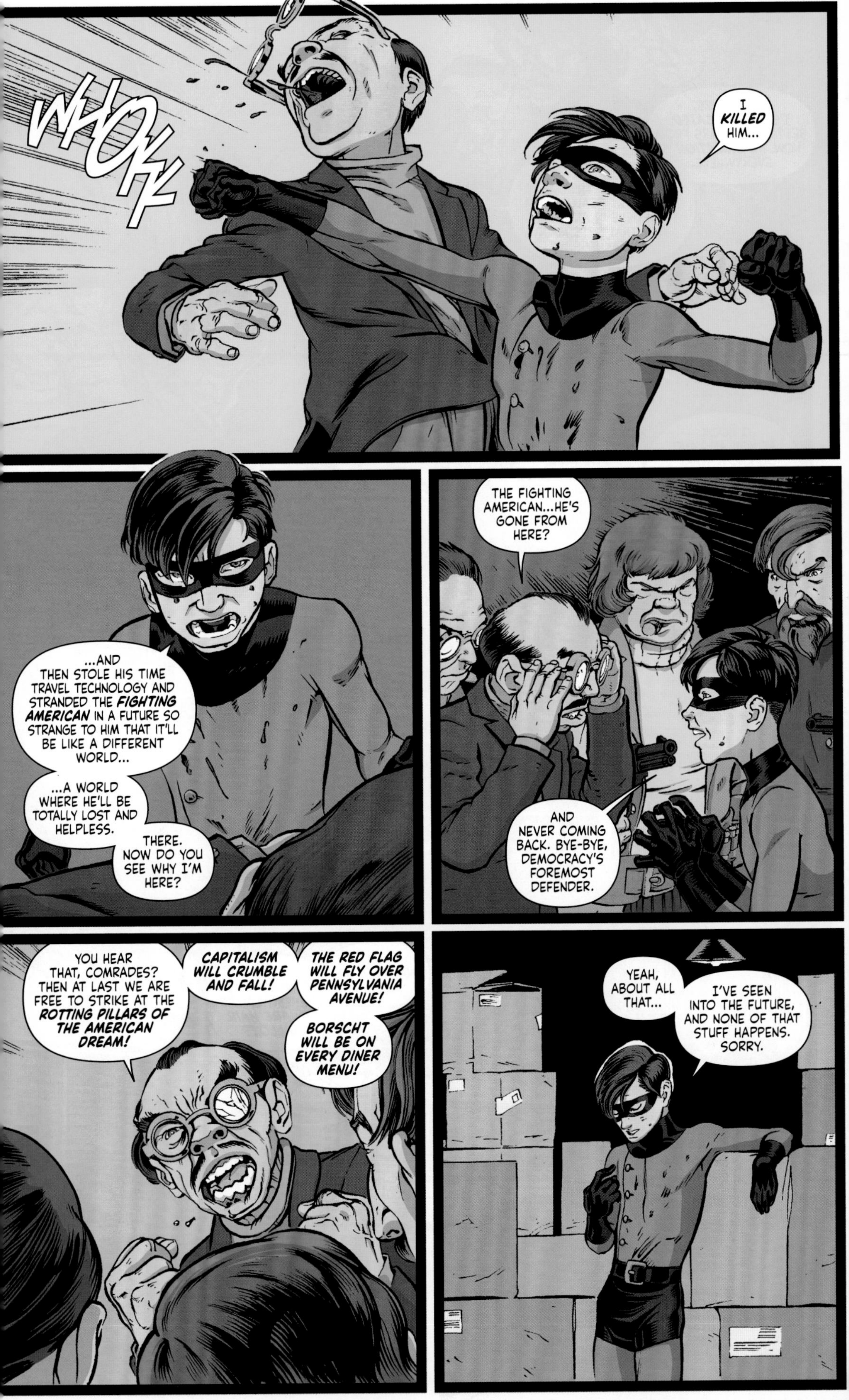

WHOKK
I KILLED HIM...
...AND THEN STOLE HIS TIME TRAVEL TECHNOLOGY AND STRANDED THE FIGHTING AMERICAN IN A FUTURE SO STRANGE TO HIM THAT IT'LL BE LIKE A DIFFERENT WORLD...
...A WORLD WHERE HE'LL BE TOTALLY LOST AND HELPLESS.
THERE. NOW DO YOU SEE WHY I'M HERE?
THE FIGHTING AMERICAN...HE'S GONE FROM HERE?
AND NEVER COMING BACK. BYE-BYE, DEMOCRACY'S FOREMOST DEFENDER.
YOU HEAR THAT, COMRADES? THEN AT LAST WE ARE FREE TO STRIKE AT THE ROTTING PILLARS OF THE AMERICAN DREAM!
CAPITALISM WILL CRUMBLE AND FALL!
THE RED FLAG WILL FLY OVER PENNSYLVANIA AVENUE!
BORSCHT WILL BE ON EVERY DINER MENU!
YEAH, ABOUT ALL THAT...
I'VE SEEN INTO THE FUTURE, AND NONE OF THAT STUFF HAPPENS. SORRY.

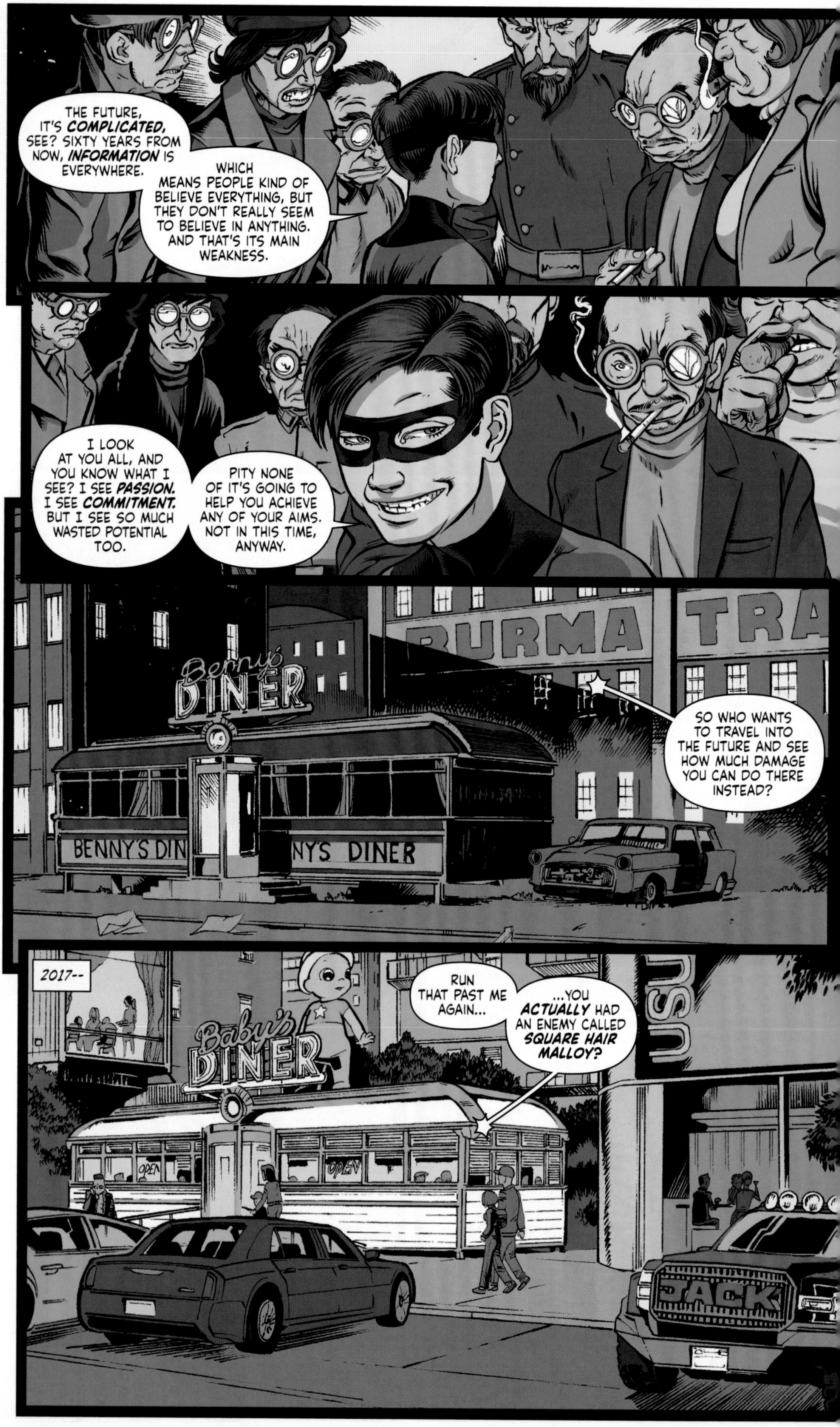
THE FUTURE, IT'S COMPLICATED, SEE? SIXTY YEARS FROM NOW, INFORMATION IS EVERYWHERE.
WHICH MEANS PEOPLE KIND OF BELIEVE EVERYTHING, BUT THEY DON'T REALLY SEEM TO BELIEVE IN ANYTHING. AND THAT'S ITS MAIN WEAKNESS.
I LOOK AT YOU ALL, AND YOU KNOW WHAT I SEE? I SEE PASSION. I SEE COMMITMENT. BUT I SEE SO MUCH WASTED POTENTIAL TOO.
PITY NONE OF IT'S GOING TO HELP YOU ACHIEVE ANY OF YOUR AIMS. NOT IN THIS TIME, ANYWAY.
Benny's DINER
BURMA TRA
BENNY'S DIN
NY'S DINER
SO WHO WANTS TO TRAVEL INTO THE FUTURE AND SEE HOW MUCH DAMAGE YOU CAN DO THERE INSTEAD?
2017--
Baby's DINER
OPEN
OPEN
RUN THAT PAST ME AGAIN...
...YOU ACTUALLY HAD AN ENEMY CALLED SQUARE HAIR MALLOY?
JACK

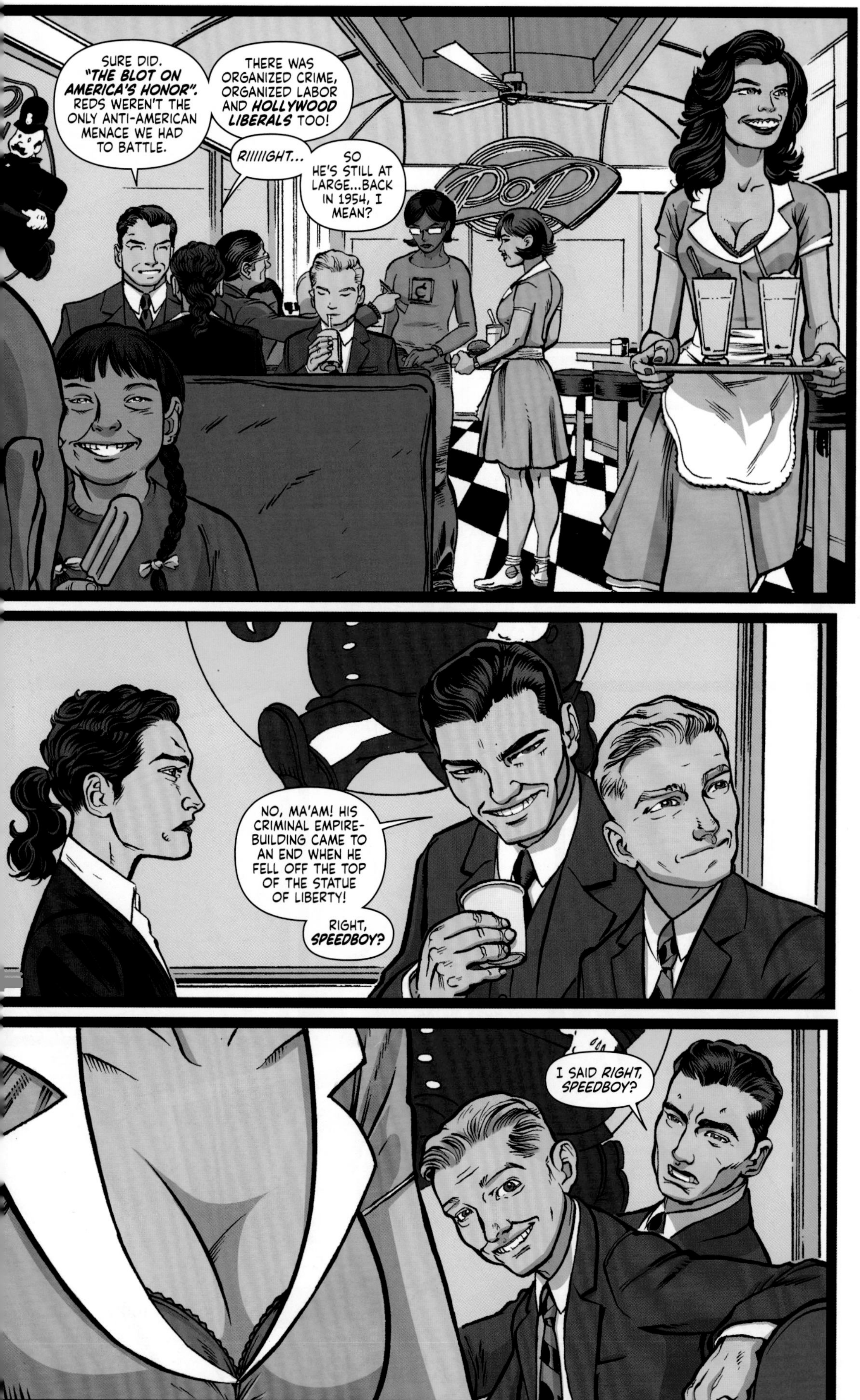
SURE DID. "THE BLOT ON AMERICA'S HONOR". REDS WEREN'T THE ONLY ANTI-AMERICAN MENACE WE HAD TO BATTLE.
THERE WAS ORGANIZED CRIME, ORGANIZED LABOR AND HOLLYWOOD LIBERALS TOO!
RIIIIIGHT...
SO HE'S STILL AT LARGE...BACK IN 1954, I MEAN?
NO, MA'AM! HIS CRIMINAL EMPIRE-BUILDING CAME TO AN END WHEN HE FELL OFF THE TOP OF THE STATUE OF LIBERTY!
RIGHT, SPEEDBOY?
I SAID RIGHT, SPEEDBOY?

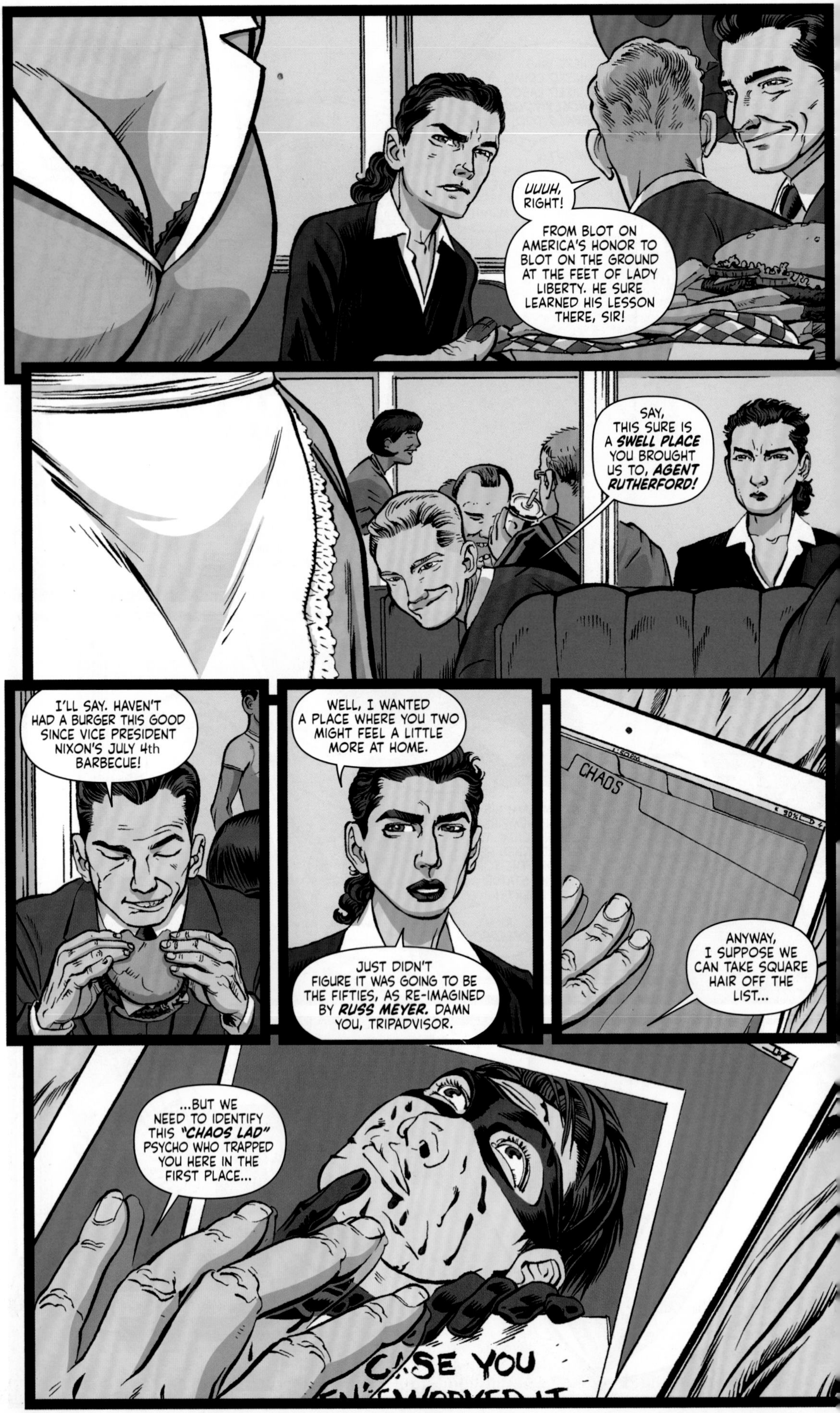
UUUH, RIGHT!
FROM BLOT ON AMERICA'S HONOR TO BLOT ON THE GROUND AT THE FEET OF LADY LIBERTY. HE SURE LEARNED HIS LESSON THERE, SIR!
SAY, THIS SURE IS A SWELL PLACE YOU BROUGHT US TO, AGENT RUTHERFORD!
I'LL SAY. HAVEN'T HAD A BURGER THIS GOOD SINCE VICE PRESIDENT NIXON'S JULY 4th BARBECUE!
WELL, I WANTED A PLACE WHERE YOU TWO MIGHT FEEL A LITTLE MORE AT HOME.
JUST DIDN'T FIGURE IT WAS GOING TO BE THE FIFTIES, AS RE-IMAGINED BY RUSS MEYER. DAMN YOU, TRIPADVISOR.
CHAOS
ANYWAY, I SUPPOSE WE CAN TAKE SQUARE HAIR OFF THE LIST...
...BUT WE NEED TO IDENTIFY THIS "CHAOS LAD" PSYCHO WHO TRAPPED YOU HERE IN THE FIRST PLACE...
CASE YOU

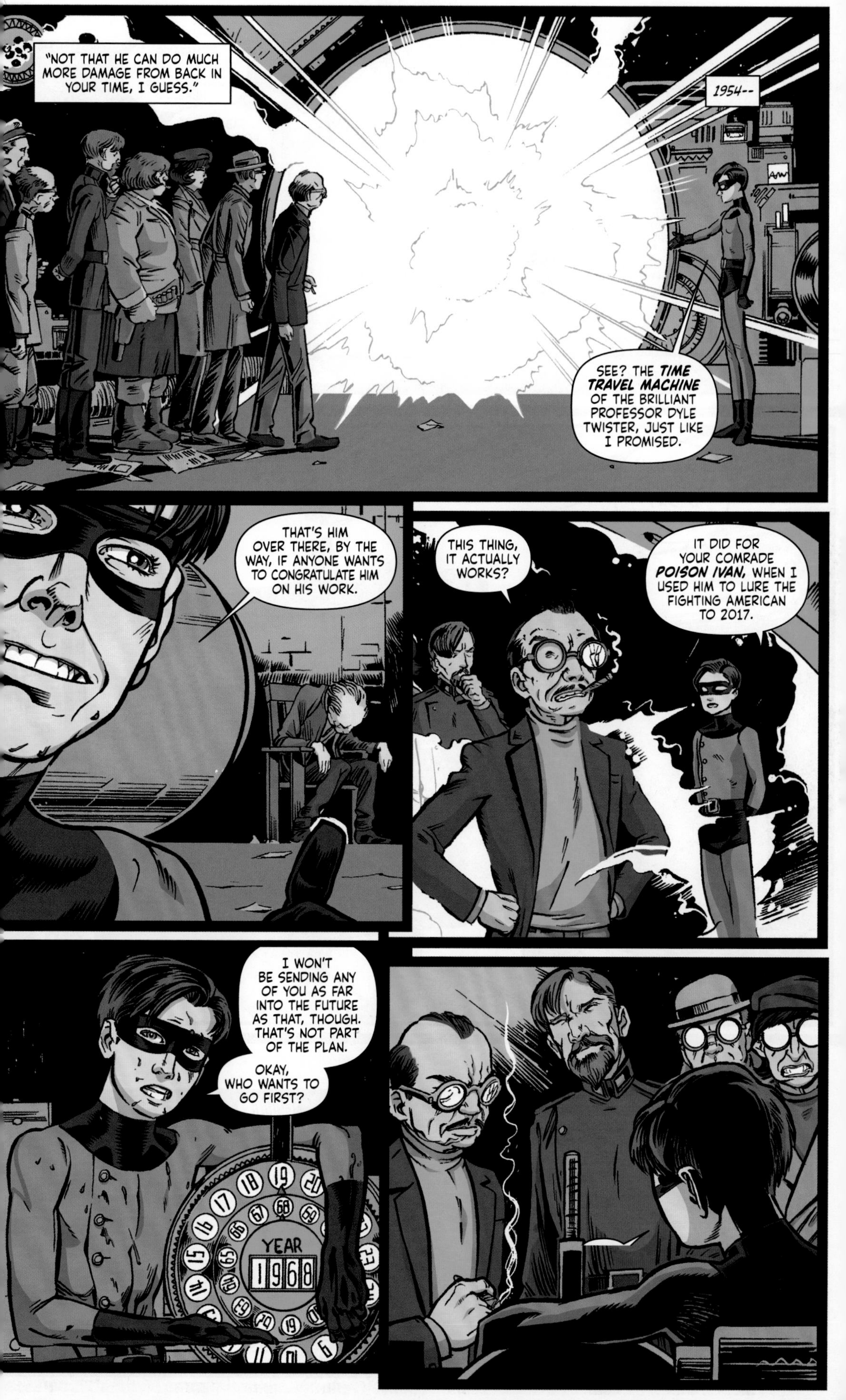
"NOT THAT HE CAN DO MUCH MORE DAMAGE FROM BACK IN YOUR TIME, I GUESS."
1954--
SEE? THE TIME TRAVEL MACHINE OF THE BRILLIANT PROFESSOR DYLE TWISTER, JUST LIKE I PROMISED.
THAT'S HIM OVER THERE, BY THE WAY, IF ANYONE WANTS TO CONGRATULATE HIM ON HIS WORK.
THIS THING, IT ACTUALLY WORKS?
IT DID FOR YOUR COMRADE POISON IVAN, WHEN I USED HIM TO LURE THE FIGHTING AMERICAN TO 2017.
I WON'T BE SENDING ANY OF YOU AS FAR INTO THE FUTURE AS THAT, THOUGH. THAT'S NOT PART OF THE PLAN.
OKAY, WHO WANTS TO GO FIRST?
YEAR
1968

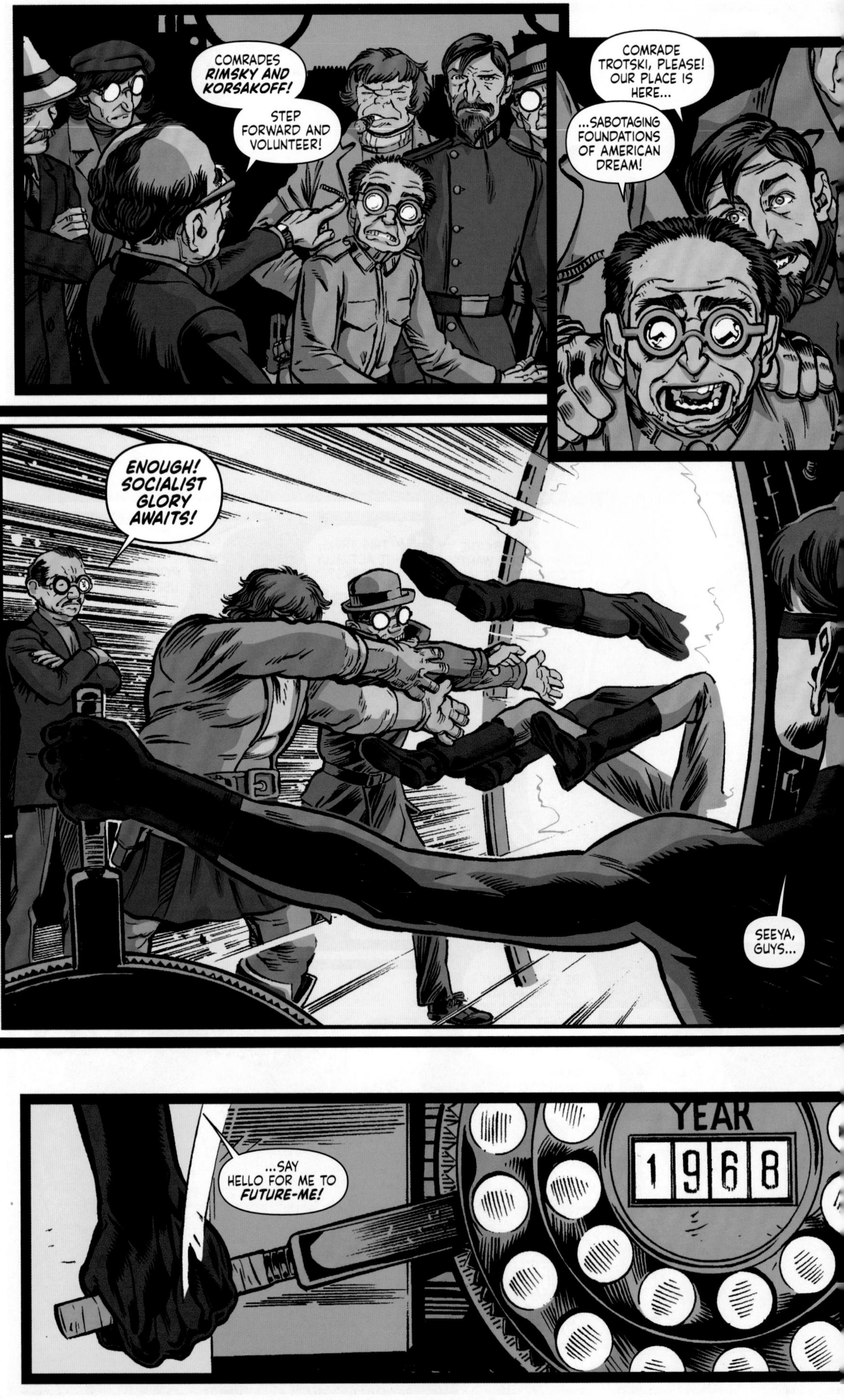
COMRADES *RIMSKY AND KORSAKOFF!*
STEP FORWARD AND VOLUNTEER!
COMRADE TROTSKI, PLEASE! OUR PLACE IS HERE...
...SABOTAGING FOUNDATIONS OF AMERICAN DREAM!
ENOUGH! SOCIALIST GLORY AWAITS!
SEEYA, GUYS...
...SAY HELLO FOR ME TO *FUTURE-ME!*
YEAR
1968

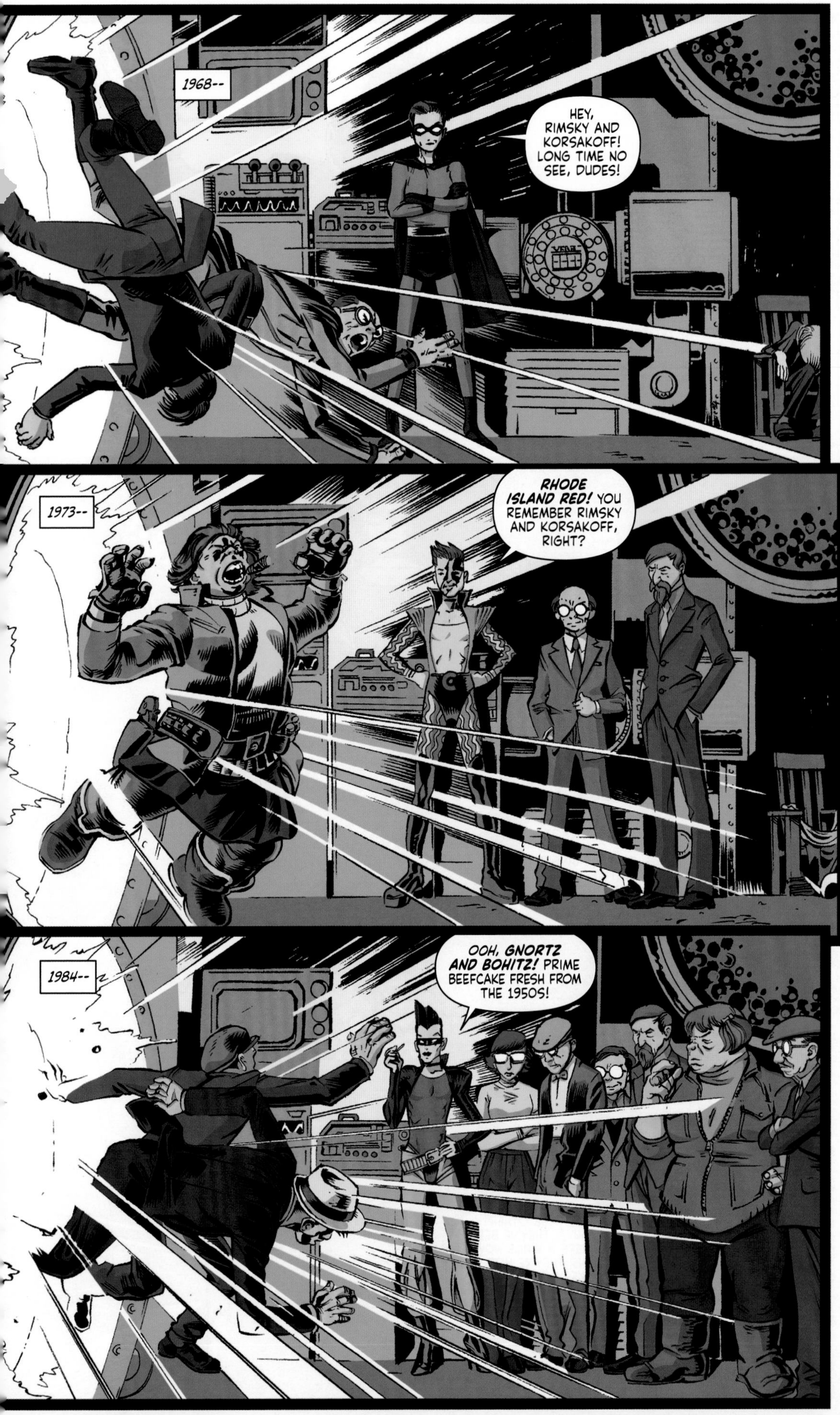
1968--
HEY, RIMSKY AND KORSAKOFF! LONG TIME NO SEE, DUDES!
1973--
RHODE ISLAND RED! YOU REMEMBER RIMSKY AND KORSAKOFF, RIGHT?
1984--
OOH, GNORTZ AND BOHITZ! PRIME BEEFCAKE FRESH FROM THE 1950S!

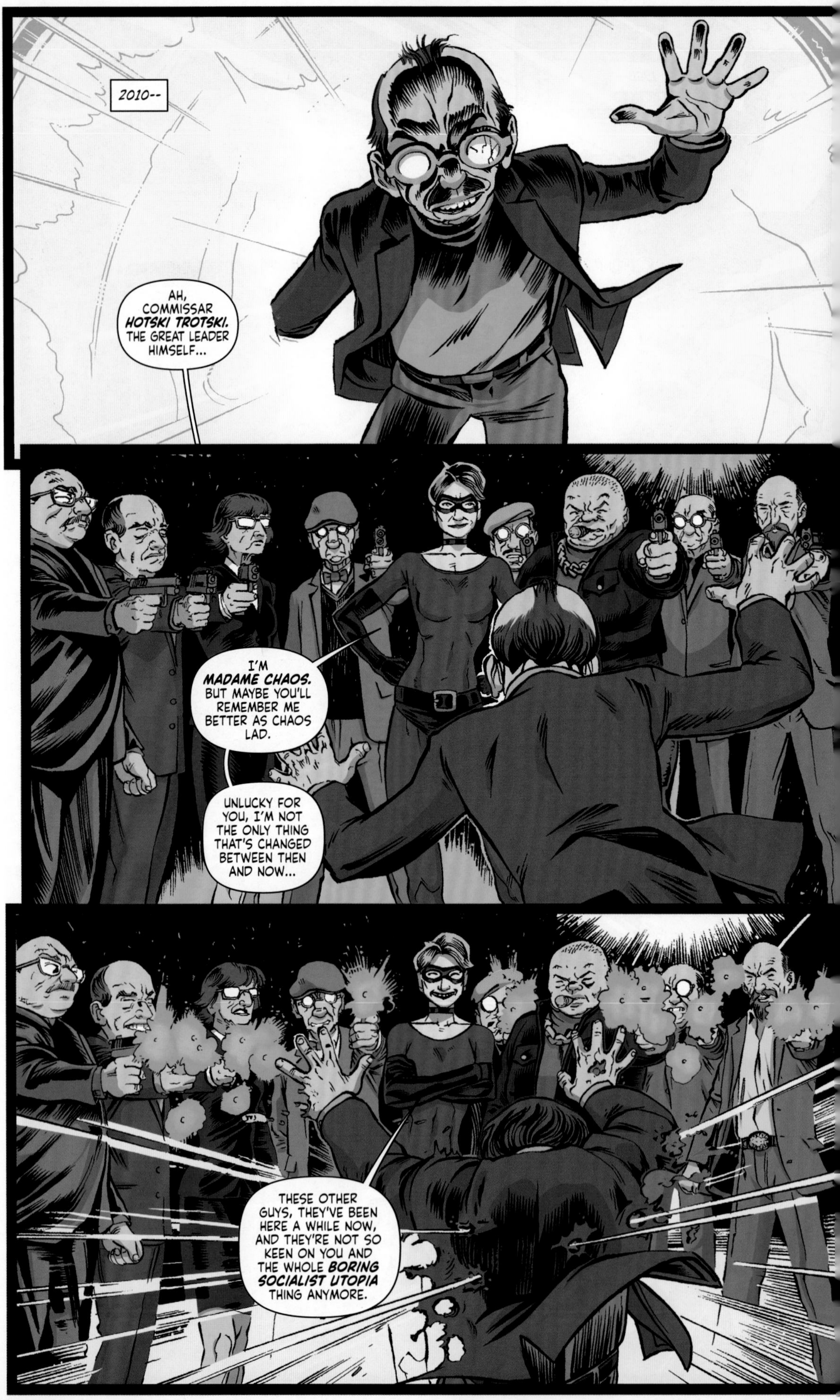
2010--
AH, COMMISSAR HOTSKI TROTSKI. THE GREAT LEADER HIMSELF...
I'M MADAME CHAOS. BUT MAYBE YOU'LL REMEMBER ME BETTER AS CHAOS LAD.
UNLUCKY FOR YOU, I'M NOT THE ONLY THING THAT'S CHANGED BETWEEN THEN AND NOW...
THESE OTHER GUYS, THEY'VE BEEN HERE A WHILE NOW, AND THEY'RE NOT SO KEEN ON YOU AND THE WHOLE BORING SOCIALIST UTOPIA THING ANYMORE.

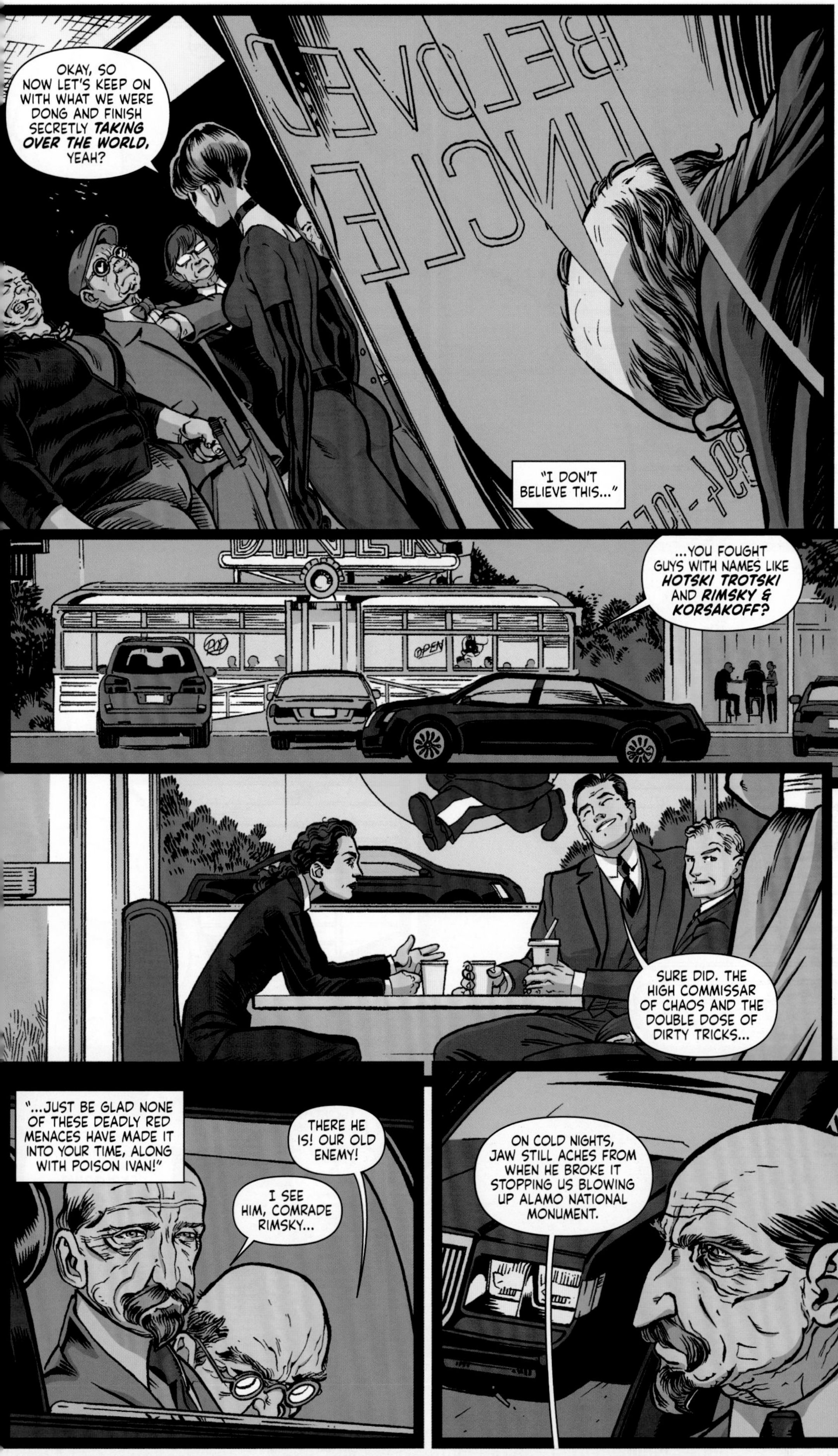

OKAY, SO NOW LET'S KEEP ON WITH WHAT WE WERE DONG AND FINISH SECRETLY TAKING OVER THE WORLD, YEAH?
BELOVED UNCLE
"I DON'T BELIEVE THIS..."
...YOU FOUGHT GUYS WITH NAMES LIKE HOTSKI TROTSKI AND RIMSKY & KORSAKOFF?
OPEN
SURE DID. THE HIGH COMMISSAR OF CHAOS AND THE DOUBLE DOSE OF DIRTY TRICKS...
"...JUST BE GLAD NONE OF THESE DEADLY RED MENACES HAVE MADE IT INTO YOUR TIME, ALONG WITH POISON IVAN!"
THERE HE IS! OUR OLD ENEMY!
I SEE HIM, COMRADE RIMSKY...
ON COLD NIGHTS, JAW STILL ACHES FROM WHEN HE BROKE IT STOPPING US BLOWING UP ALAMO NATIONAL MONUMENT.

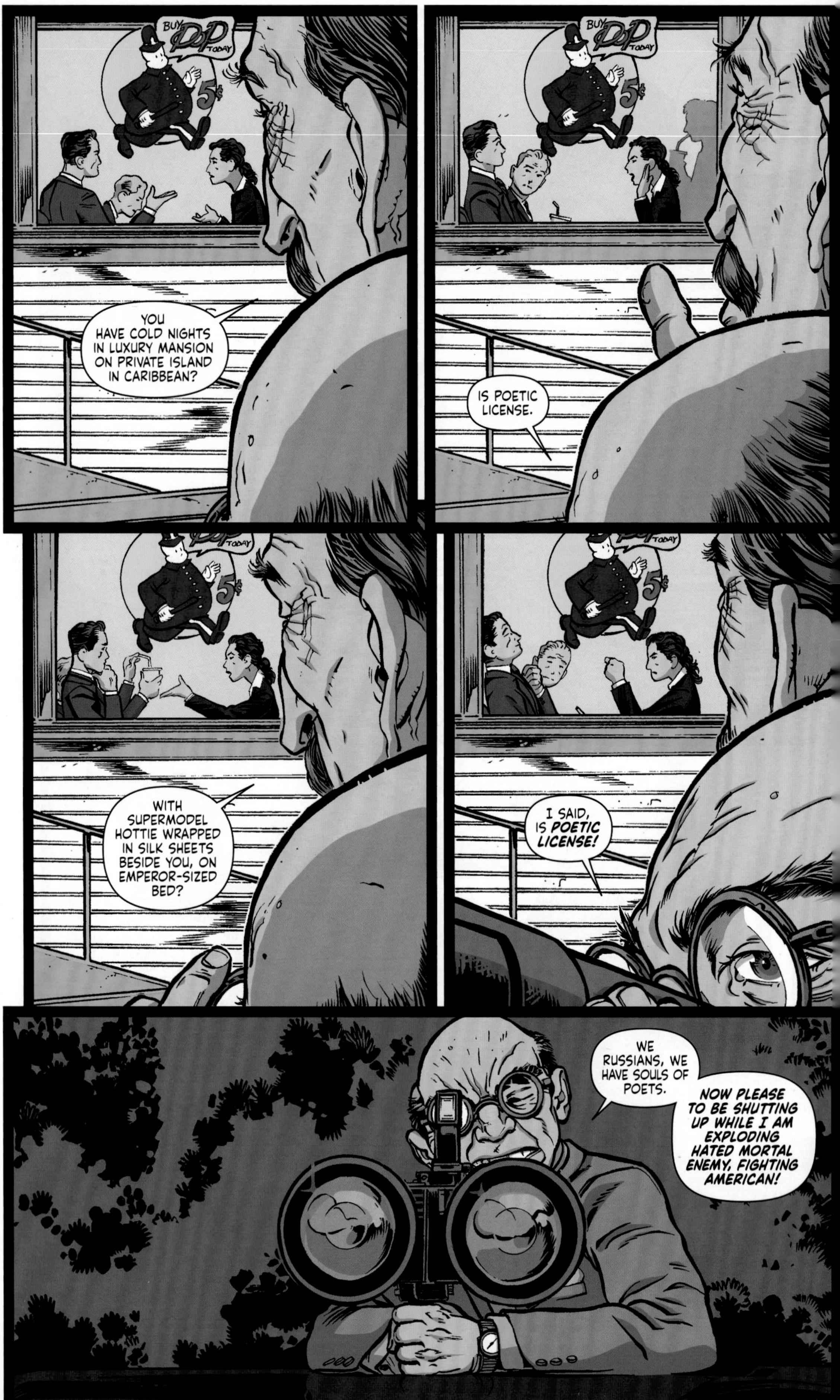
BUY DoP TODAY
5¢
YOU HAVE COLD NIGHTS IN LUXURY MANSION ON PRIVATE ISLAND IN CARIBBEAN?
IS POETIC LICENSE.
WITH SUPERMODEL HOTTIE WRAPPED IN SILK SHEETS BESIDE YOU, ON EMPEROR-SIZED BED?
I SAID, IS *POETIC LICENSE!*
WE RUSSIANS, WE HAVE SOULS OF POETS.
NOW PLEASE TO BE SHUTTING UP WHILE I AM EXPLODING HATED MORTAL ENEMY, FIGHTING AMERICAN!

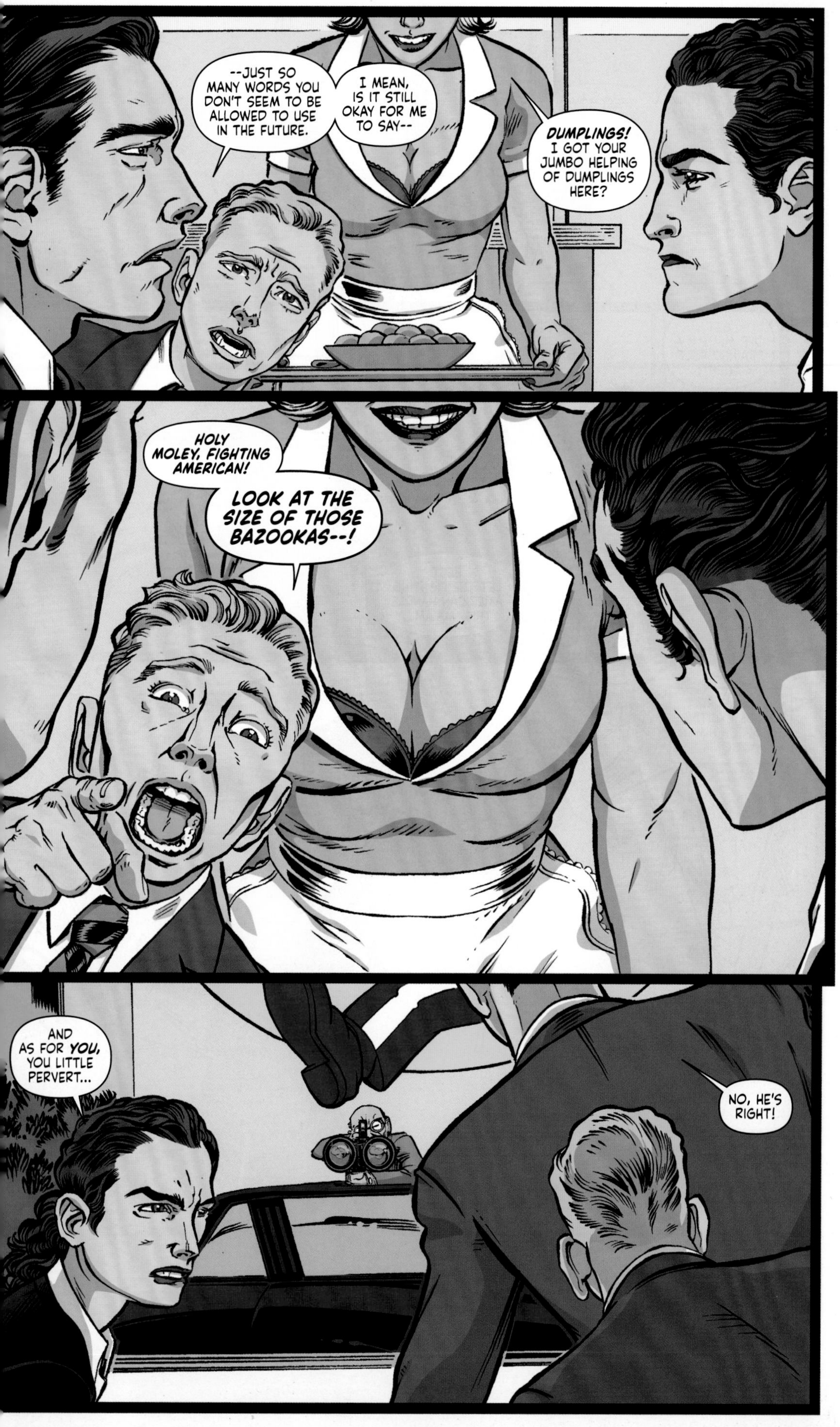
--JUST SO MANY WORDS YOU DON'T SEEM TO BE ALLOWED TO USE IN THE FUTURE.
I MEAN, IS IT STILL OKAY FOR ME TO SAY--
DUMPLINGS! I GOT YOUR JUMBO HELPING OF DUMPLINGS HERE?
HOLY MOLEY, FIGHTING AMERICAN!
LOOK AT THE SIZE OF THOSE BAZOOKAS--!
AND AS FOR YOU, YOU LITTLE PERVERT...
NO, HE'S RIGHT!

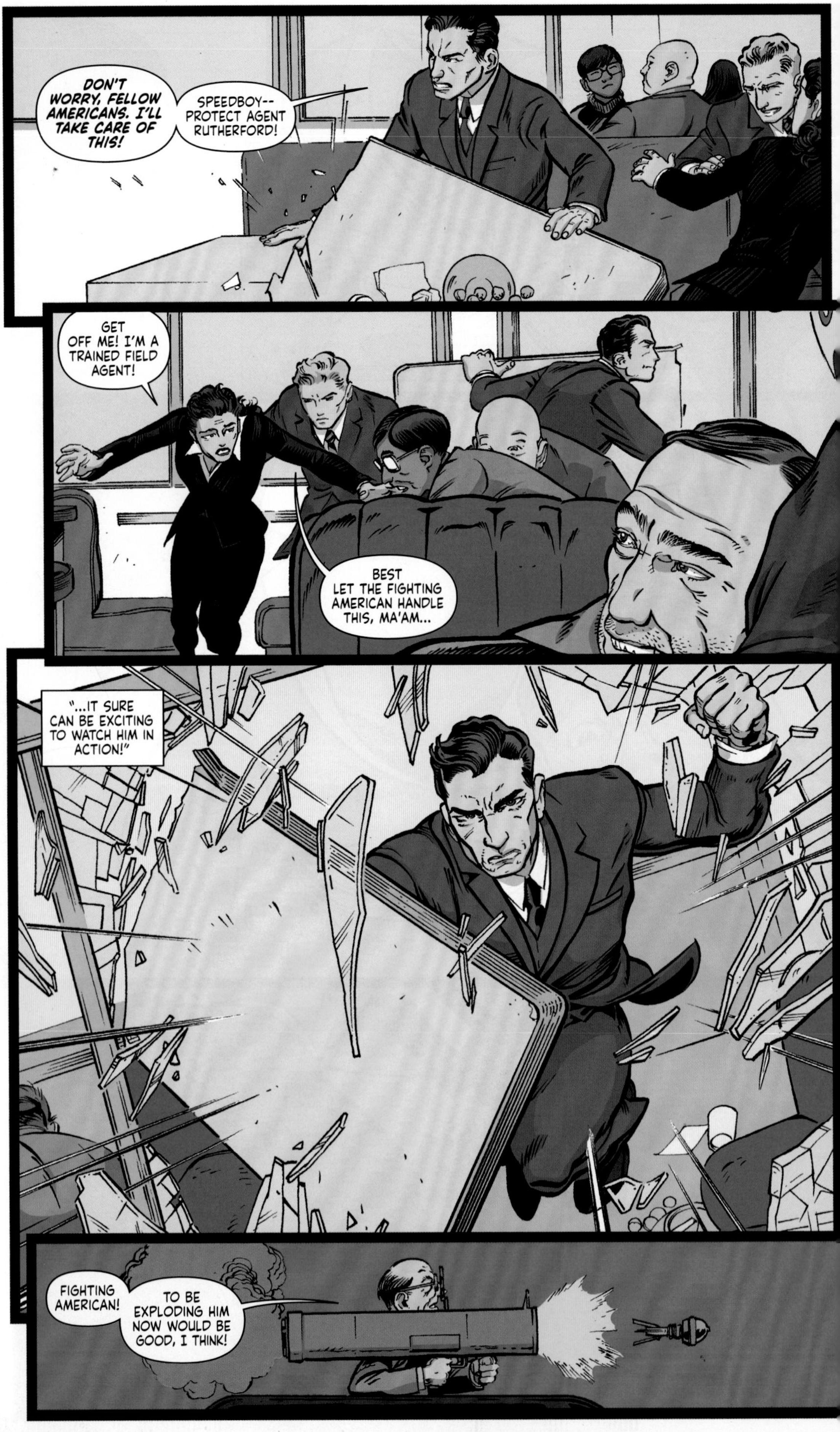
DON'T WORRY, FELLOW AMERICANS. I'LL TAKE CARE OF THIS!
SPEEDBOY-- PROTECT AGENT RUTHERFORD!
GET OFF ME! I'M A TRAINED FIELD AGENT!
BEST LET THE FIGHTING AMERICAN HANDLE THIS, MA'AM...
"...IT SURE CAN BE EXCITING TO WATCH HIM IN ACTION!"
FIGHTING AMERICAN!
TO BE EXPLODING HIM NOW WOULD BE GOOD, I THINK!

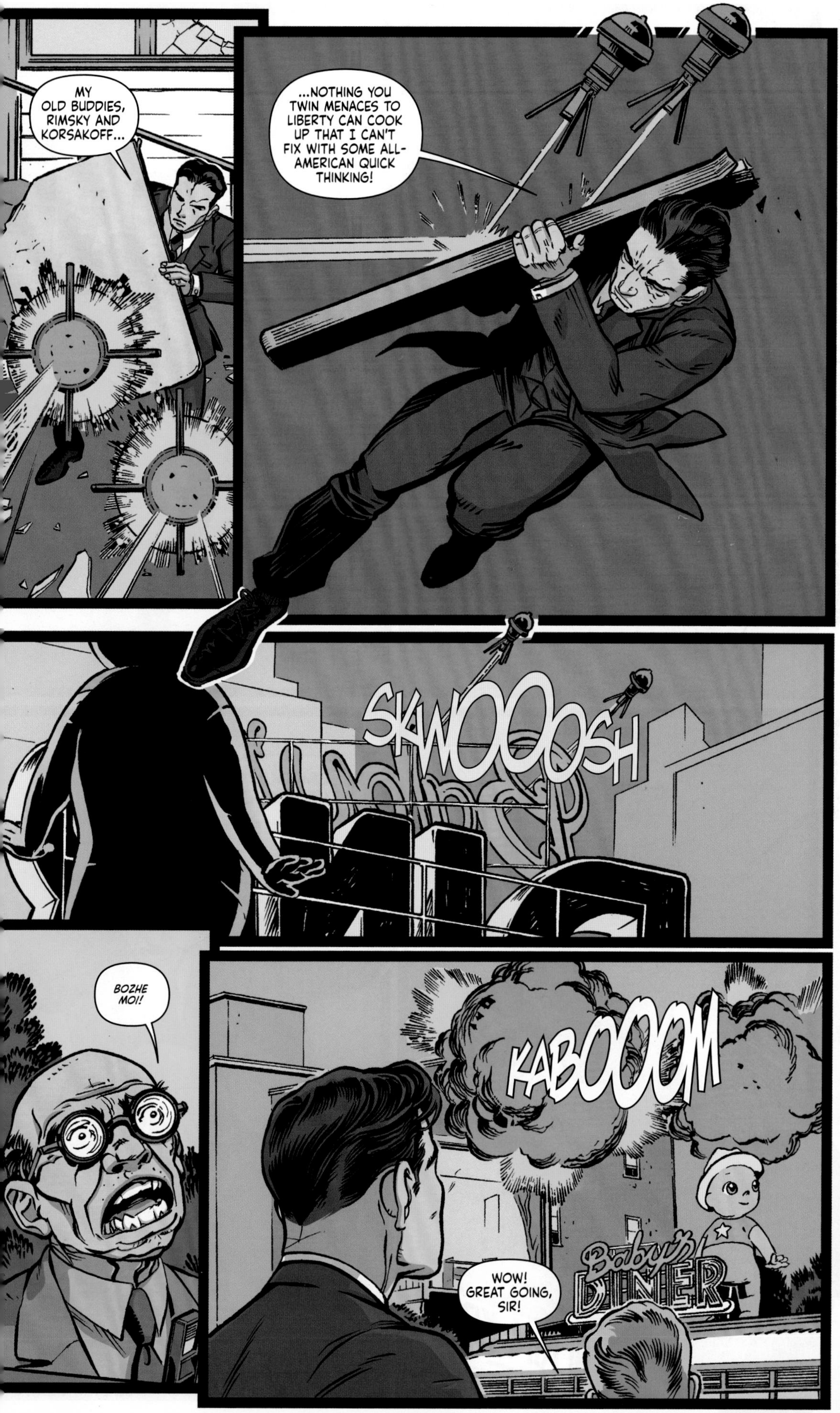
MY OLD BUDDIES, RIMSKY AND KORSAKOFF...
...NOTHING YOU TWIN MENACES TO LIBERTY CAN COOK UP THAT I CAN'T FIX WITH SOME ALL-AMERICAN QUICK THINKING!
SKWOOOSH
BOZHE MOI!
KABOOOM
Baby's DINER
WOW! GREAT GOING, SIR!

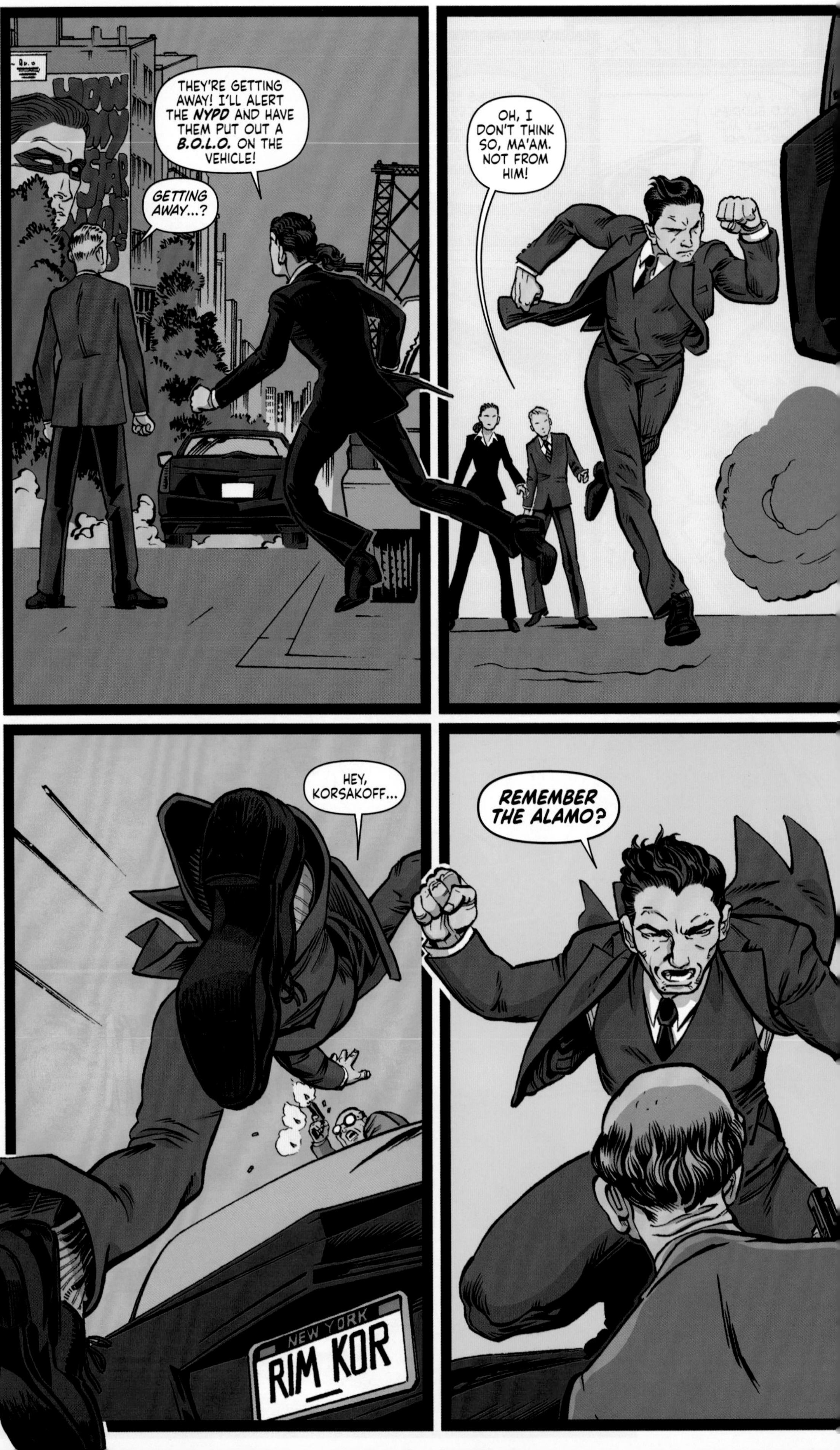
THEY'RE GETTING AWAY! I'LL ALERT THE NYPD AND HAVE THEM PUT OUT A B.O.L.O. ON THE VEHICLE!
GETTING AWAY...?
OH, I DON'T THINK SO, MA'AM. NOT FROM HIM!
HEY, KORSAKOFF...
NEW YORK
RIM KOR
REMEMBER THE ALAMO?

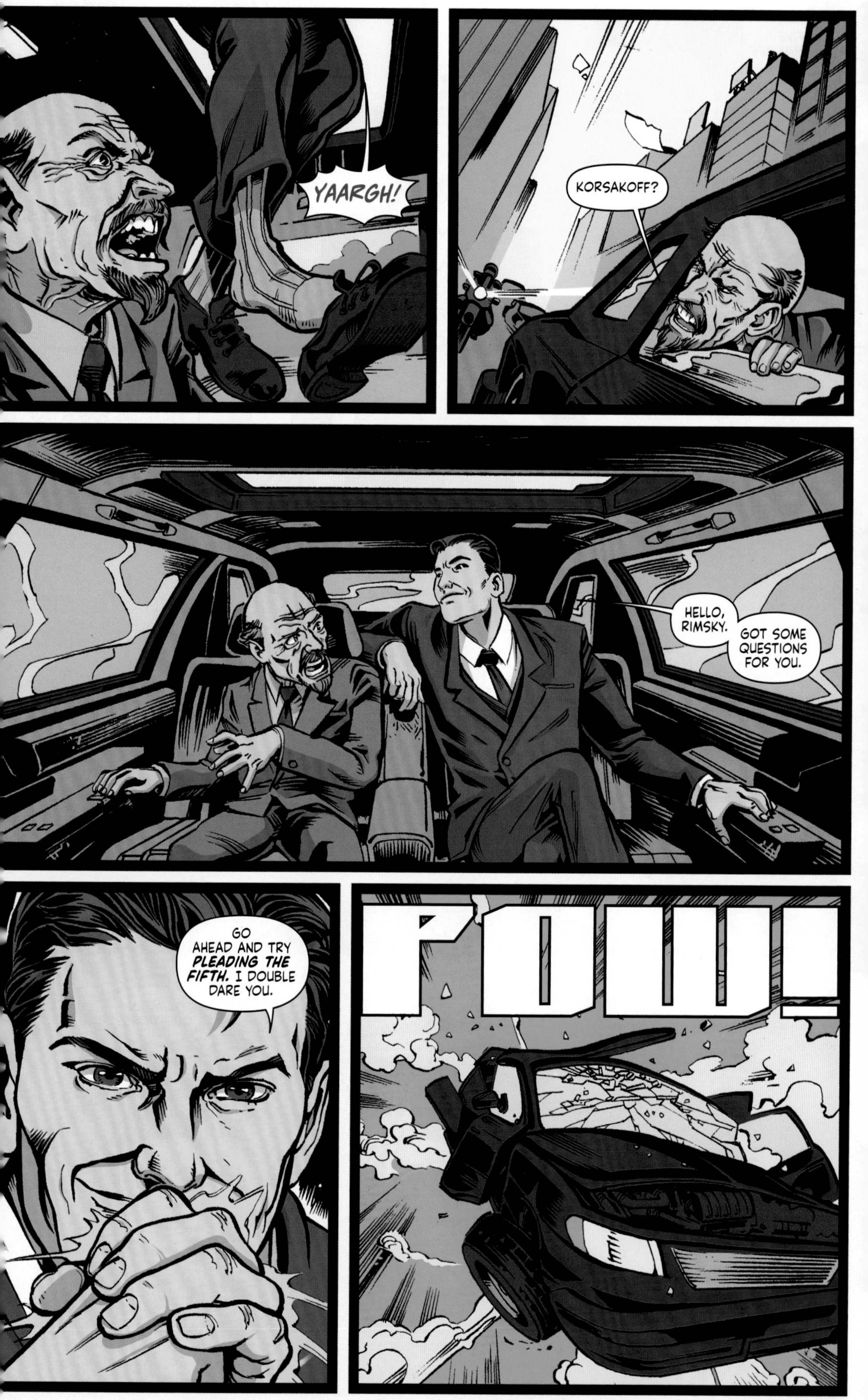
YAARGH!
KORSAKOFF?
HELLO, RIMSKY.
GOT SOME QUESTIONS FOR YOU.
GO AHEAD AND TRY *PLEADING THE FIFTH.* I DOUBLE DARE YOU.
POW!

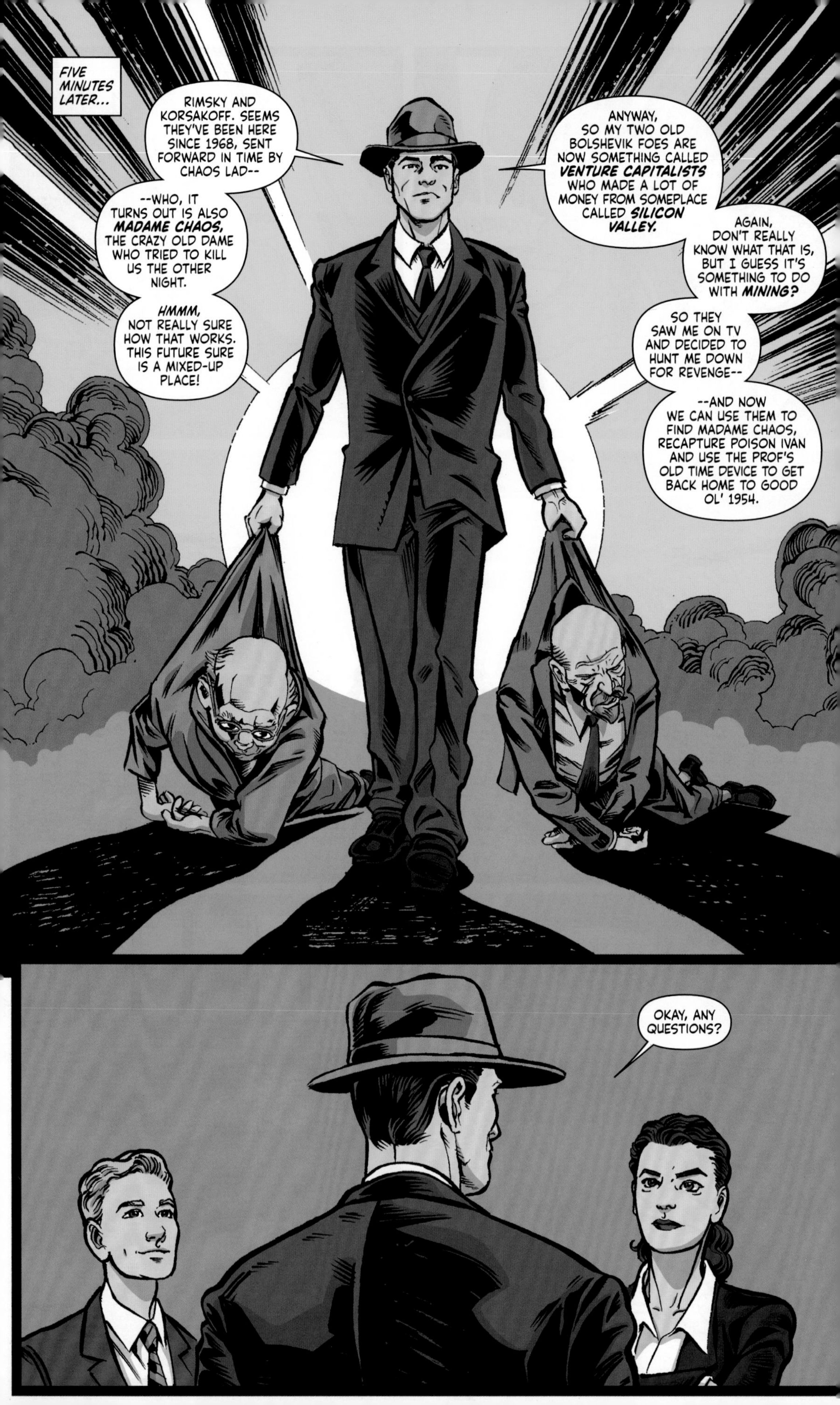
FIVE MINUTES LATER...
RIMSKY AND KORSAKOFF. SEEMS THEY'VE BEEN HERE SINCE 1968, SENT FORWARD IN TIME BY CHAOS LAD--
--WHO, IT TURNS OUT IS ALSO **MADAME CHAOS,** THE CRAZY OLD DAME WHO TRIED TO KILL US THE OTHER NIGHT.
HMMM, NOT REALLY SURE HOW THAT WORKS. THIS FUTURE SURE IS A MIXED-UP PLACE!
ANYWAY, SO MY TWO OLD BOLSHEVIK FOES ARE NOW SOMETHING CALLED **VENTURE CAPITALISTS** WHO MADE A LOT OF MONEY FROM SOMEPLACE CALLED **SILICON VALLEY.**
AGAIN, DON'T REALLY KNOW WHAT THAT IS, BUT I GUESS IT'S SOMETHING TO DO WITH **MINING?**
SO THEY SAW ME ON TV AND DECIDED TO HUNT ME DOWN FOR REVENGE--
--AND NOW WE CAN USE THEM TO FIND MADAME CHAOS, RECAPTURE POISON IVAN AND USE THE PROF'S OLD TIME DEVICE TO GET BACK HOME TO GOOD OL' 1954.
OKAY, ANY QUESTIONS?

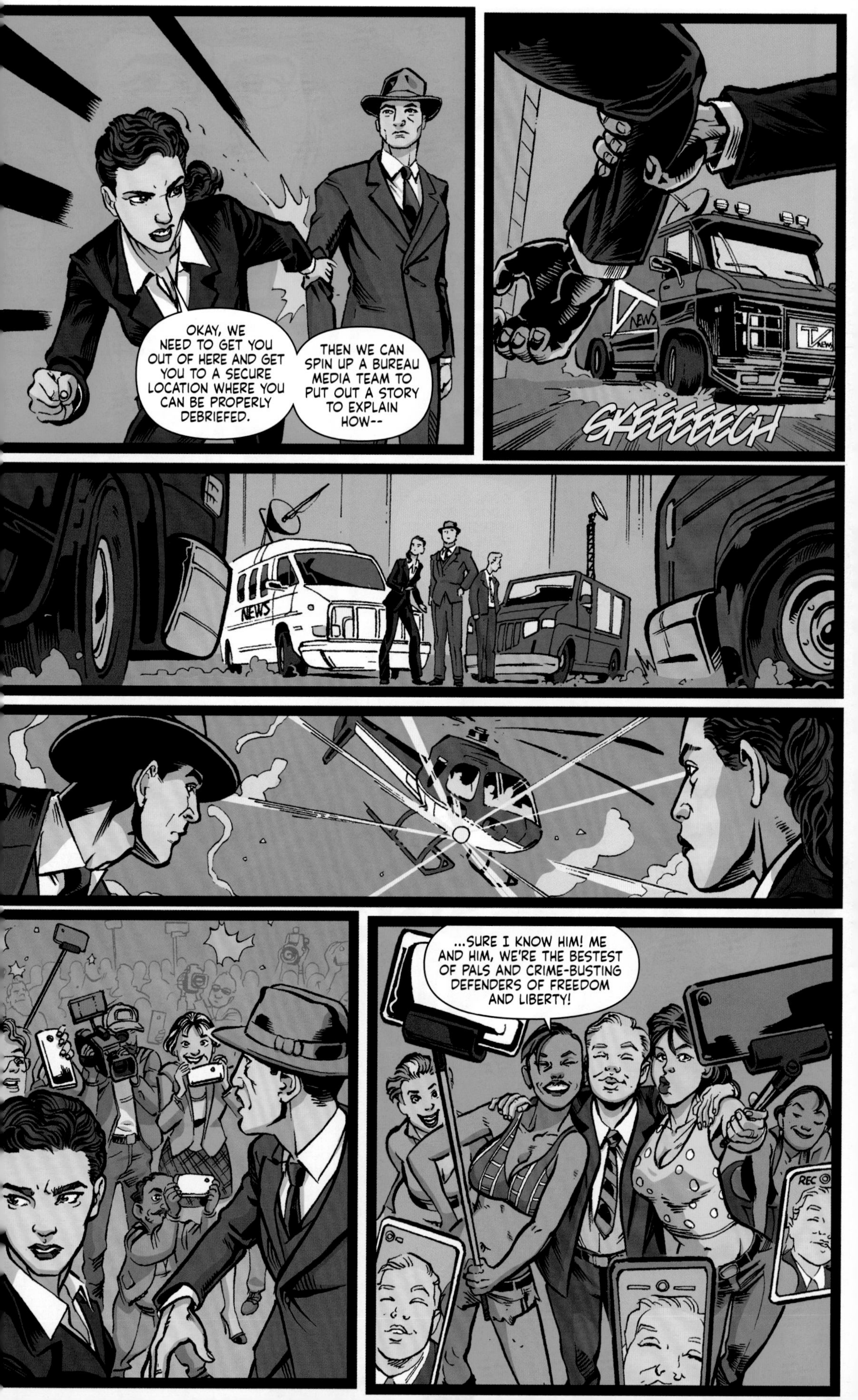
OKAY, WE NEED TO GET YOU OUT OF HERE AND GET YOU TO A SECURE LOCATION WHERE YOU CAN BE PROPERLY DEBRIEFED.
THEN WE CAN SPIN UP A BUREAU MEDIA TEAM TO PUT OUT A STORY TO EXPLAIN HOW--
NEWS
SKEEEEEECH
NEWS
...SURE I KNOW HIM! ME AND HIM, WE'RE THE BESTEST OF PALS AND CRIME-BUSTING DEFENDERS OF FREEDOM AND LIBERTY!
REC

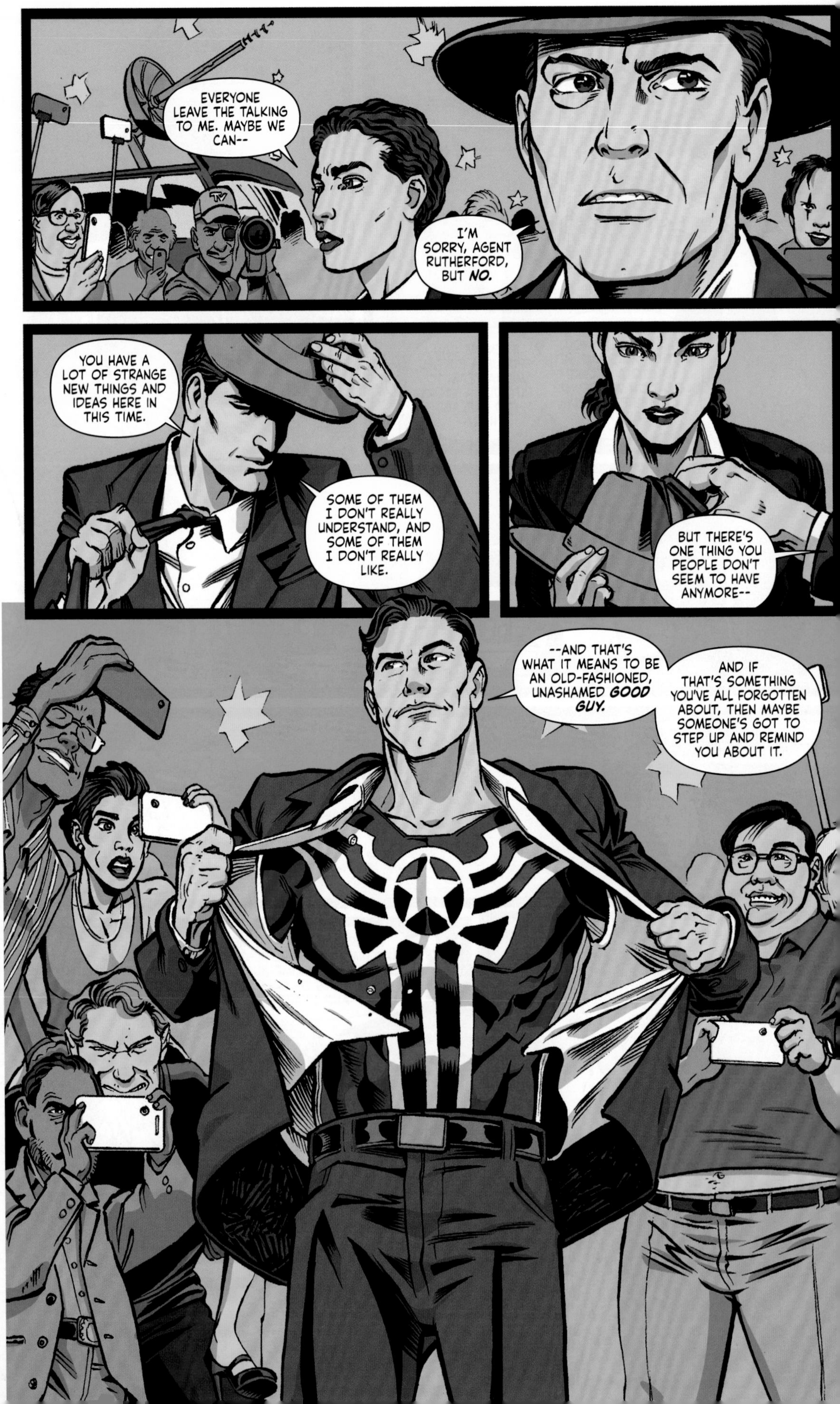
EVERYONE LEAVE THE TALKING TO ME. MAYBE WE CAN--
I'M SORRY, AGENT RUTHERFORD, BUT **NO.**
YOU HAVE A LOT OF STRANGE NEW THINGS AND IDEAS HERE IN THIS TIME.
SOME OF THEM I DON'T REALLY UNDERSTAND, AND SOME OF THEM I DON'T REALLY LIKE.
BUT THERE'S ONE THING YOU PEOPLE DON'T SEEM TO HAVE ANYMORE--
--AND THAT'S WHAT IT MEANS TO BE AN OLD-FASHIONED, UNASHAMED ***GOOD GUY.***
AND IF THAT'S SOMETHING YOU'VE ALL FORGOTTEN ABOUT, THEN MAYBE SOMEONE'S GOT TO STEP UP AND REMIND YOU ABOUT IT.

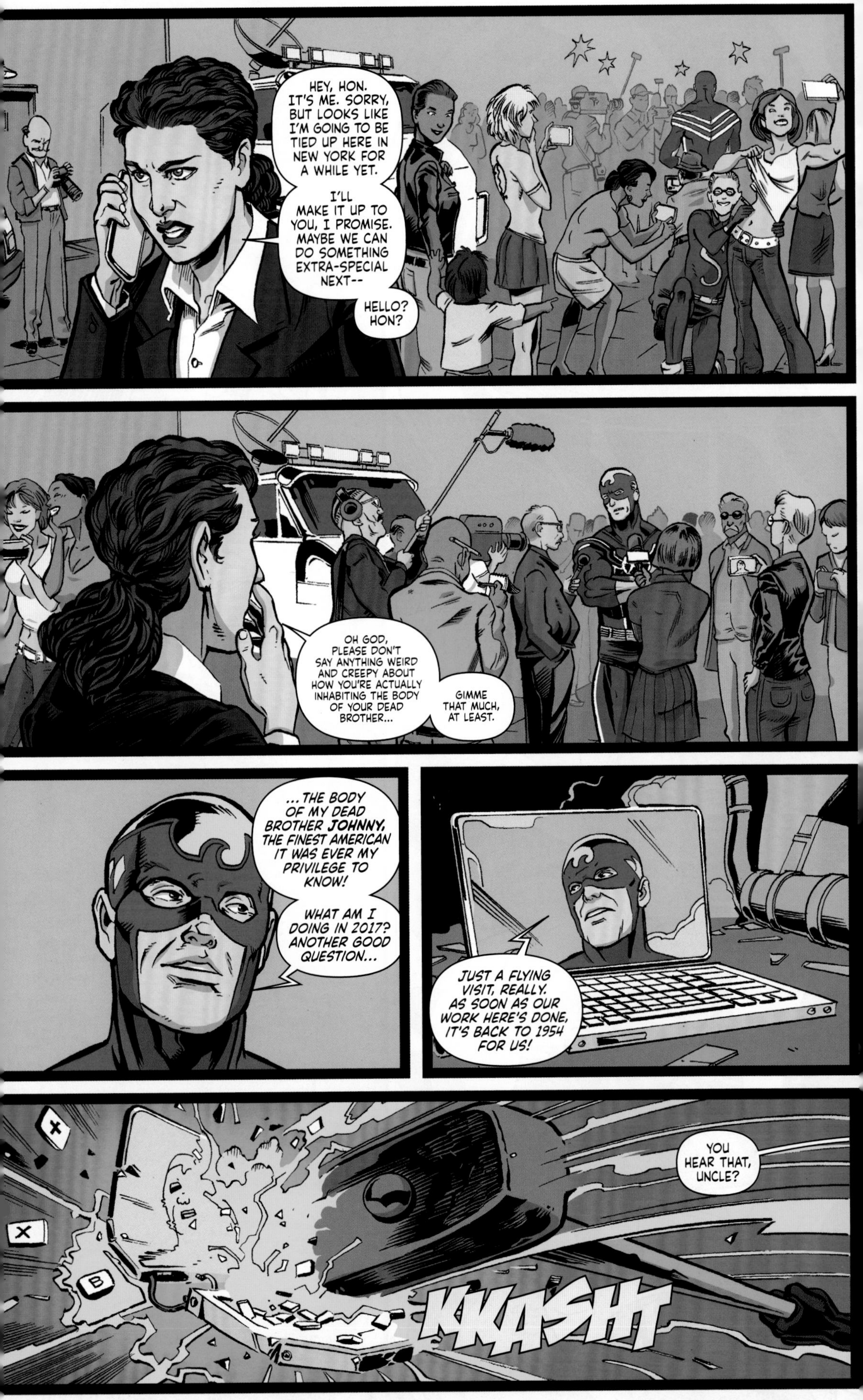
HEY, HON. IT'S ME. SORRY, BUT LOOKS LIKE I'M GOING TO BE TIED UP HERE IN NEW YORK FOR A WHILE YET.
I'LL MAKE IT UP TO YOU, I PROMISE. MAYBE WE CAN DO SOMETHING EXTRA-SPECIAL NEXT--
HELLO? HON?
OH GOD, PLEASE DON'T SAY ANYTHING WEIRD AND CREEPY ABOUT HOW YOU'RE ACTUALLY INHABITING THE BODY OF YOUR DEAD BROTHER...
GIMME THAT MUCH, AT LEAST.
...THE BODY OF MY DEAD BROTHER JOHNNY, THE FINEST AMERICAN IT WAS EVER MY PRIVILEGE TO KNOW!
WHAT AM I DOING IN 2017? ANOTHER GOOD QUESTION...
JUST A FLYING VISIT, REALLY. AS SOON AS OUR WORK HERE'S DONE, IT'S BACK TO 1954 FOR US!
YOU HEAR THAT, UNCLE?
KKASHT

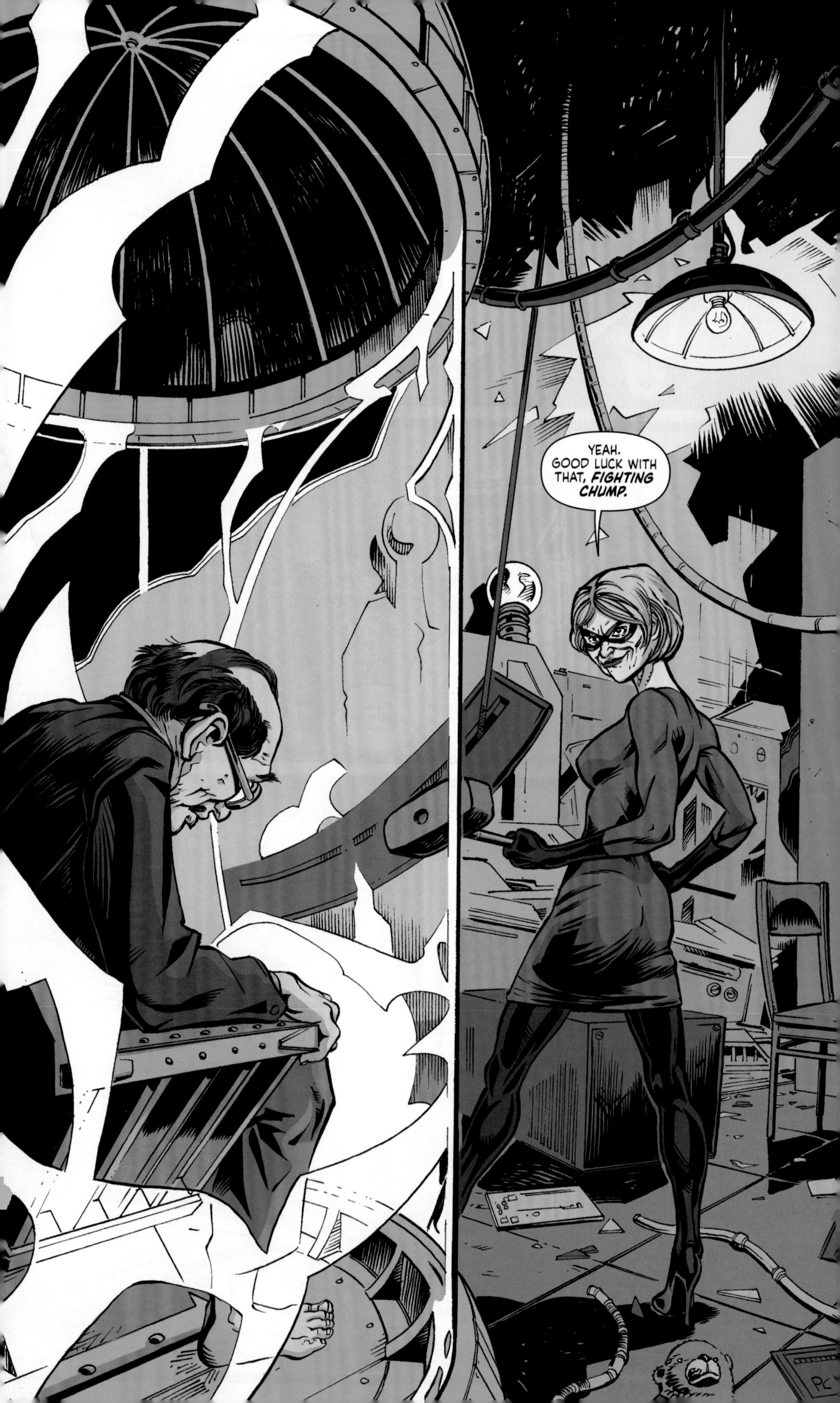
YEAH. GOOD LUCK WITH THAT, *FIGHTING CHUMP.*
PC

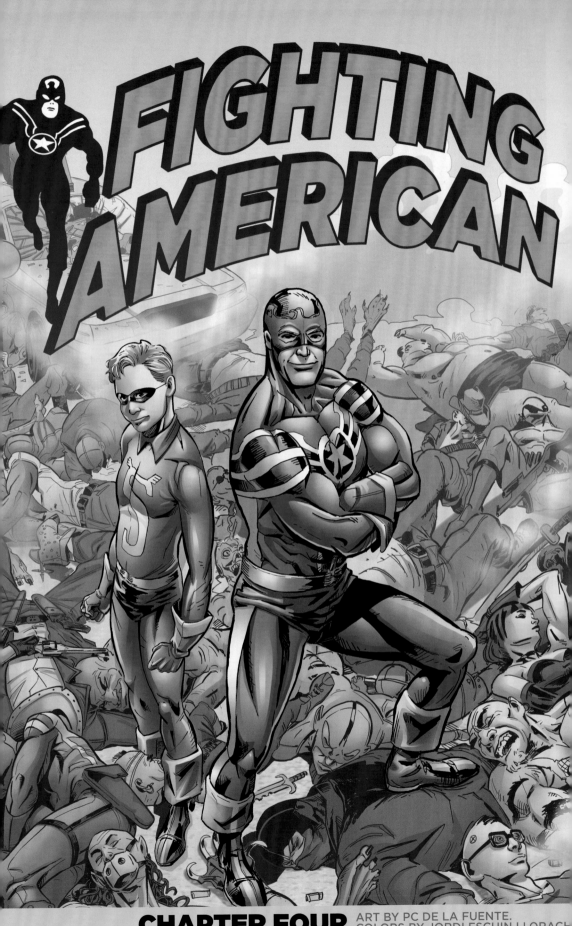

FIGHTING AMERICAN

CHAPTER FOUR ART BY PC DE LA FUENTE.
COLORS BY JORDI ESCUIN LLORACH.

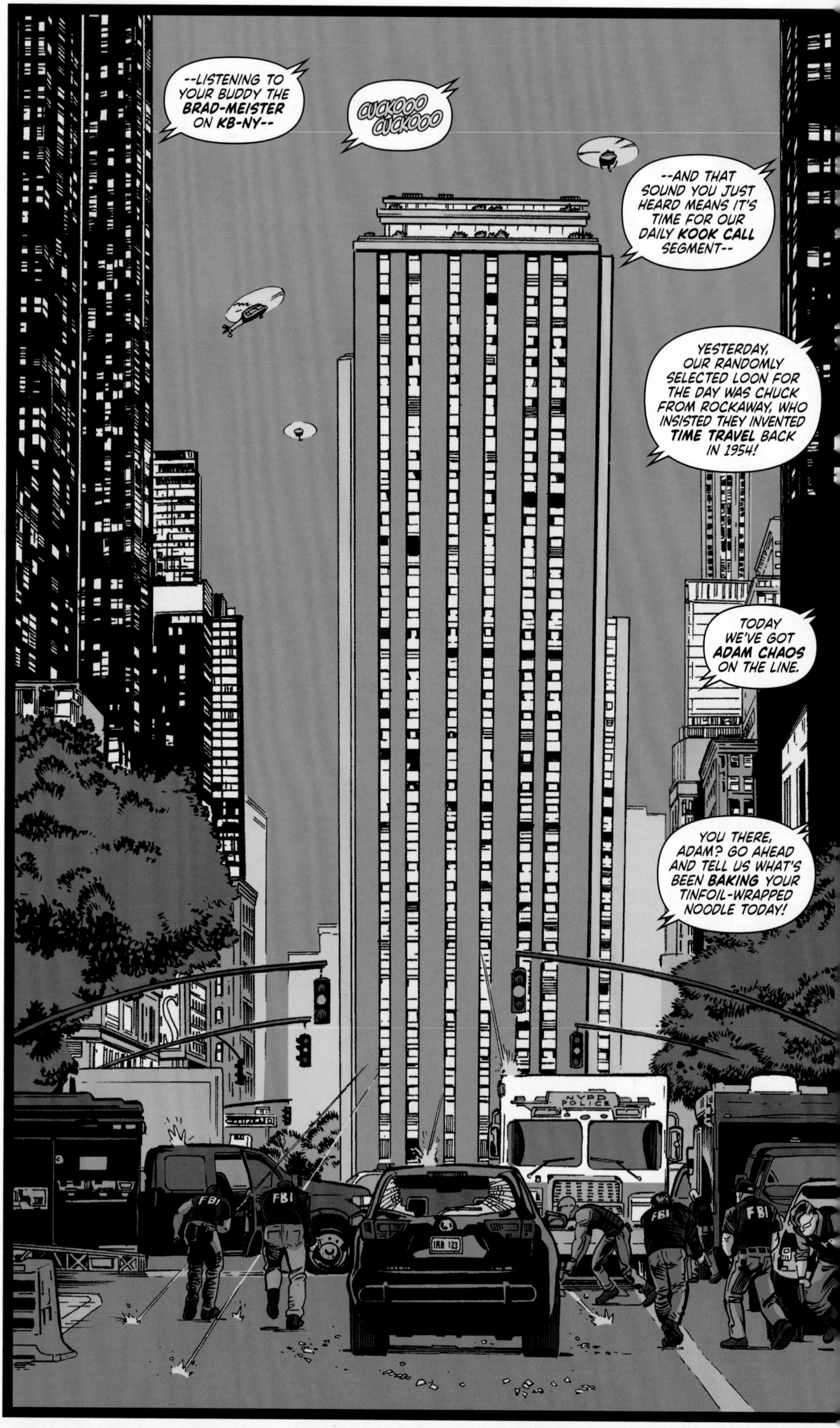
--LISTENING TO YOUR BUDDY THE BRAD-MEISTER ON KB-NY--
CUCKOOO CUCKOOO
--AND THAT SOUND YOU JUST HEARD MEANS IT'S TIME FOR OUR DAILY KOOK CALL SEGMENT--
YESTERDAY, OUR RANDOMLY SELECTED LOON FOR THE DAY WAS CHUCK FROM ROCKAWAY, WHO INSISTED THEY INVENTED TIME TRAVEL BACK IN 1954!
TODAY WE'VE GOT ADAM CHAOS ON THE LINE.
YOU THERE, ADAM? GO AHEAD AND TELL US WHAT'S BEEN BAKING YOUR TINFOIL-WRAPPED NOODLE TODAY!
NYPD POLICE
FBI
FBI
FBI
FBI

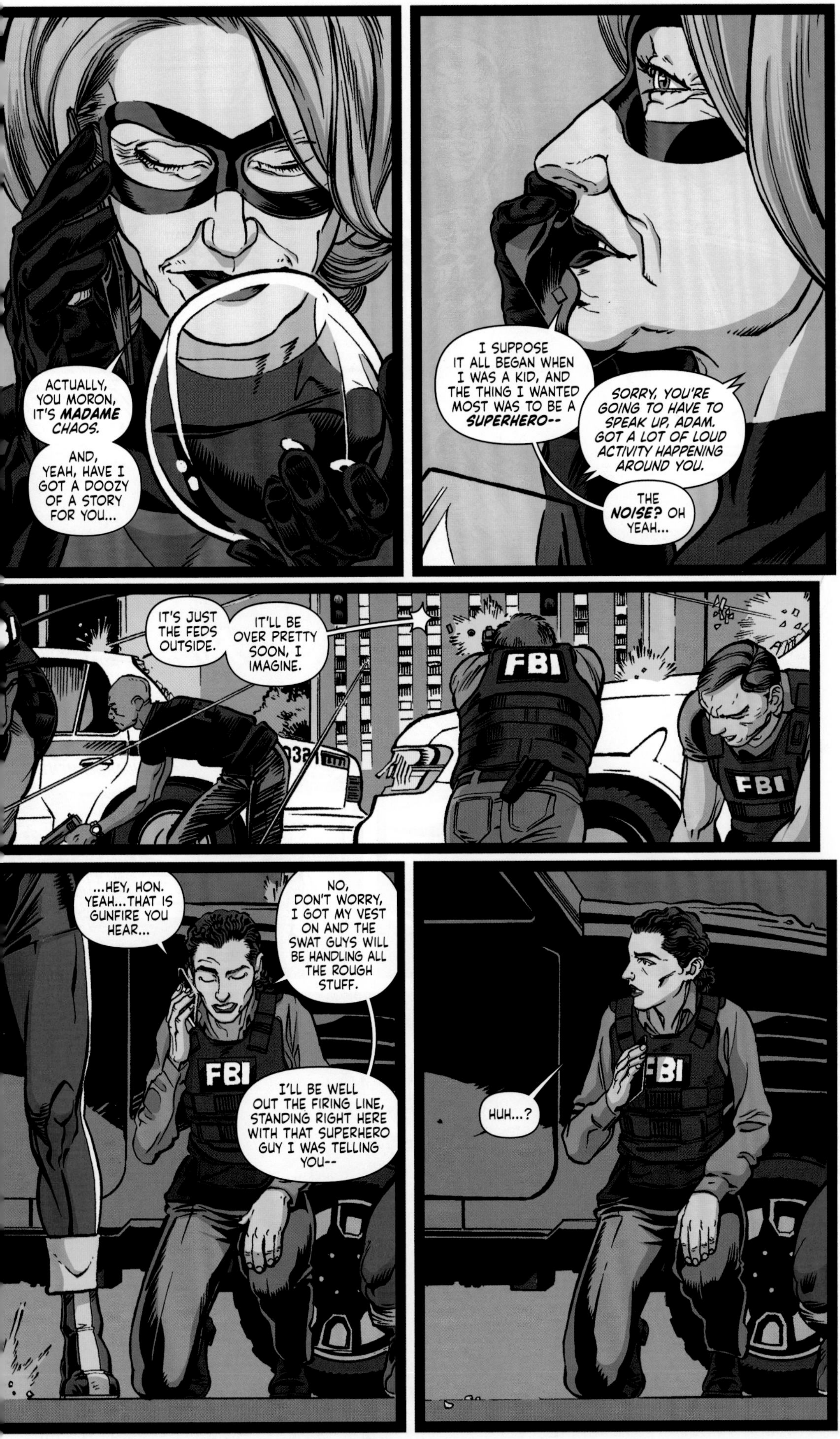
ACTUALLY, YOU MORON, IT'S MADAME CHAOS.
AND, YEAH, HAVE I GOT A DOOZY OF A STORY FOR YOU...
I SUPPOSE IT ALL BEGAN WHEN I WAS A KID, AND THE THING I WANTED MOST WAS TO BE A SUPERHERO--
SORRY, YOU'RE GOING TO HAVE TO SPEAK UP, ADAM. GOT A LOT OF LOUD ACTIVITY HAPPENING AROUND YOU.
THE NOISE? OH YEAH...
IT'S JUST THE FEDS OUTSIDE.
IT'LL BE OVER PRETTY SOON, I IMAGINE.
FBI
FBI
...HEY, HON. YEAH...THAT IS GUNFIRE YOU HEAR...
NO, DON'T WORRY, I GOT MY VEST ON AND THE SWAT GUYS WILL BE HANDLING ALL THE ROUGH STUFF.
I'LL BE WELL OUT THE FIRING LINE, STANDING RIGHT HERE WITH THAT SUPERHERO GUY I WAS TELLING YOU--
FBI
HUH...?
FBI

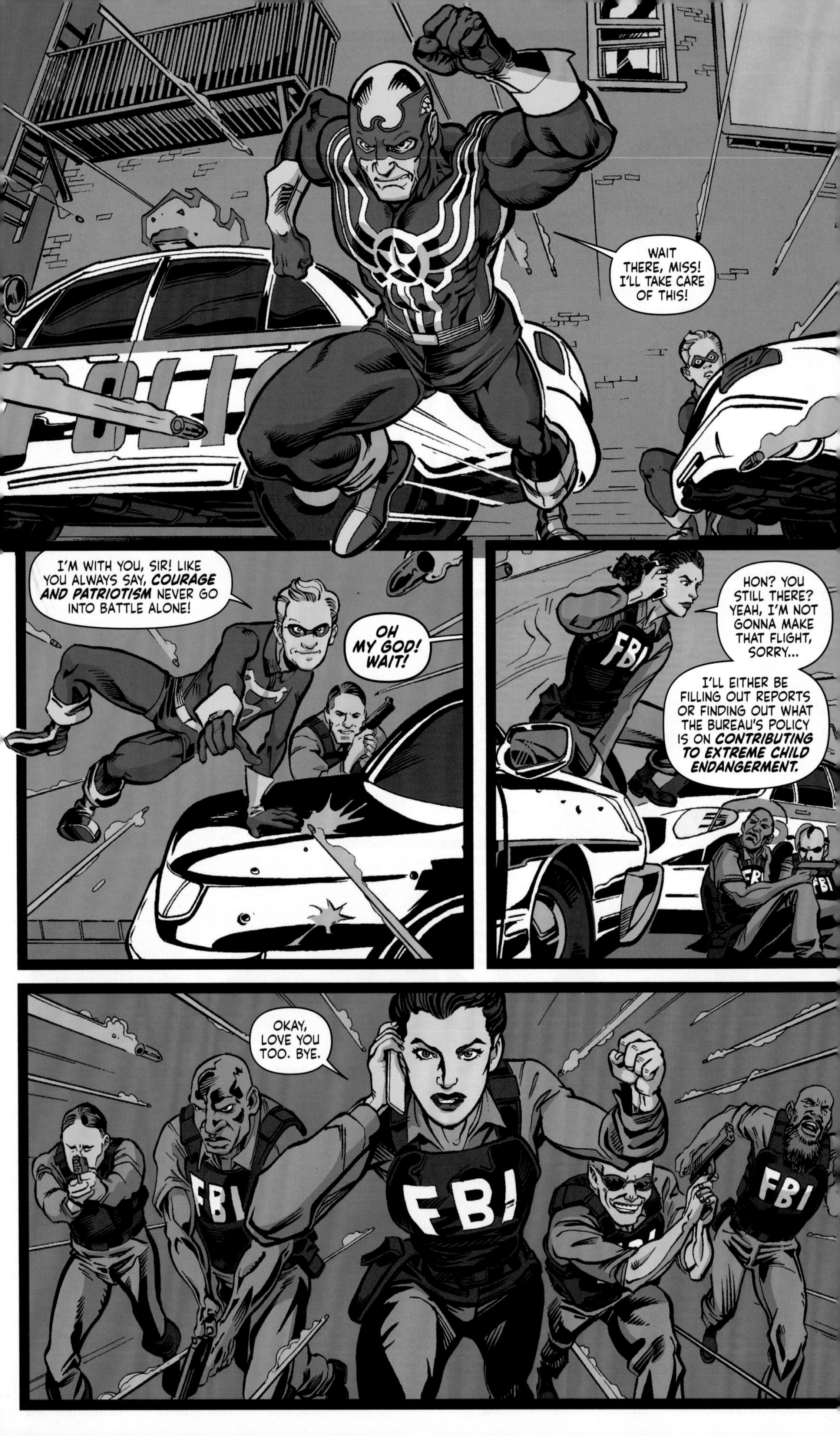
WAIT THERE, MISS! I'LL TAKE CARE OF THIS!
I'M WITH YOU, SIR! LIKE YOU ALWAYS SAY, **COURAGE AND PATRIOTISM** NEVER GO INTO BATTLE ALONE!
OH MY GOD! WAIT!
HON? YOU STILL THERE? YEAH, I'M NOT GONNA MAKE THAT FLIGHT, SORRY...
I'LL EITHER BE FILLING OUT REPORTS OR FINDING OUT WHAT THE BUREAU'S POLICY IS ON **CONTRIBUTING TO EXTREME CHILD ENDANGERMENT.**
OKAY, LOVE YOU TOO. BYE.

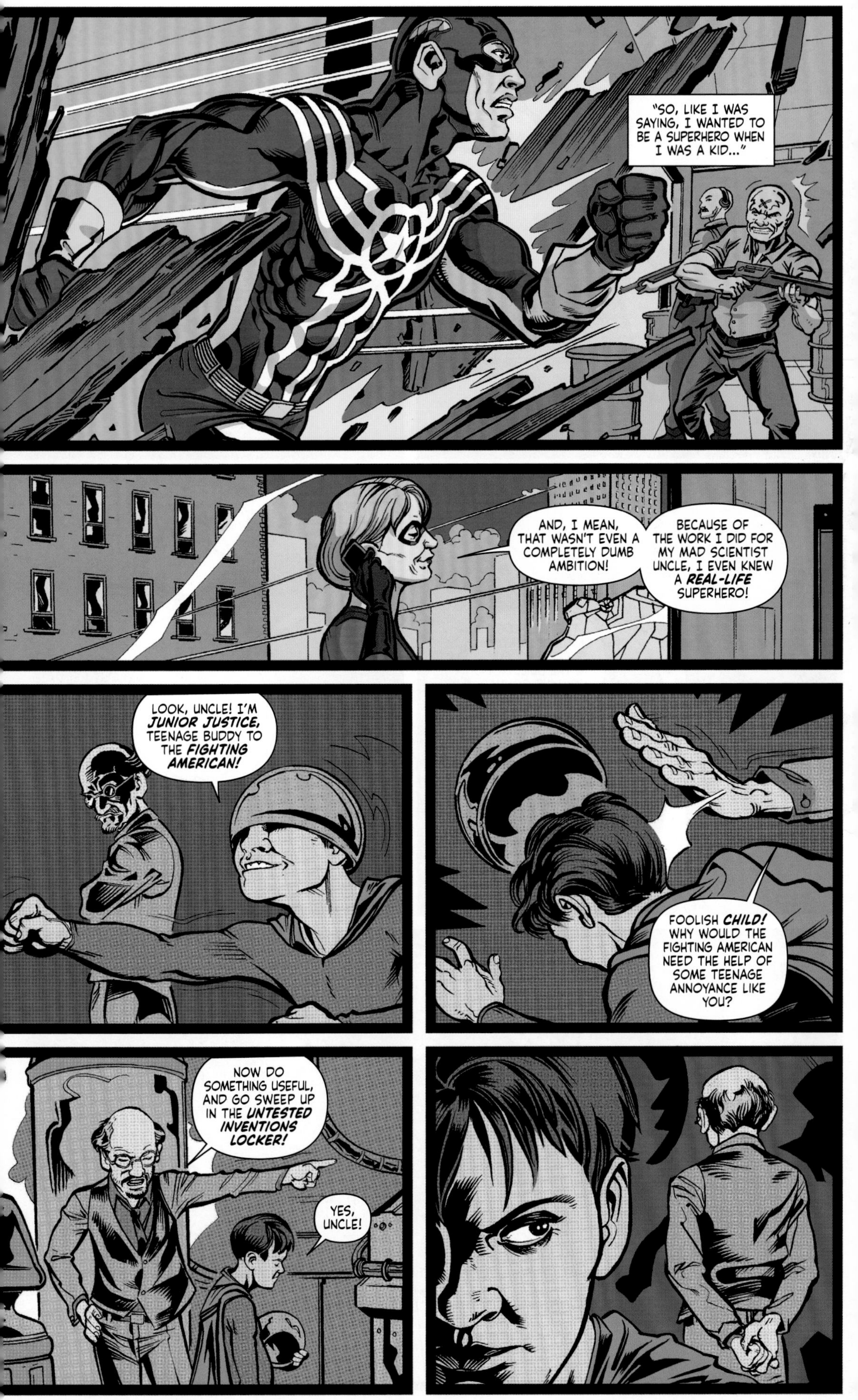
"SO, LIKE I WAS SAYING, I WANTED TO BE A SUPERHERO WHEN I WAS A KID..."
AND, I MEAN, THAT WASN'T EVEN A COMPLETELY DUMB AMBITION!
BECAUSE OF THE WORK I DID FOR MY MAD SCIENTIST UNCLE, I EVEN KNEW A REAL-LIFE SUPERHERO!
LOOK, UNCLE! I'M JUNIOR JUSTICE, TEENAGE BUDDY TO THE FIGHTING AMERICAN!
FOOLISH CHILD! WHY WOULD THE FIGHTING AMERICAN NEED THE HELP OF SOME TEENAGE ANNOYANCE LIKE YOU?
NOW DO SOMETHING USEFUL, AND GO SWEEP UP IN THE UNTESTED INVENTIONS LOCKER!
YES, UNCLE!

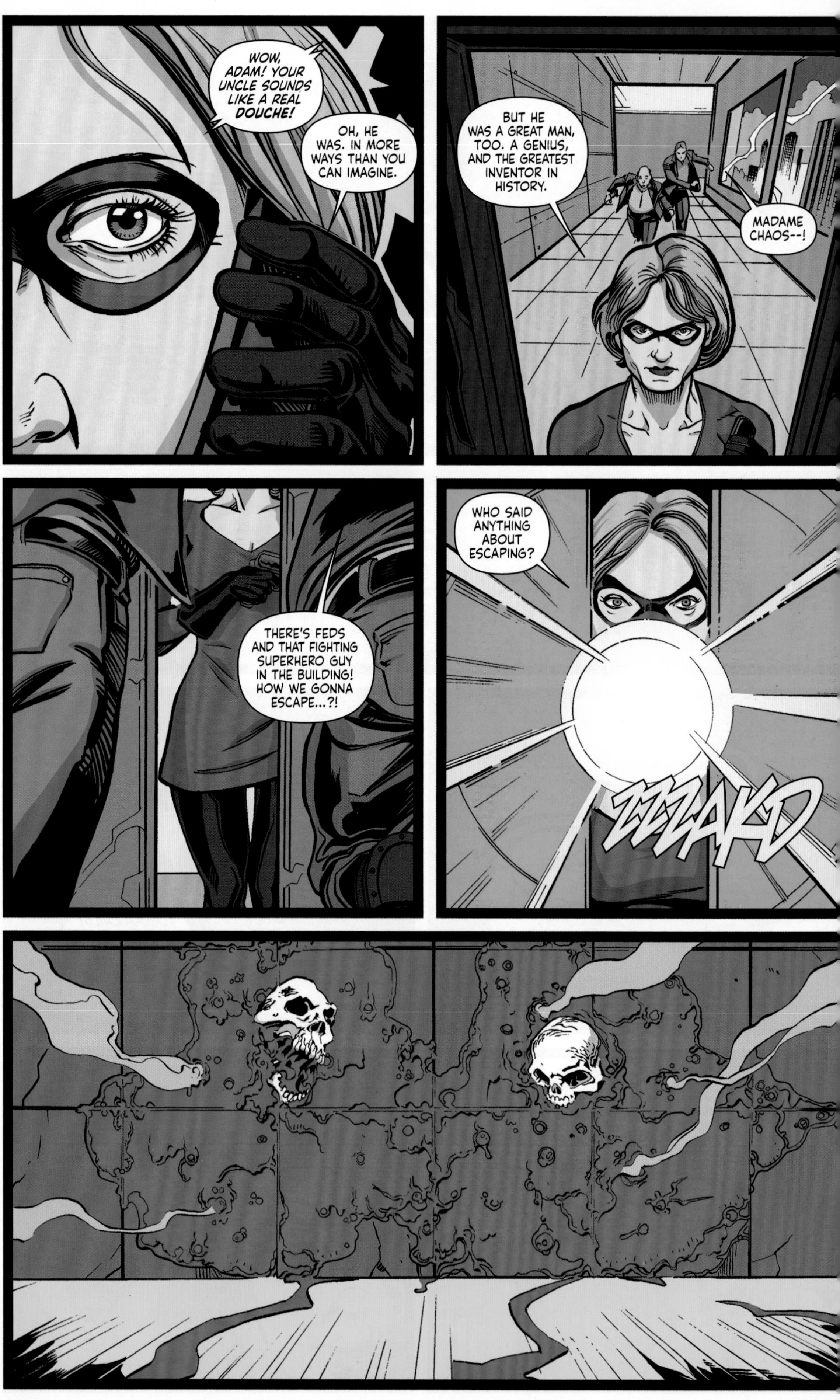
WOW, ADAM! YOUR UNCLE SOUNDS LIKE A REAL DOUCHE!
OH, HE WAS. IN MORE WAYS THAN YOU CAN IMAGINE.
BUT HE WAS A GREAT MAN, TOO. A GENIUS, AND THE GREATEST INVENTOR IN HISTORY.
MADAME CHAOS--!
THERE'S FEDS AND THAT FIGHTING SUPERHERO GUY IN THE BUILDING! HOW WE GONNA ESCAPE...?!
WHO SAID ANYTHING ABOUT ESCAPING?
ZZZAKD

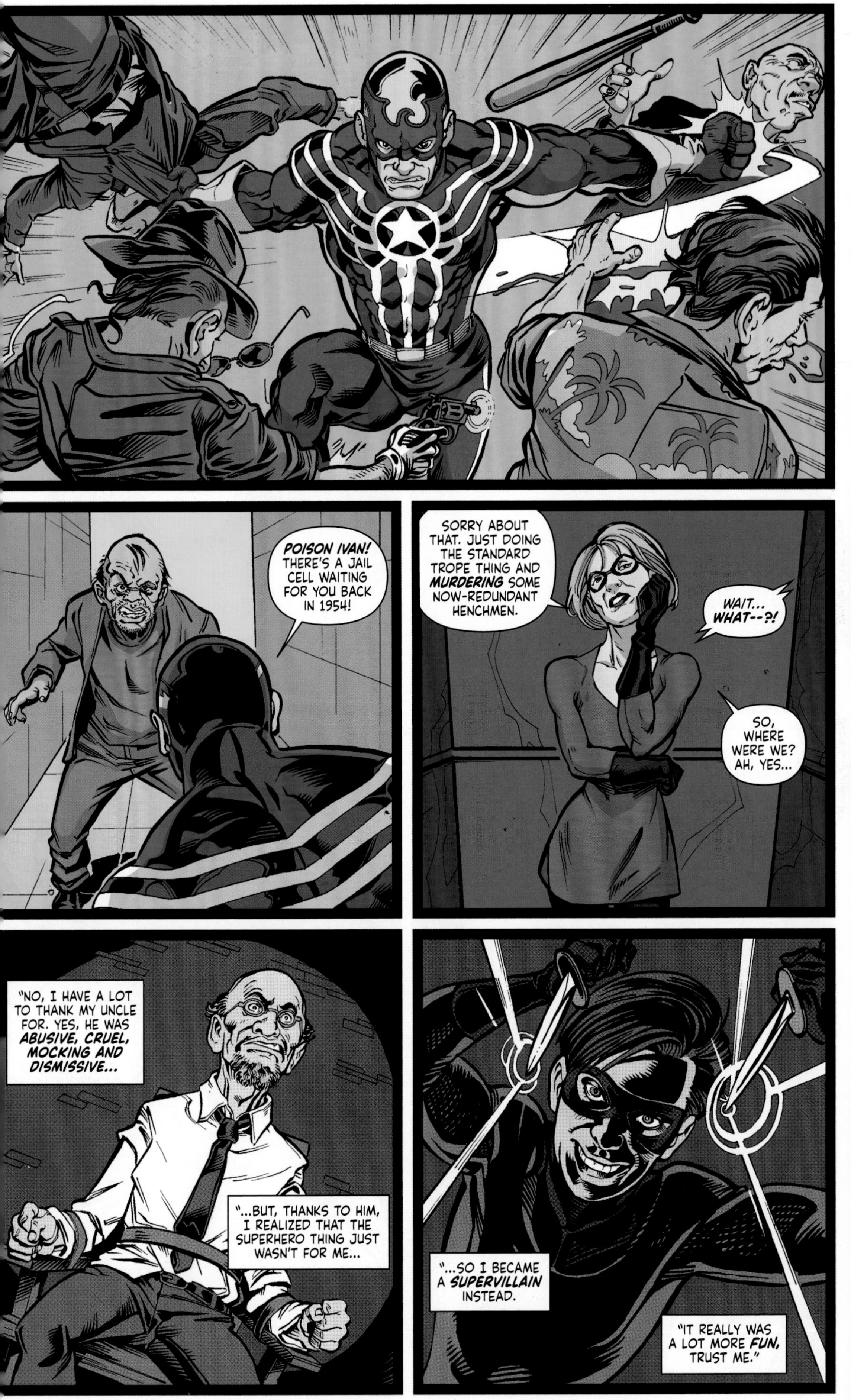
POISON IVAN! THERE'S A JAIL CELL WAITING FOR YOU BACK IN 1954!
SORRY ABOUT THAT. JUST DOING THE STANDARD TROPE THING AND MURDERING SOME NOW-REDUNDANT HENCHMEN.
WAIT... WHAT--?!
SO, WHERE WERE WE? AH, YES...
"NO, I HAVE A LOT TO THANK MY UNCLE FOR. YES, HE WAS ABUSIVE, CRUEL, MOCKING AND DISMISSIVE...
"...BUT, THANKS TO HIM, I REALIZED THAT THE SUPERHERO THING JUST WASN'T FOR ME...
"...SO I BECAME A SUPERVILLAIN INSTEAD.
"IT REALLY WAS A LOT MORE FUN, TRUST ME."

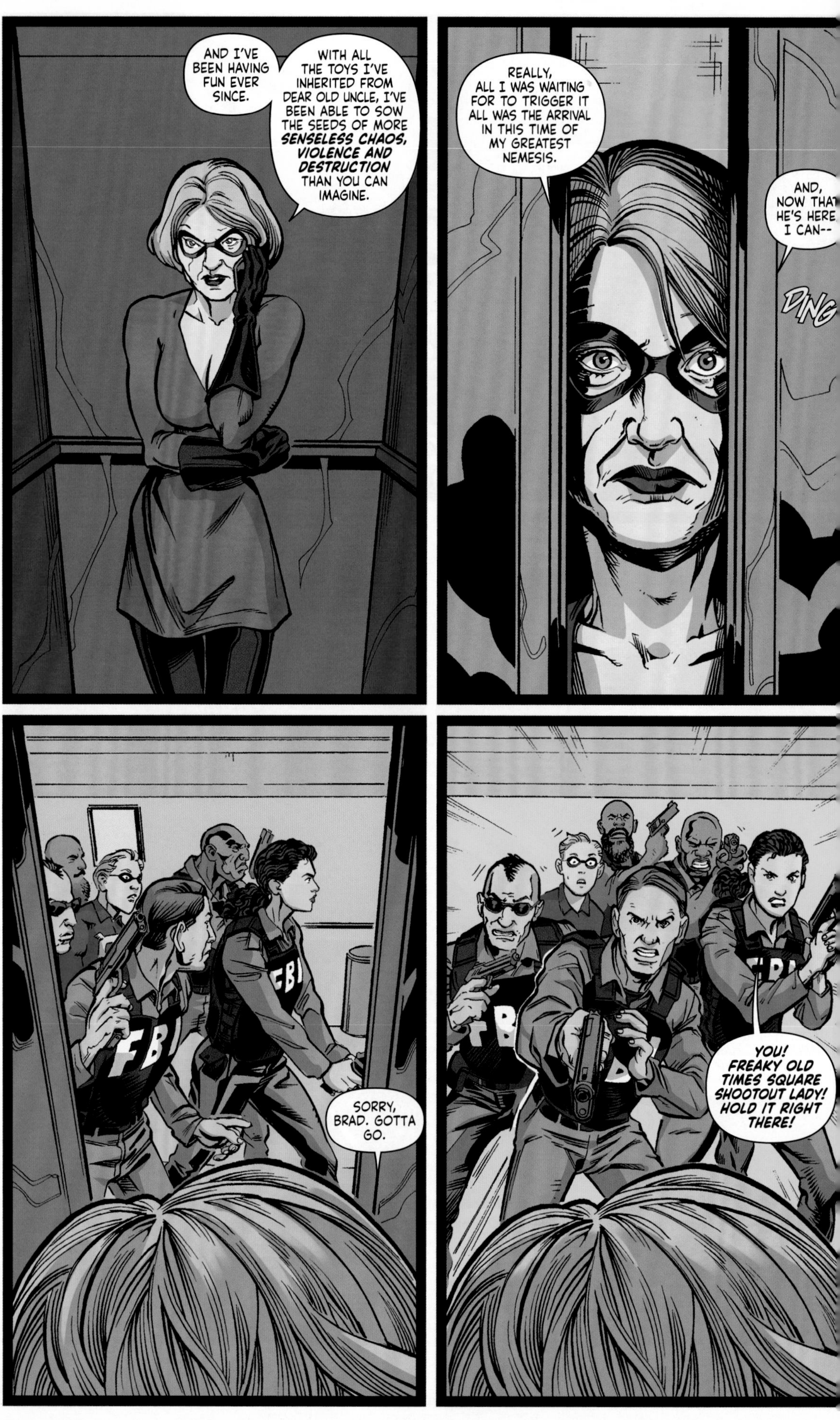
AND I'VE BEEN HAVING FUN EVER SINCE.
WITH ALL THE TOYS I'VE INHERITED FROM DEAR OLD UNCLE, I'VE BEEN ABLE TO SOW THE SEEDS OF MORE SENSELESS CHAOS, VIOLENCE AND DESTRUCTION THAN YOU CAN IMAGINE.
REALLY, ALL I WAS WAITING FOR TO TRIGGER IT ALL WAS THE ARRIVAL IN THIS TIME OF MY GREATEST NEMESIS.
AND, NOW THAT HE'S HERE I CAN--
DING
SORRY, BRAD. GOTTA GO.
YOU! FREAKY OLD TIMES SQUARE SHOOTOUT LADY! HOLD IT RIGHT THERE!

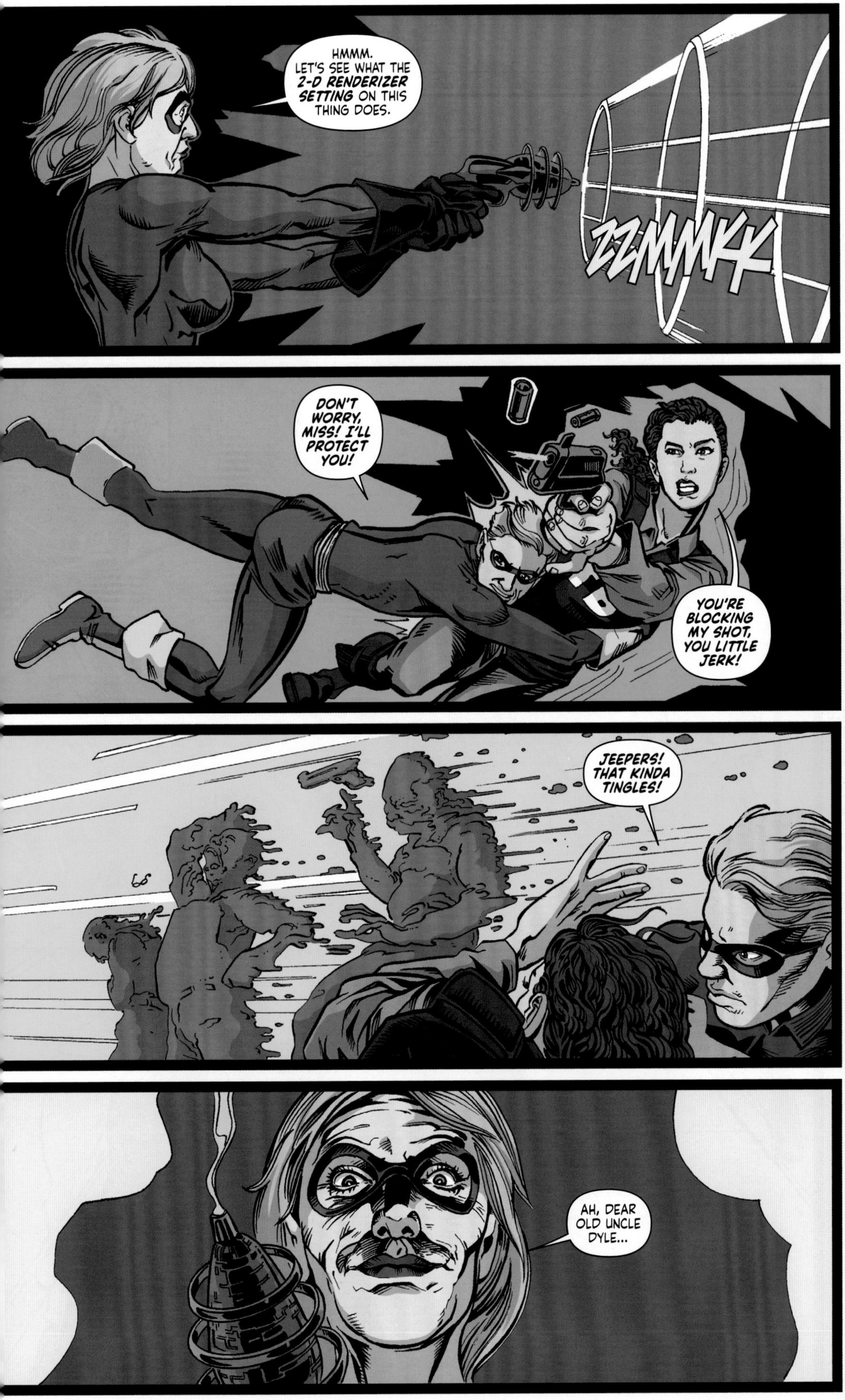
HMMM. LET'S SEE WHAT THE 2-D RENDERIZER SETTING ON THIS THING DOES.
ZZMMKK
DON'T WORRY, MISS! I'LL PROTECT YOU!
YOU'RE BLOCKING MY SHOT, YOU LITTLE JERK!
JEEPERS! THAT KINDA TINGLES!
AH, DEAR OLD UNCLE DYLE...

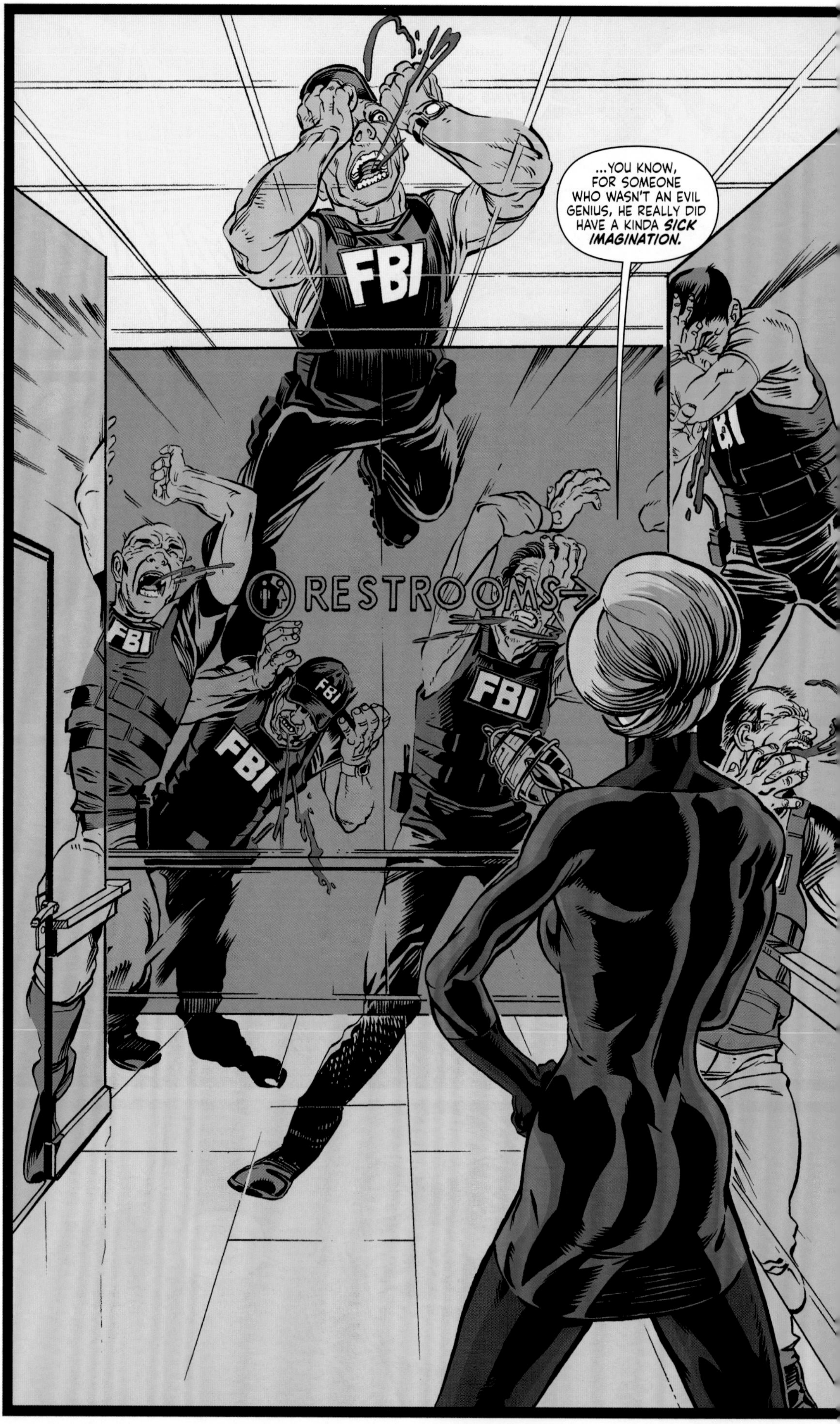
...YOU KNOW, FOR SOMEONE WHO WASN'T AN EVIL GENIUS, HE REALLY DID HAVE A KINDA SICK IMAGINATION.
FBI
RESTROOMS
FBI
FBI
FBI
FBI
FBI

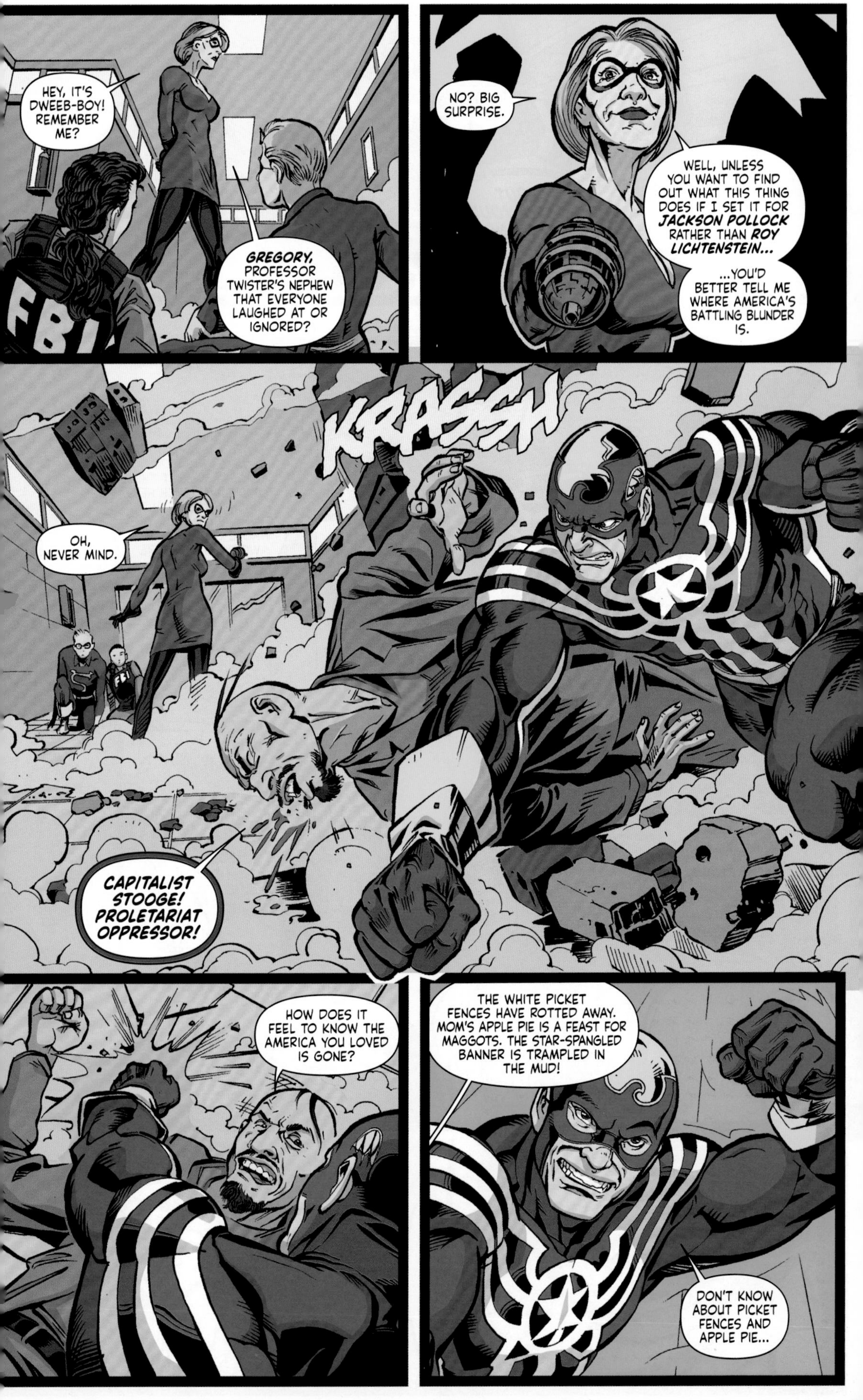
HEY, IT'S DWEEB-BOY! REMEMBER ME?
GREGORY, PROFESSOR TWISTER'S NEPHEW THAT EVERYONE LAUGHED AT OR IGNORED?
NO? BIG SURPRISE.
WELL, UNLESS YOU WANT TO FIND OUT WHAT THIS THING DOES IF I SET IT FOR JACKSON POLLOCK RATHER THAN ROY LICHTENSTEIN...
...YOU'D BETTER TELL ME WHERE AMERICA'S BATTLING BLUNDER IS.
KRASSH
OH, NEVER MIND.
CAPITALIST STOOGE! PROLETARIAT OPPRESSOR!
HOW DOES IT FEEL TO KNOW THE AMERICA YOU LOVED IS GONE?
THE WHITE PICKET FENCES HAVE ROTTED AWAY. MOM'S APPLE PIE IS A FEAST FOR MAGGOTS. THE STAR-SPANGLED BANNER IS TRAMPLED IN THE MUD!
DON'T KNOW ABOUT PICKET FENCES AND APPLE PIE...

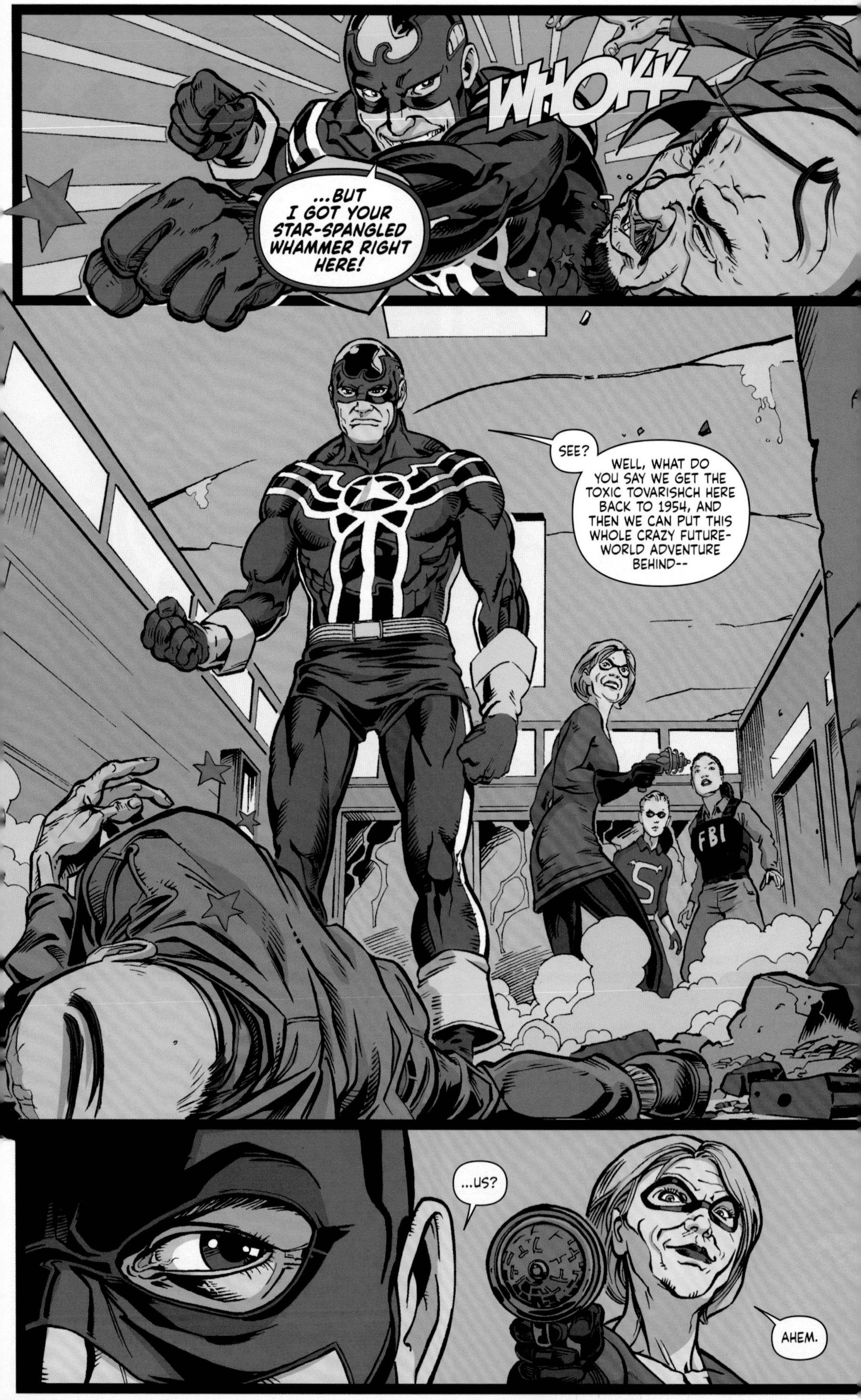
WHOKK
...BUT I GOT YOUR STAR-SPANGLED WHAMMER RIGHT HERE!
SEE?
WELL, WHAT DO YOU SAY WE GET THE TOXIC TOVARISHCH HERE BACK TO 1954, AND THEN WE CAN PUT THIS WHOLE CRAZY FUTURE-WORLD ADVENTURE BEHIND--
FBI
...US?
AHEM.

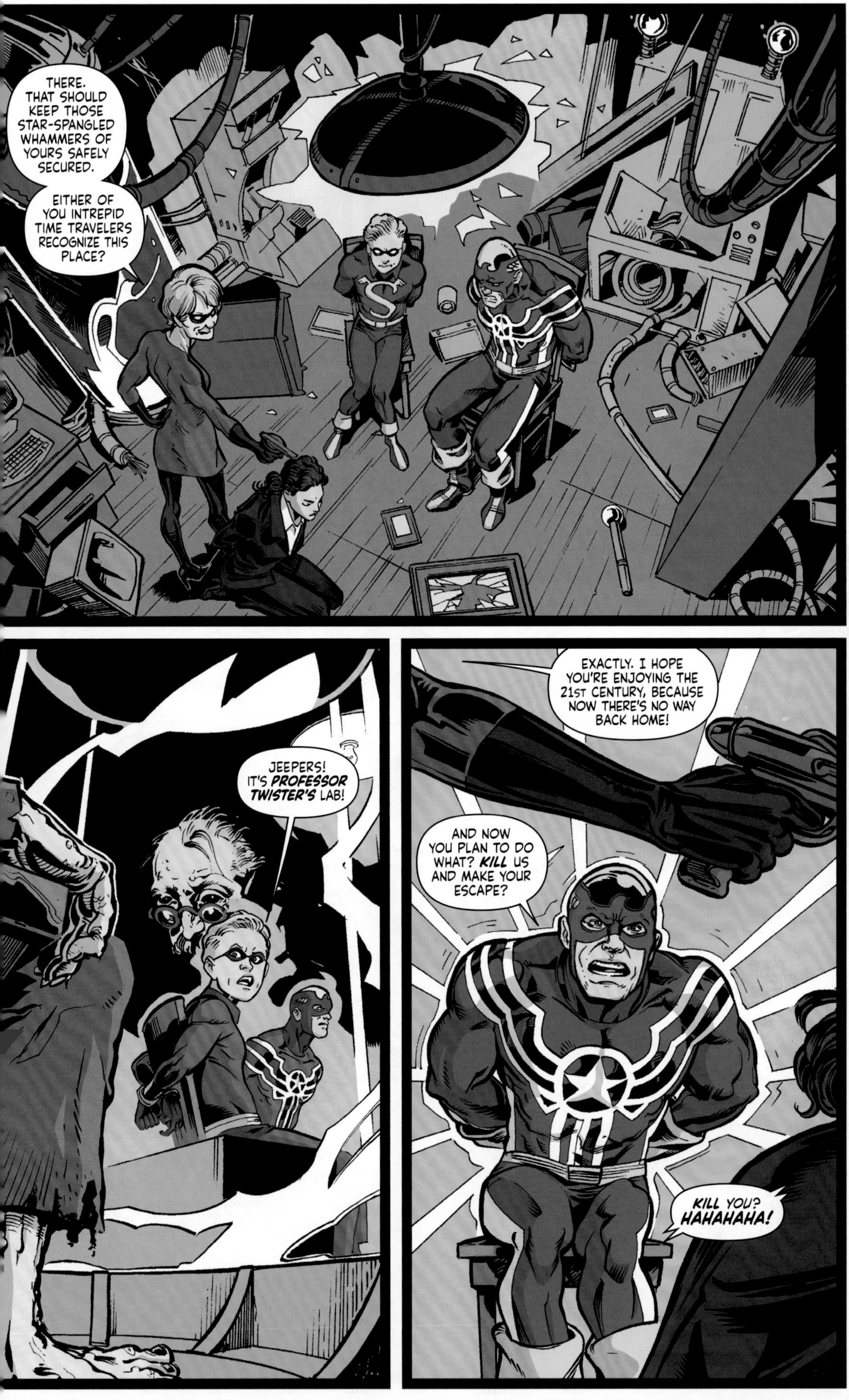
THERE. THAT SHOULD KEEP THOSE STAR-SPANGLED WHAMMERS OF YOURS SAFELY SECURED.
EITHER OF YOU INTREPID TIME TRAVELERS RECOGNIZE THIS PLACE?
JEEPERS! IT'S PROFESSOR TWISTER'S LAB!
EXACTLY. I HOPE YOU'RE ENJOYING THE 21ST CENTURY, BECAUSE NOW THERE'S NO WAY BACK HOME!
AND NOW YOU PLAN TO DO WHAT? KILL US AND MAKE YOUR ESCAPE?
KILL YOU? HAHAHAHA!

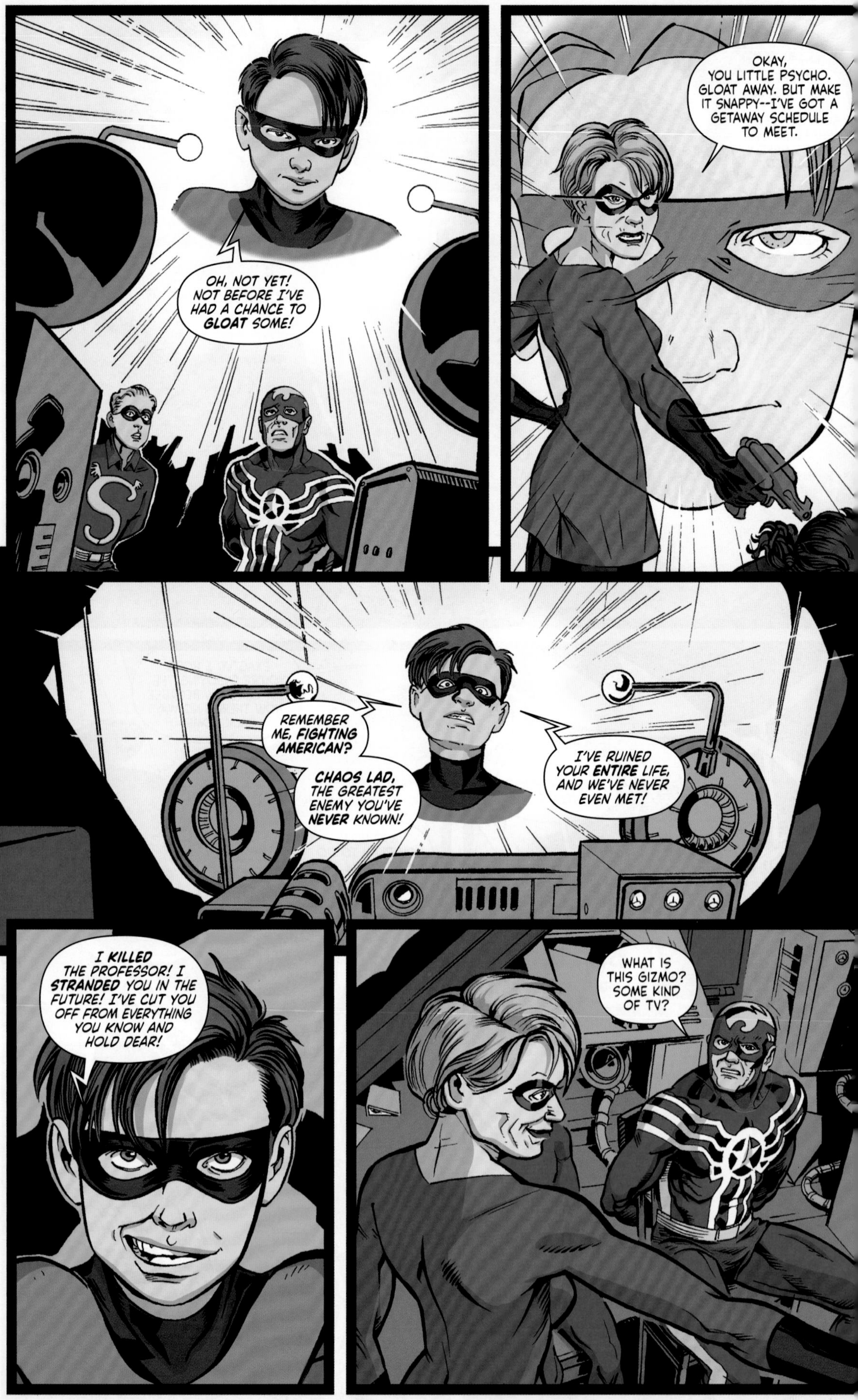

OH, NOT YET! NOT BEFORE I'VE HAD A CHANCE TO GLOAT SOME!
OKAY, YOU LITTLE PSYCHO. GLOAT AWAY. BUT MAKE IT SNAPPY--I'VE GOT A GETAWAY SCHEDULE TO MEET.
REMEMBER ME, FIGHTING AMERICAN?
CHAOS LAD, THE GREATEST ENEMY YOU'VE NEVER KNOWN!
I'VE RUINED YOUR ENTIRE LIFE, AND WE'VE NEVER EVEN MET!
I KILLED THE PROFESSOR! I STRANDED YOU IN THE FUTURE! I'VE CUT YOU OFF FROM EVERYTHING YOU KNOW AND HOLD DEAR!
WHAT IS THIS GIZMO? SOME KIND OF TV?

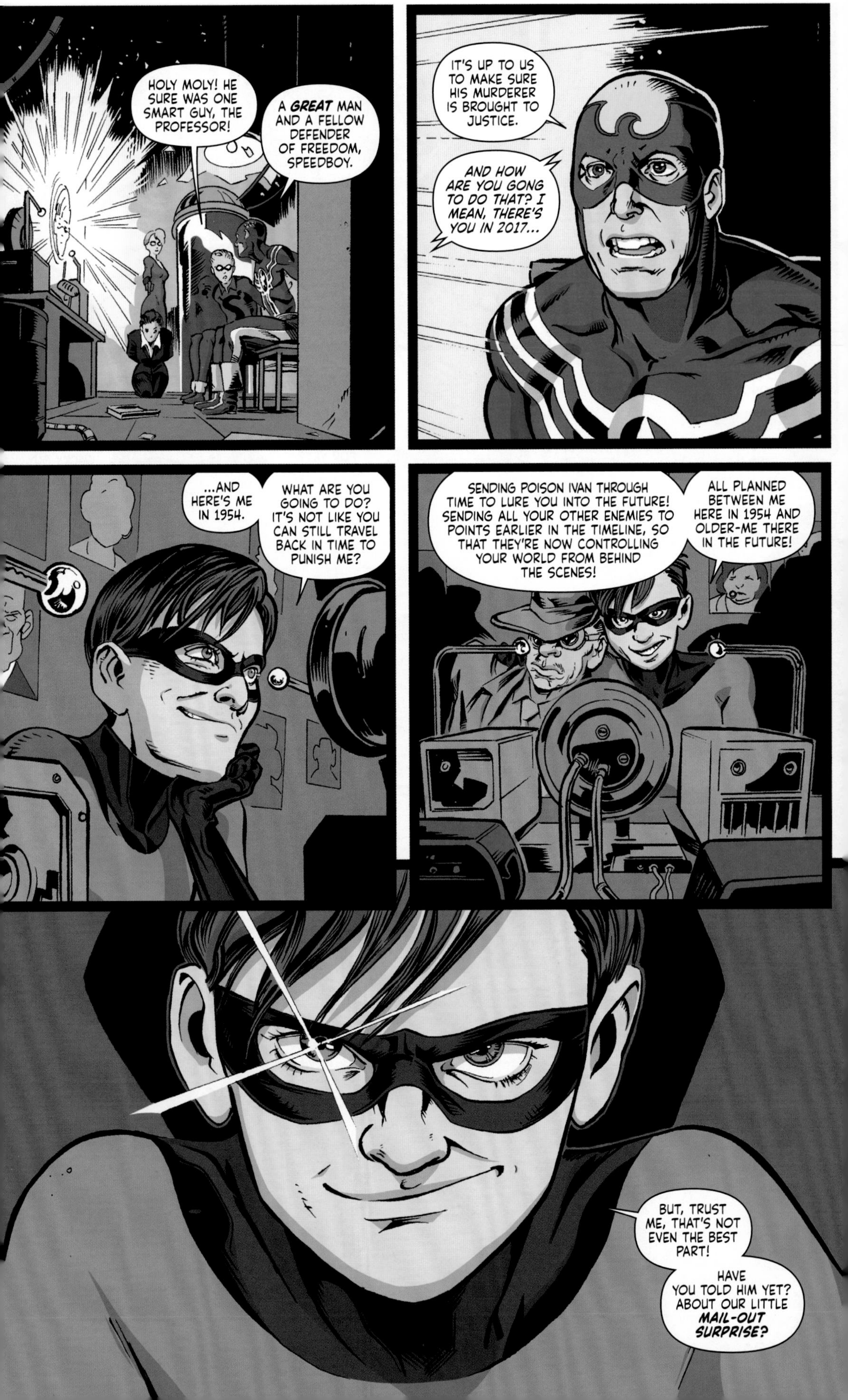
HOLY MOLY! HE SURE WAS ONE SMART GUY, THE PROFESSOR!
A **GREAT** MAN AND A FELLOW DEFENDER OF FREEDOM, SPEEDBOY.
IT'S UP TO US TO MAKE SURE HIS MURDERER IS BROUGHT TO JUSTICE.
AND HOW ARE YOU GONG TO DO THAT? I MEAN, THERE'S YOU IN 2017...
...AND HERE'S ME IN 1954.
WHAT ARE YOU GOING TO DO? IT'S NOT LIKE YOU CAN STILL TRAVEL BACK IN TIME TO PUNISH ME?
SENDING POISON IVAN THROUGH TIME TO LURE YOU INTO THE FUTURE! SENDING ALL YOUR OTHER ENEMIES TO POINTS EARLIER IN THE TIMELINE, SO THAT THEY'RE NOW CONTROLLING YOUR WORLD FROM BEHIND THE SCENES!
ALL PLANNED BETWEEN ME HERE IN 1954 AND OLDER-ME THERE IN THE FUTURE!
BUT, TRUST ME, THAT'S NOT EVEN THE BEST PART!
HAVE YOU TOLD HIM YET? ABOUT OUR LITTLE ***MAIL-OUT SURPRISE?***

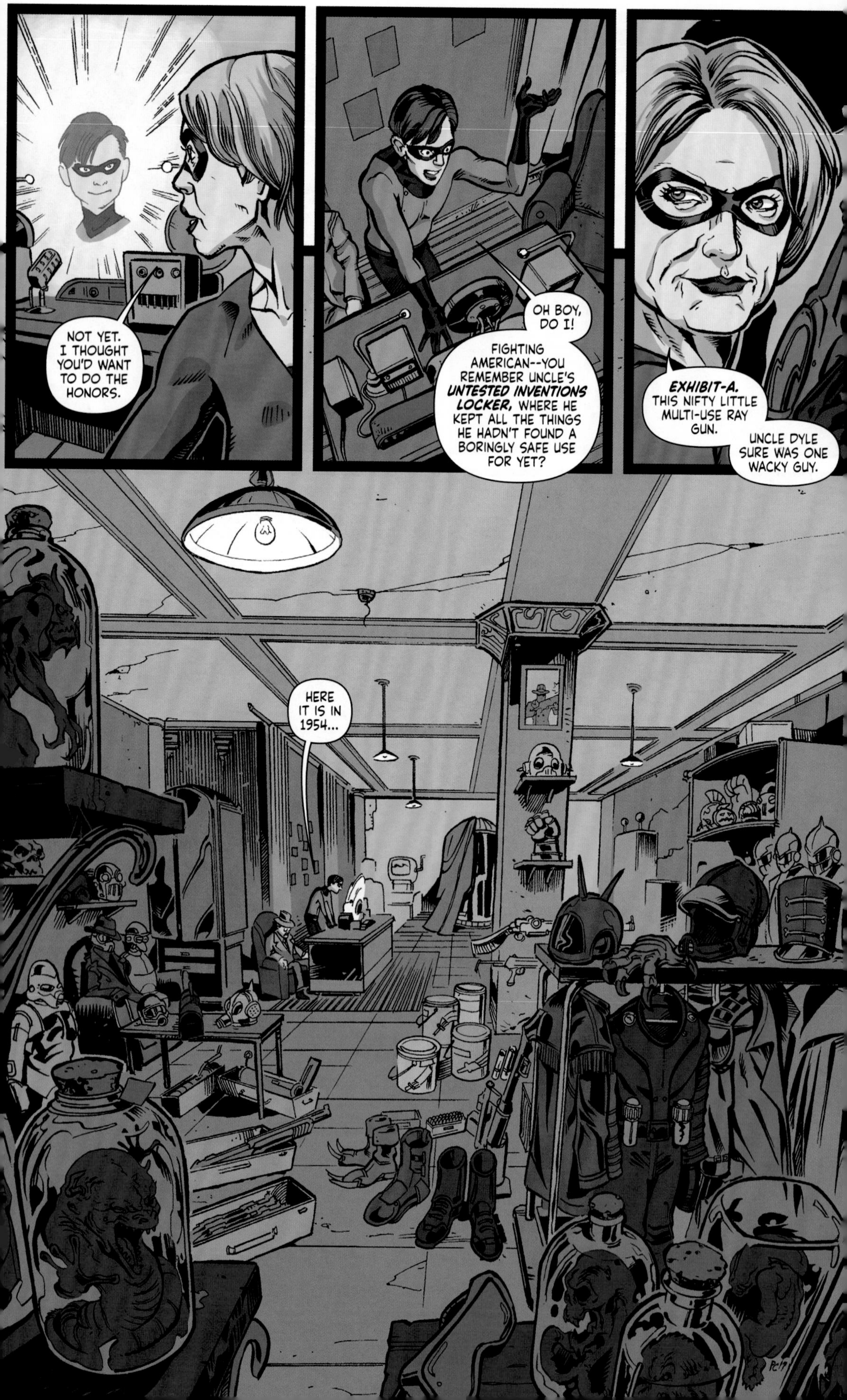
NOT YET. I THOUGHT YOU'D WANT TO DO THE HONORS.
OH BOY, DO I!
FIGHTING AMERICAN--YOU REMEMBER UNCLE'S ***UNTESTED INVENTIONS LOCKER,*** WHERE HE KEPT ALL THE THINGS HE HADN'T FOUND A BORINGLY SAFE USE FOR YET?
EXHIBIT-A. THIS NIFTY LITTLE MULTI-USE RAY GUN.
UNCLE DYLE SURE WAS ONE WACKY GUY.
HERE IT IS IN 1954...

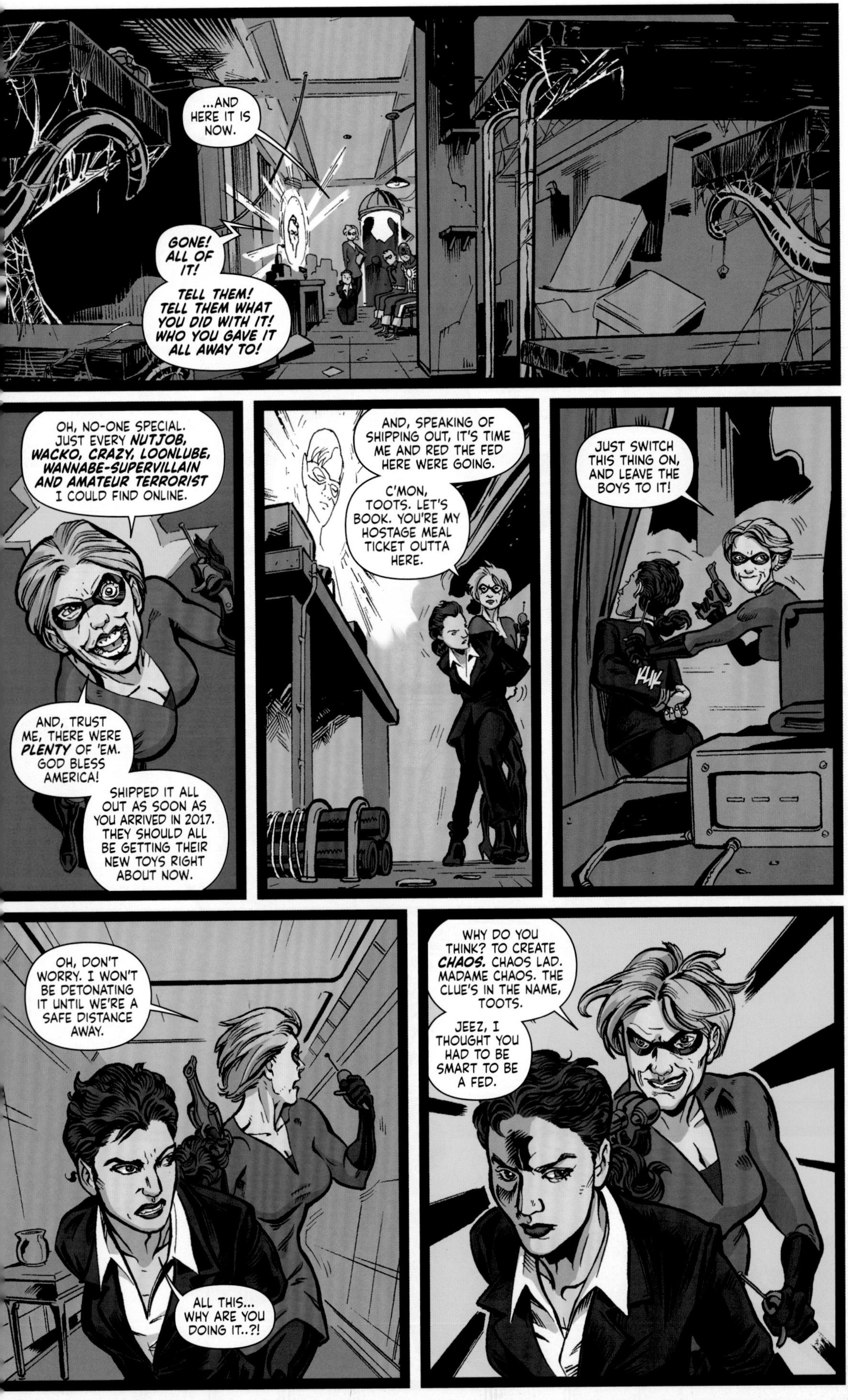
...AND HERE IT IS NOW.
GONE! ALL OF IT!
TELL THEM! TELL THEM WHAT YOU DID WITH IT! WHO YOU GAVE IT ALL AWAY TO!
OH, NO-ONE SPECIAL. JUST EVERY NUTJOB, WACKO, CRAZY, LOONLUBE, WANNABE-SUPERVILLAIN AND AMATEUR TERRORIST I COULD FIND ONLINE.
AND, TRUST ME, THERE WERE PLENTY OF 'EM. GOD BLESS AMERICA!
SHIPPED IT ALL OUT AS SOON AS YOU ARRIVED IN 2017. THEY SHOULD ALL BE GETTING THEIR NEW TOYS RIGHT ABOUT NOW.
AND, SPEAKING OF SHIPPING OUT, IT'S TIME ME AND RED THE FED HERE WERE GOING.
C'MON, TOOTS. LET'S BOOK. YOU'RE MY HOSTAGE MEAL TICKET OUTTA HERE.
JUST SWITCH THIS THING ON, AND LEAVE THE BOYS TO IT!
KLIK
OH, DON'T WORRY. I WON'T BE DETONATING IT UNTIL WE'RE A SAFE DISTANCE AWAY.
ALL THIS... WHY ARE YOU DOING IT..?!
WHY DO YOU THINK? TO CREATE CHAOS. CHAOS LAD. MADAME CHAOS. THE CLUE'S IN THE NAME, TOOTS.
JEEZ, I THOUGHT YOU HAD TO BE SMART TO BE A FED.

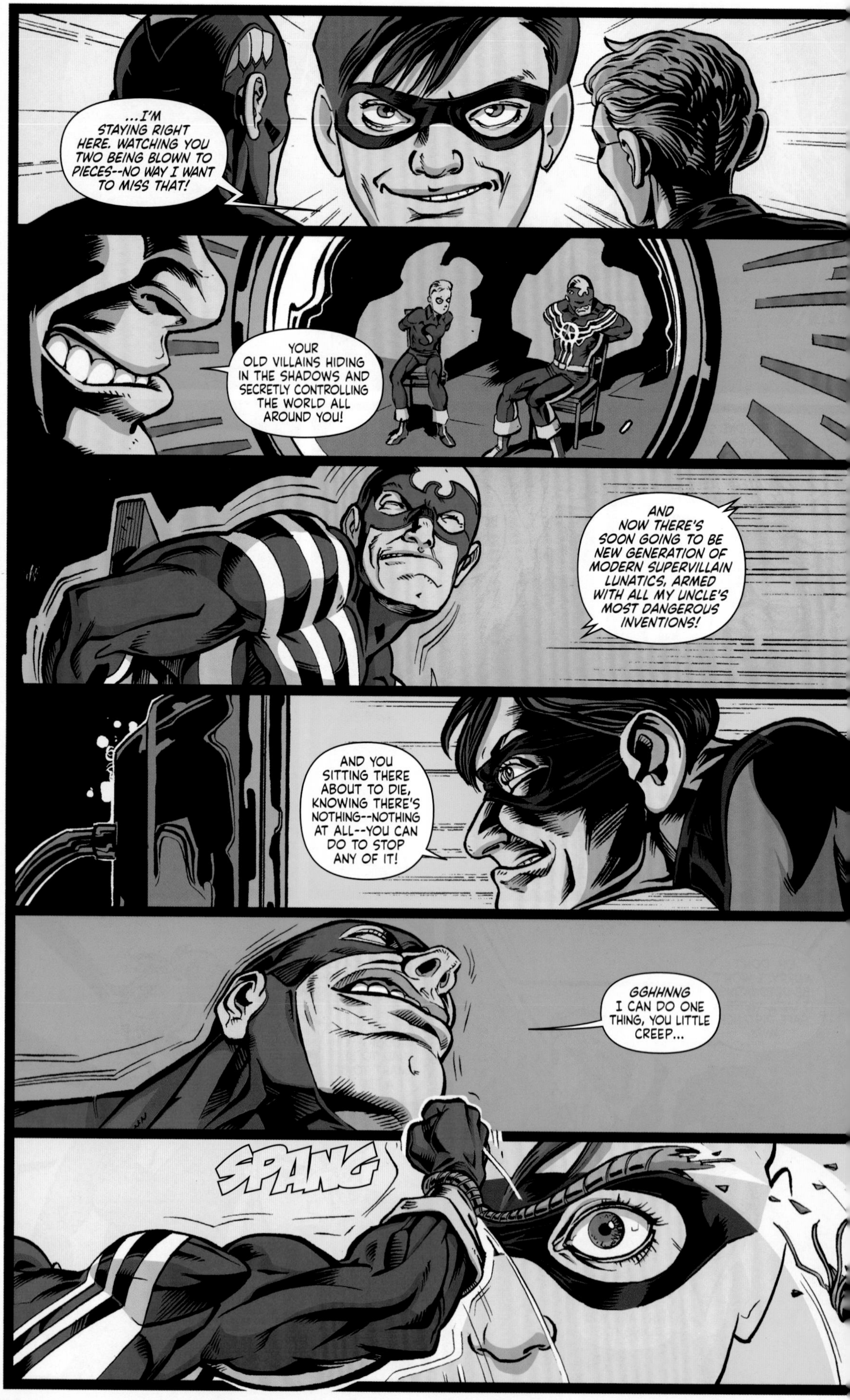
...I'M STAYING RIGHT HERE. WATCHING YOU TWO BEING BLOWN TO PIECES--NO WAY I WANT TO MISS THAT!
YOUR OLD VILLAINS HIDING IN THE SHADOWS AND SECRETLY CONTROLLING THE WORLD ALL AROUND YOU!
AND NOW THERE'S SOON GOING TO BE NEW GENERATION OF MODERN SUPERVILLAIN LUNATICS, ARMED WITH ALL MY UNCLE'S MOST DANGEROUS INVENTIONS!
AND YOU SITTING THERE ABOUT TO DIE, KNOWING THERE'S NOTHING--NOTHING AT ALL--YOU CAN DO TO STOP ANY OF IT!
GGHHNNG I CAN DO ONE THING, YOU LITTLE CREEP...
SPANG

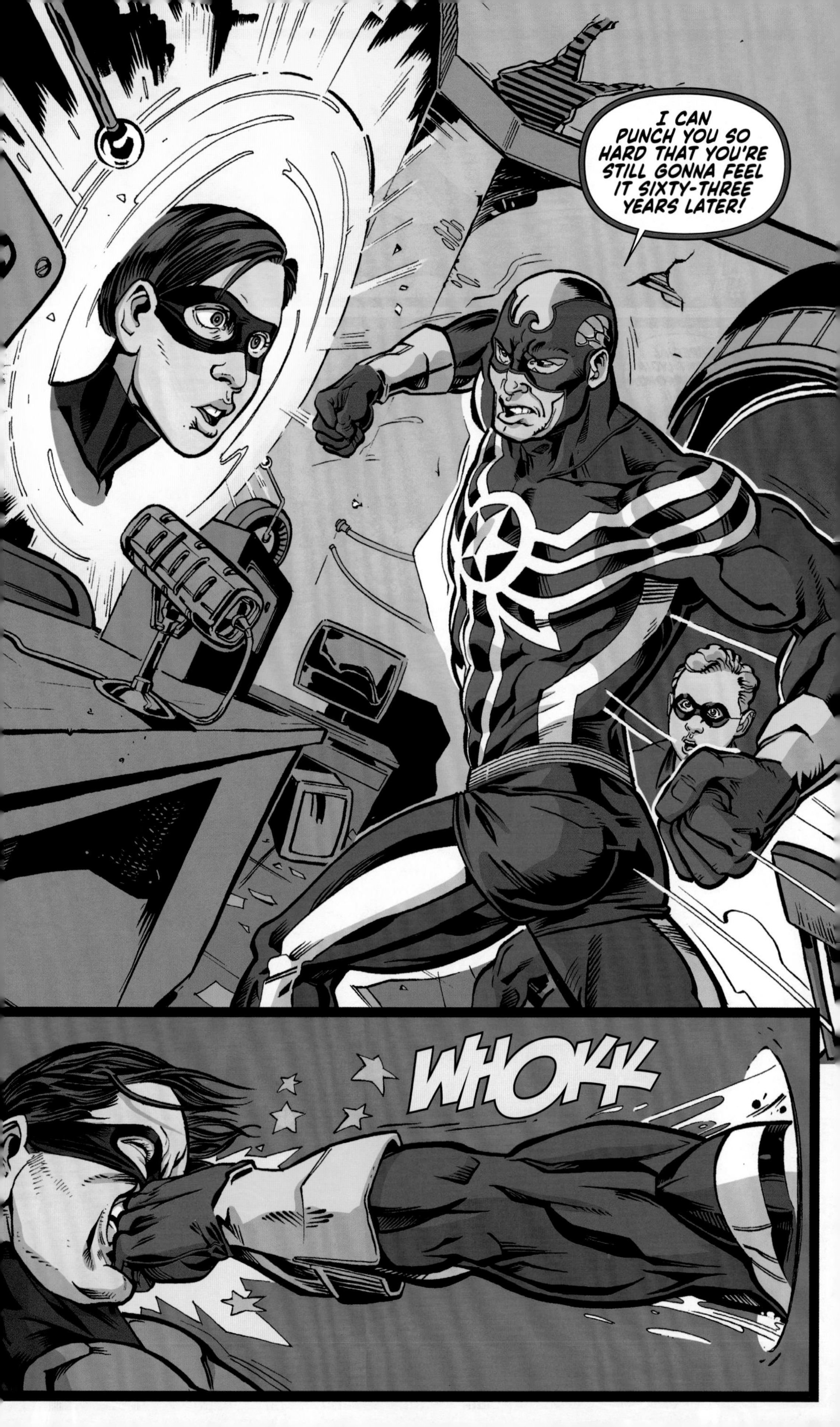
I CAN PUNCH YOU SO HARD THAT YOU'RE STILL GONNA FEEL IT SIXTY-THREE YEARS LATER!
WHOKK

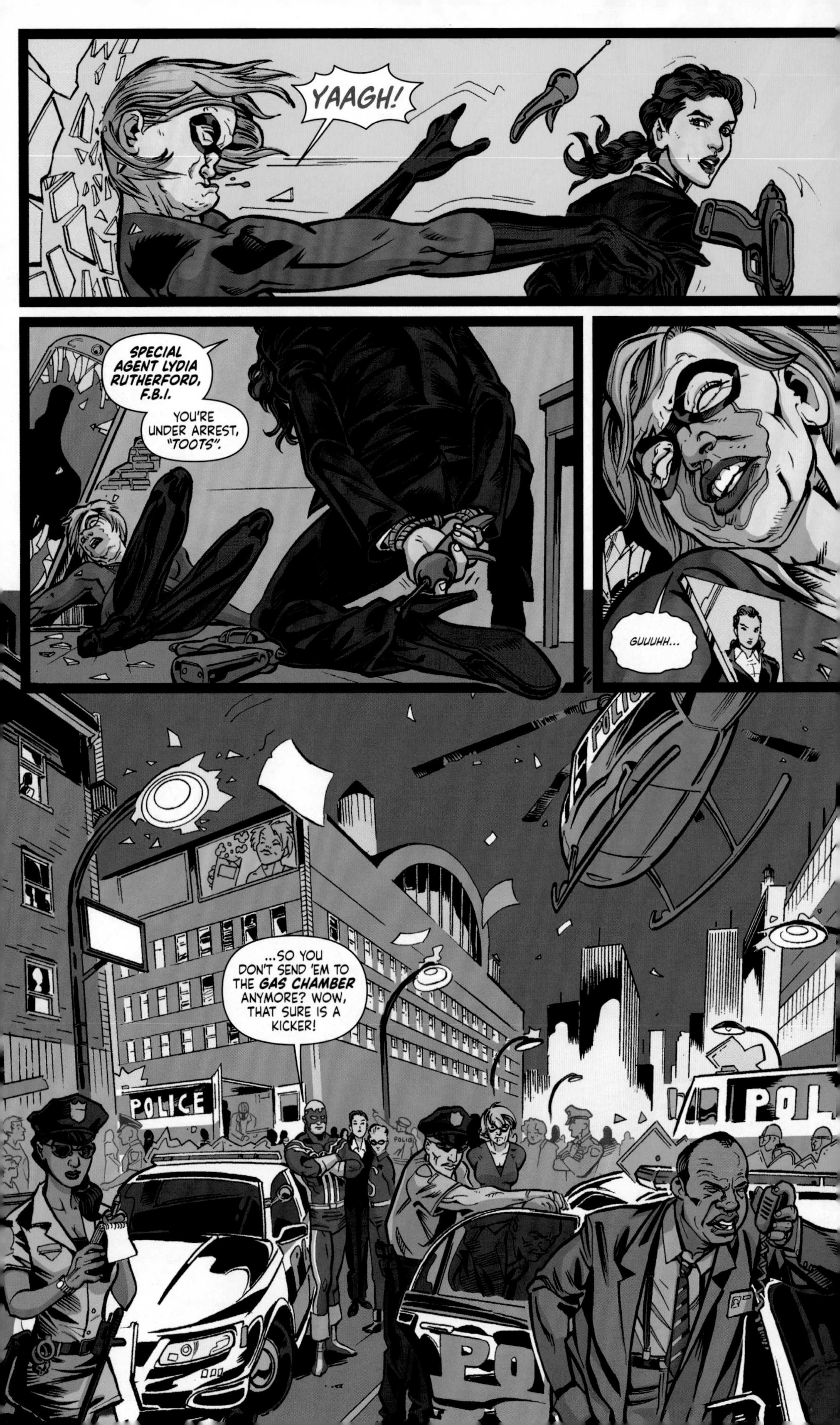
YAAGH!
SPECIAL AGENT LYDIA RUTHERFORD, F.B.I.
YOU'RE UNDER ARREST, "TOOTS".
GUUUHH...
POLICE
...SO YOU DON'T SEND 'EM TO THE GAS CHAMBER ANYMORE? WOW, THAT SURE IS A KICKER!
POL
PO

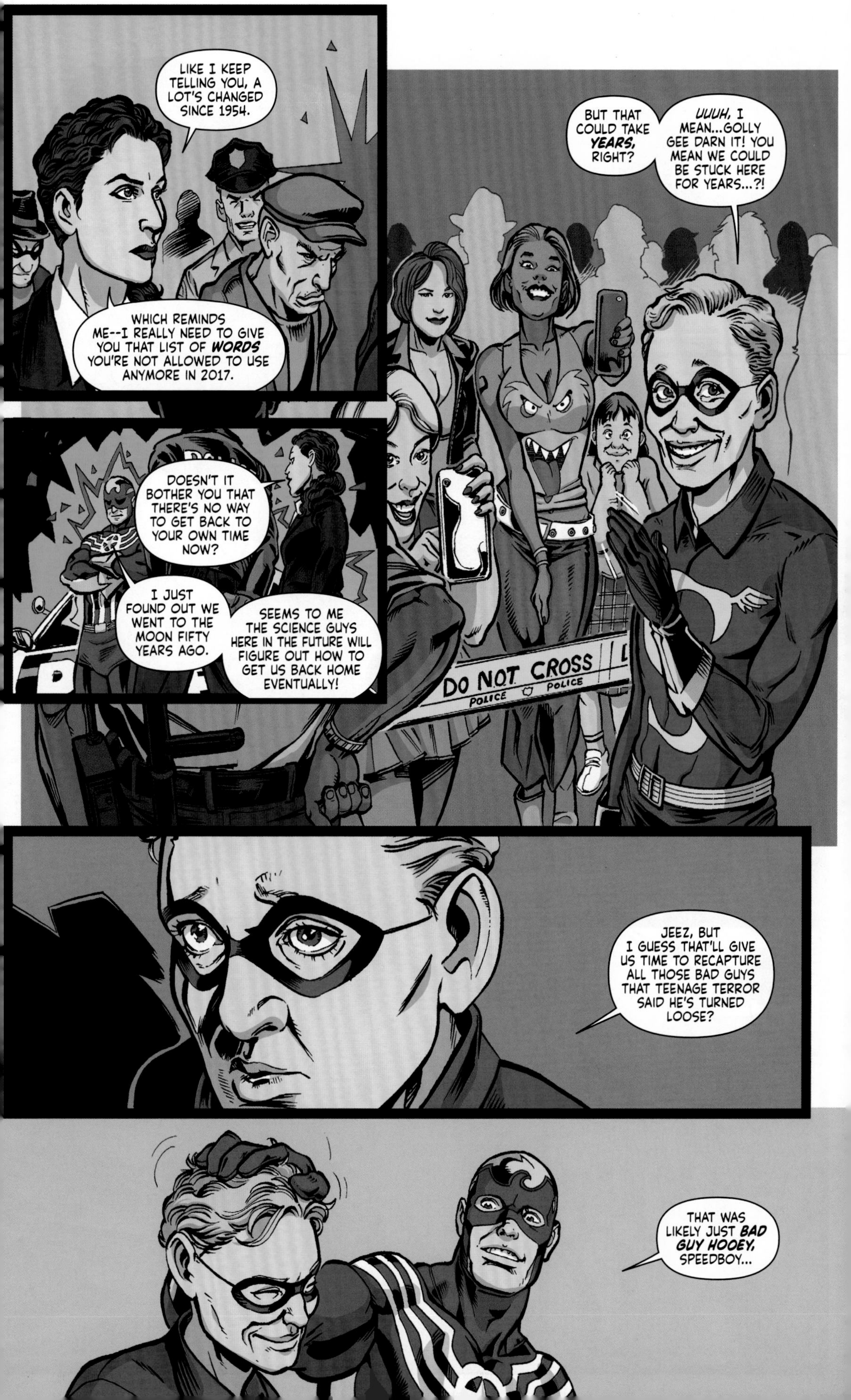

LIKE I KEEP TELLING YOU, A LOT'S CHANGED SINCE 1954.
WHICH REMINDS ME--I REALLY NEED TO GIVE YOU THAT LIST OF **WORDS** YOU'RE NOT ALLOWED TO USE ANYMORE IN 2017.
DOESN'T IT BOTHER YOU THAT THERE'S NO WAY TO GET BACK TO YOUR OWN TIME NOW?
I JUST FOUND OUT WE WENT TO THE MOON FIFTY YEARS AGO.
SEEMS TO ME THE SCIENCE GUYS HERE IN THE FUTURE WILL FIGURE OUT HOW TO GET US BACK HOME EVENTUALLY!
DO NOT CROSS
POLICE
POLICE
BUT THAT COULD TAKE **YEARS,** RIGHT?
UUUH, I MEAN...GOLLY GEE DARN IT! YOU MEAN WE COULD BE STUCK HERE FOR YEARS...?!
JEEZ, BUT I GUESS THAT'LL GIVE US TIME TO RECAPTURE ALL THOSE BAD GUYS THAT TEENAGE TERROR SAID HE'S TURNED LOOSE?
THAT WAS LIKELY JUST ***BAD GUY HOOEY,*** SPEEDBOY...

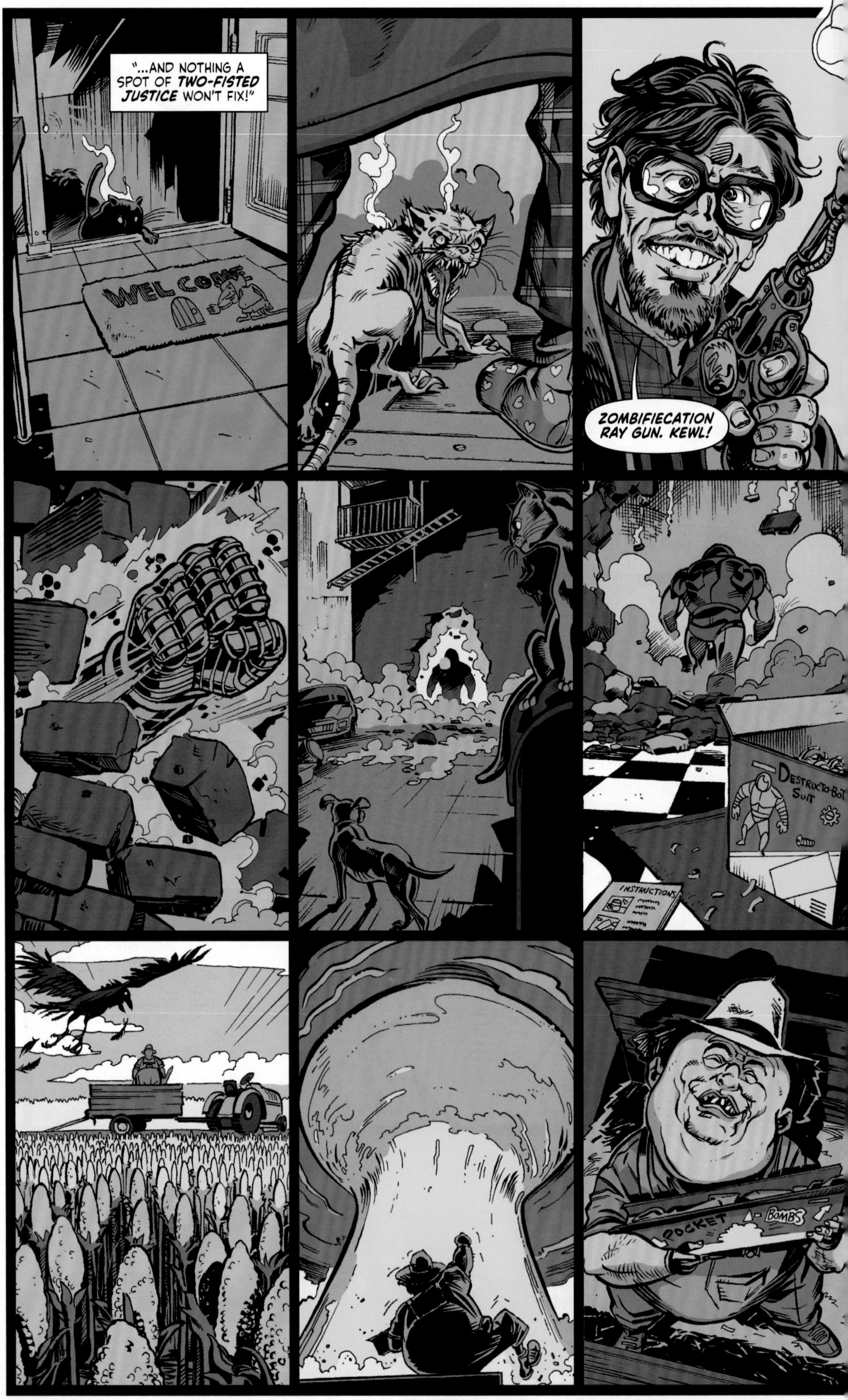
"...AND NOTHING A SPOT OF TWO-FISTED JUSTICE WON'T FIX!"
WELCOME
ZOMBIFIECATION RAY GUN. KEWL!
DESTRUCTO-BOT SUIT
INSTRUCTIONS
POCKET A-BOMBS

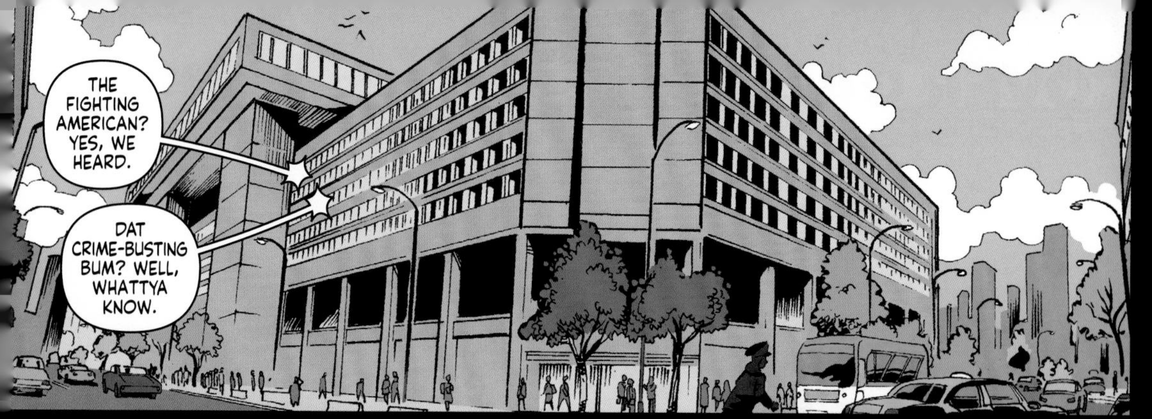
THE FIGHTING AMERICAN? YES, WE HEARD.
DAT CRIME-BUSTING BUM? WELL, WHATTYA KNOW.

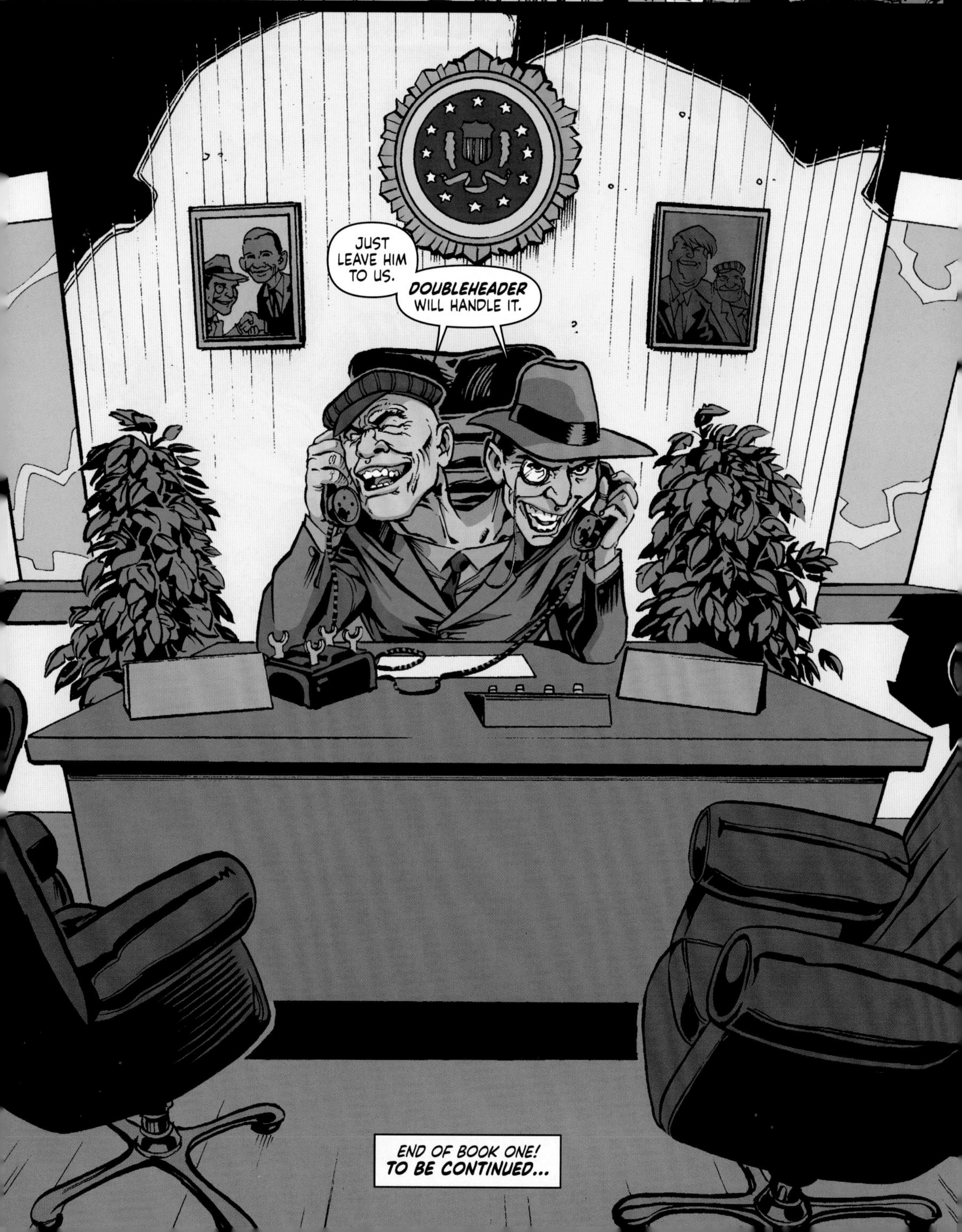
JUST LEAVE HIM TO US.
DOUBLEHEADER WILL HANDLE IT.
END OF BOOK ONE!
TO BE CONTINUED...

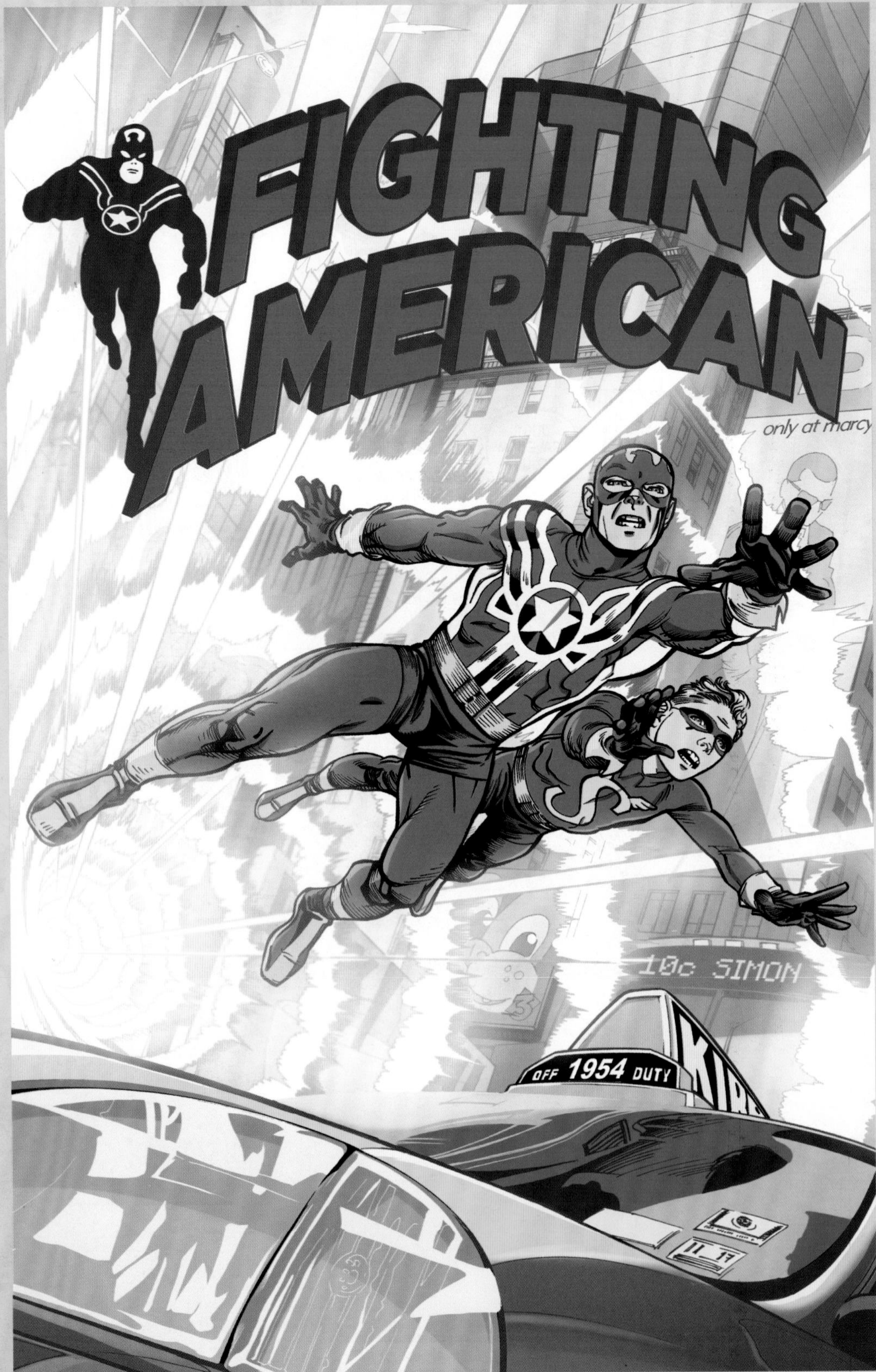
FIGHTING AMERICAN
only at marcy
10c SIMON
OFF 1954 DUTY
KIRB

ISSUE 1 VARIANT COVER D Art by Duke Mighten. Color by Tracy Bailey

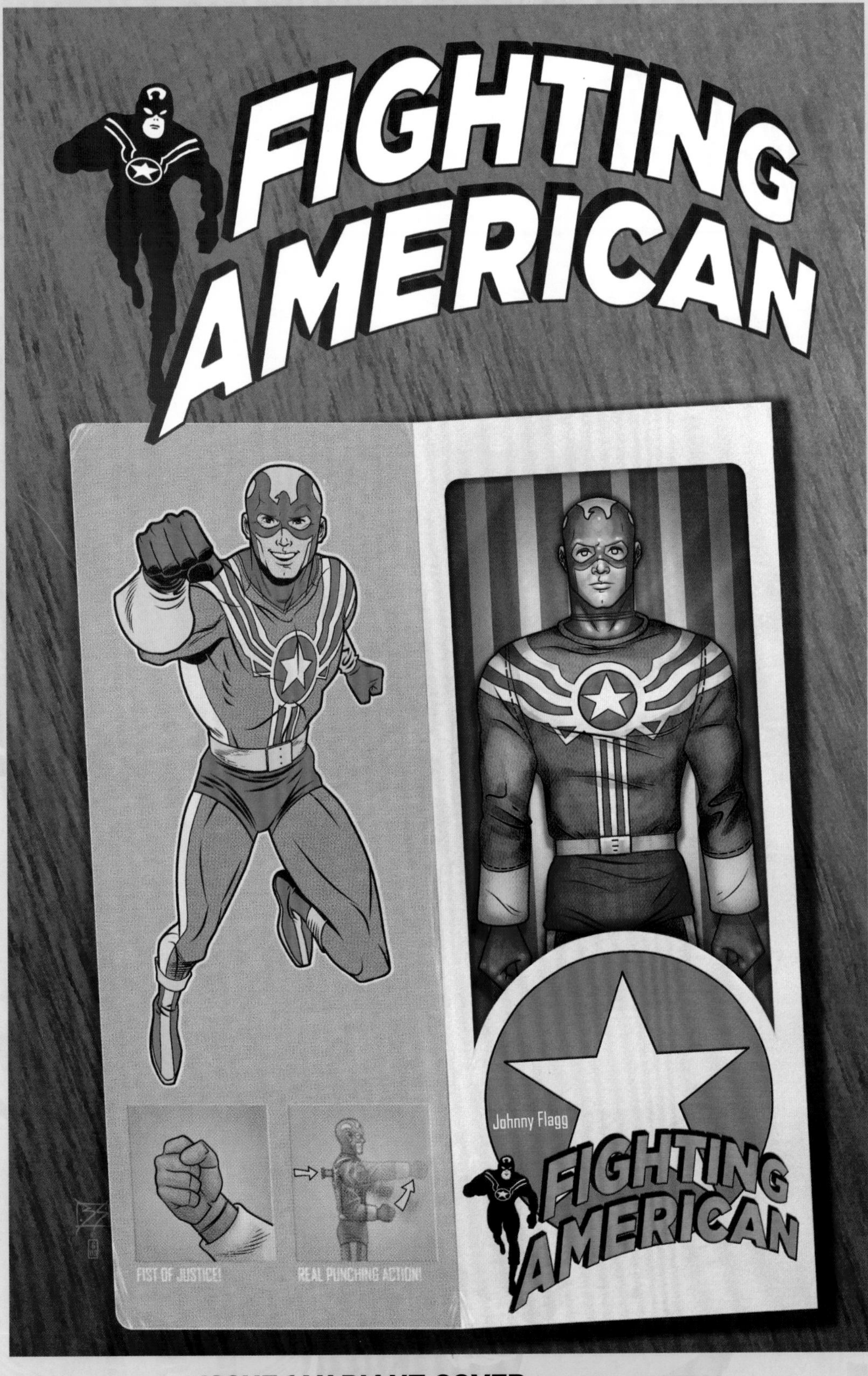
FIGHTING AMERICAN
Johnny Flagg
FIGHTING AMERICAN
FIST OF JUSTICE!
REAL PUNCHING ACTION!

ISSUE 1 VARIANT COVER Art by Blair Shedd

COVER GALLERY

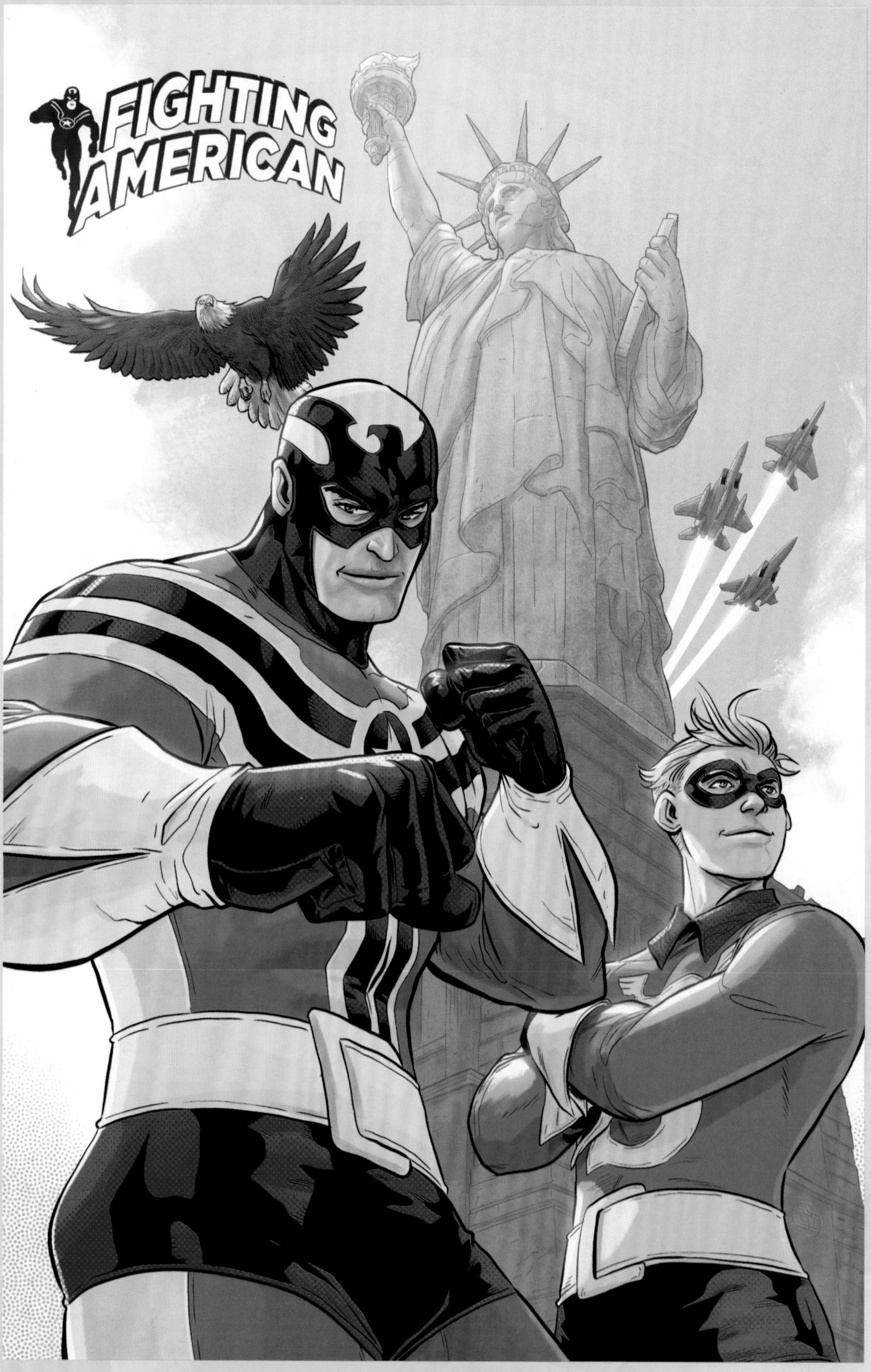

FIGHTING AMERICAN

ISSUE 1 NYCC VARIANT COVER Art by Andie Tong

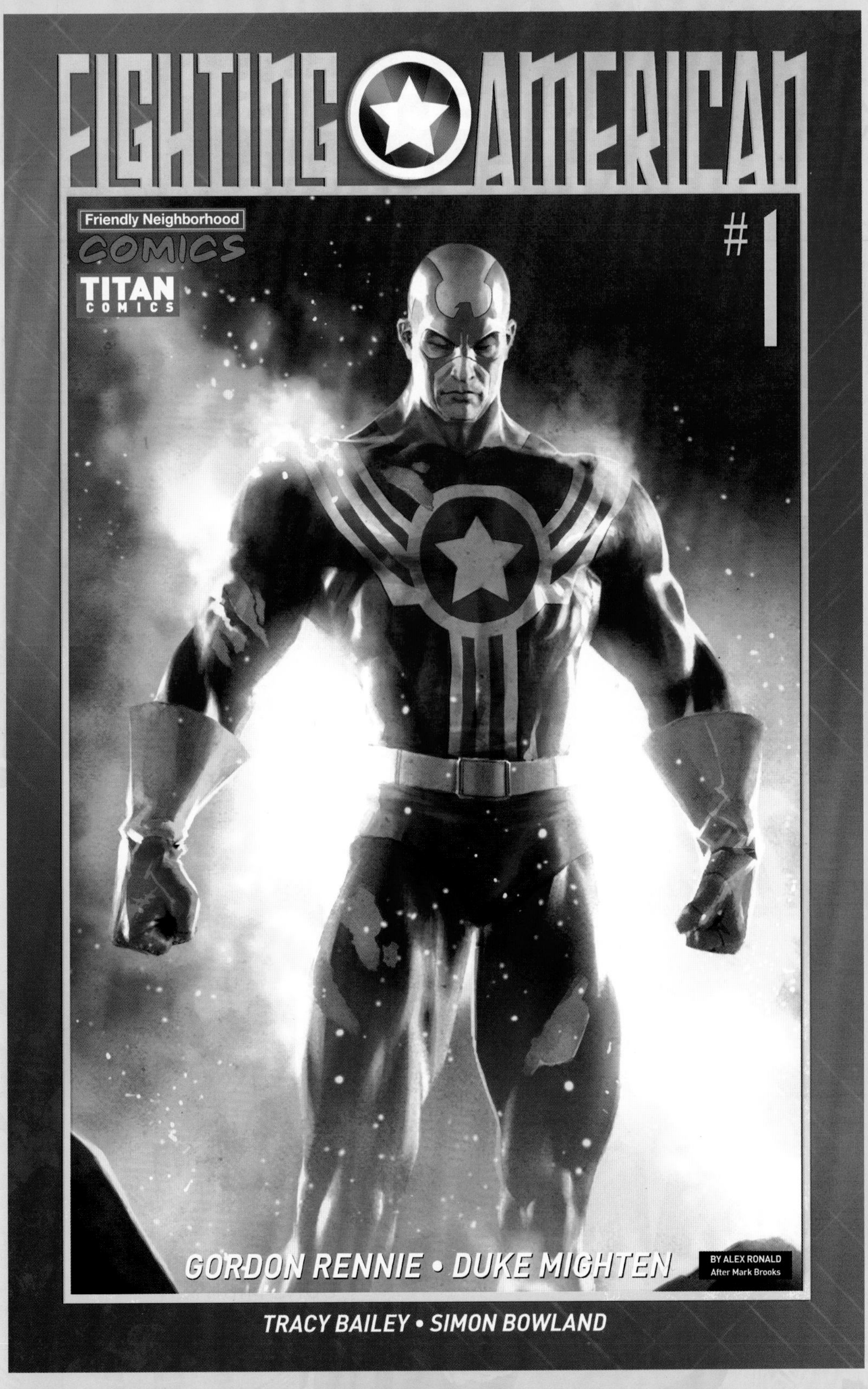
FIGHTING AMERICAN
Friendly Neighborhood
COMICS
TITAN
COMICS
#1
GORDON RENNIE • DUKE MIGHTEN
BY ALEX RONALD
After Mark Brooks
TRACY BAILEY • SIMON BOWLAND

ISSUE 1 FRIENDLY NEIGHBORHOOD COMICS EXCLUSIVE Art by Alex Ronald

COVER GALLERY

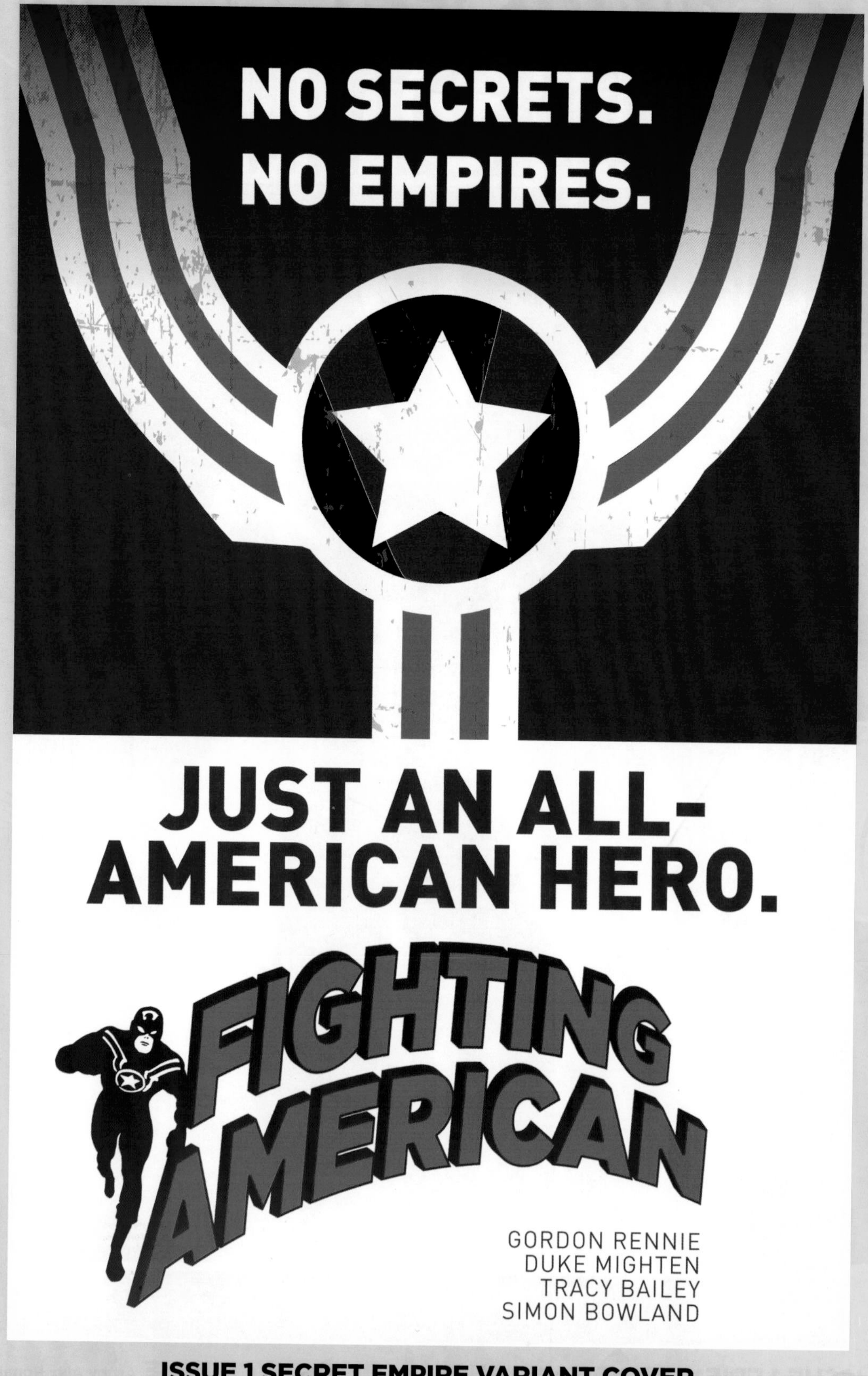
NO SECRETS.
NO EMPIRES.
JUST AN ALL-
AMERICAN HERO.
FIGHTING
AMERICAN
GORDON RENNIE
DUKE MIGHTEN
TRACY BAILEY
SIMON BOWLAND

ISSUE 1 SECRET EMPIRE VARIANT COVER

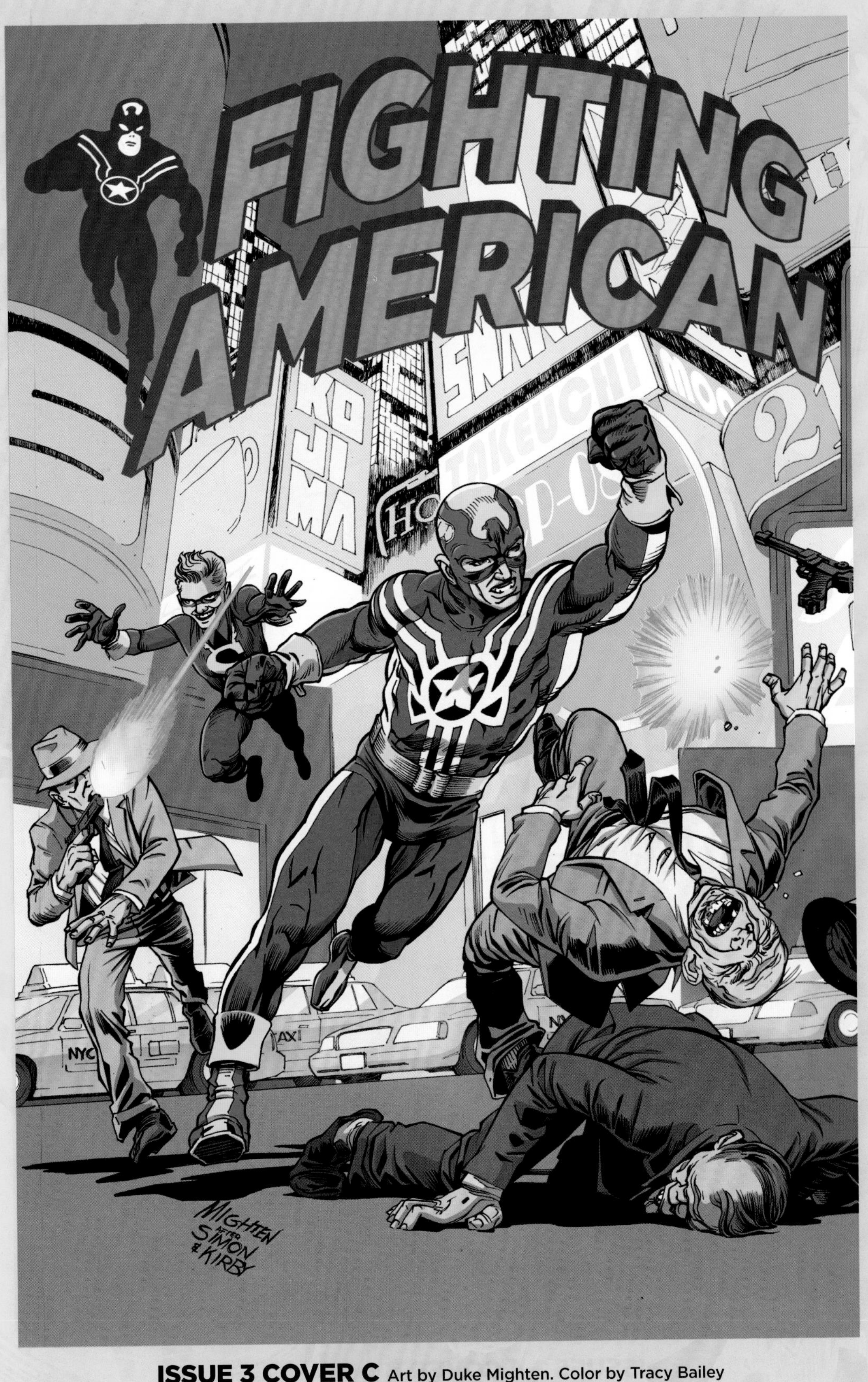
FIGHTING AMERICAN
KOJIMA
TAKEUCHI
NYC
TAXI
MIGHTEN AFTER SIMON & KIRBY

ISSUE 3 COVER C Art by Duke Mighten. Color by Tracy Bailey

COVER GALLERY

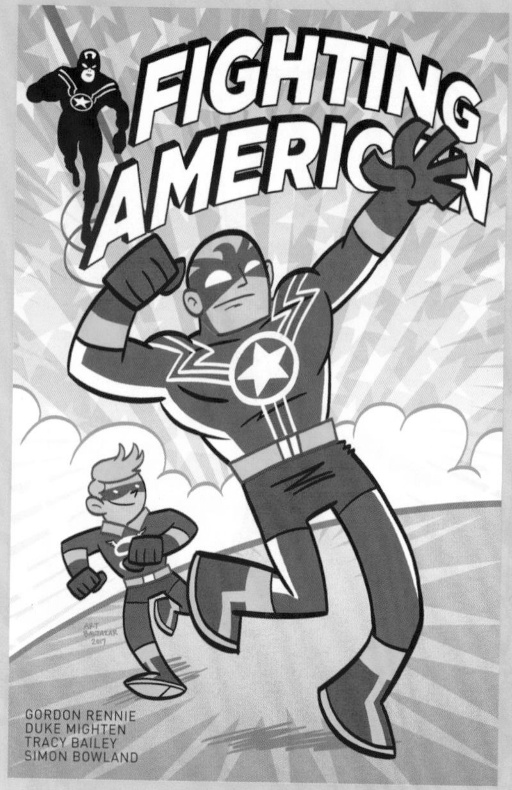
FIGHTING AMERICAN
GORDON RENNIE
DUKE MIGHTEN
TRACY BAILEY
SIMON BOWLAND

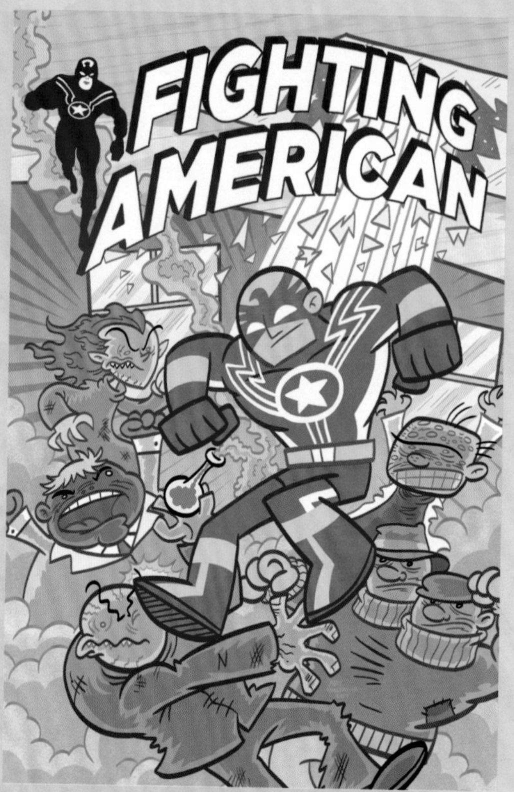
FIGHTING AMERICAN

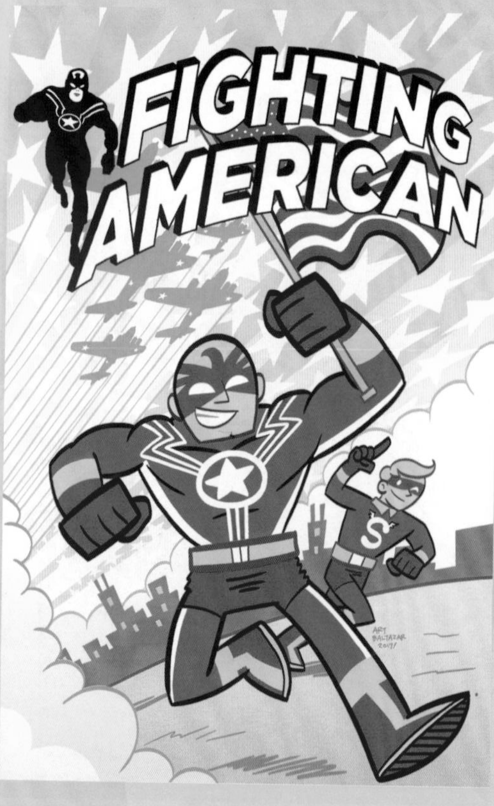
FIGHTING AMERICAN

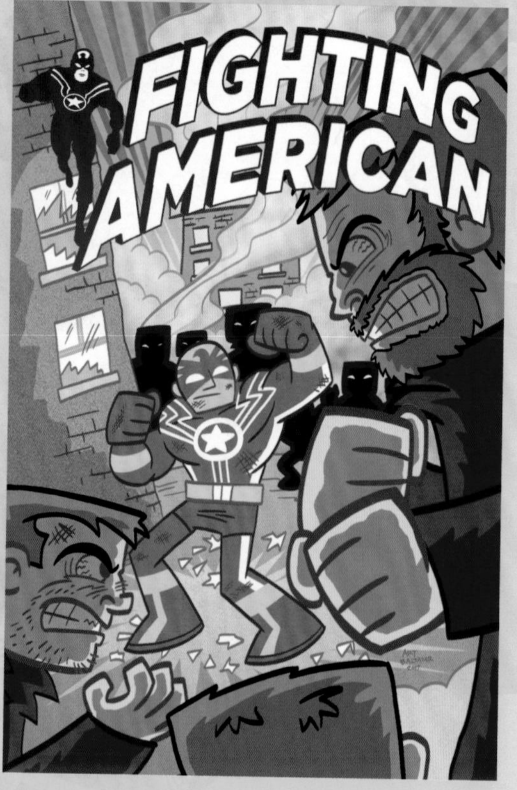
FIGHTING AMERICAN

ISSUES 1-4 COVER B Art by Art Baltazar

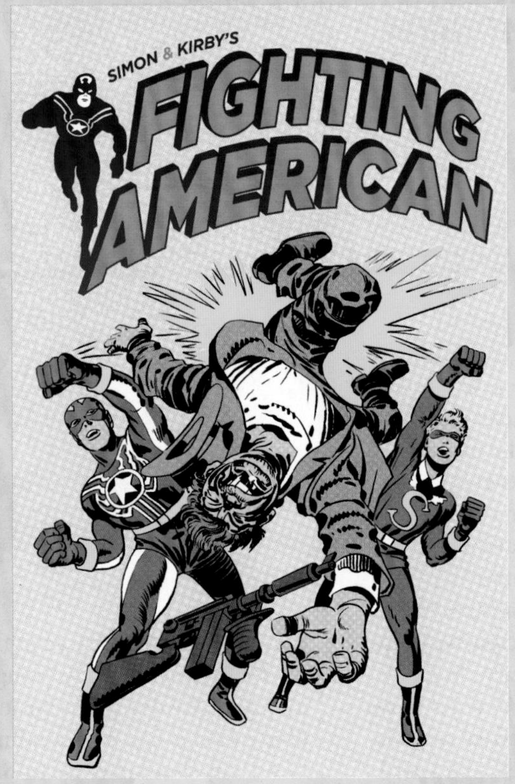
SIMON & KIRBY'S
FIGHTING AMERICAN

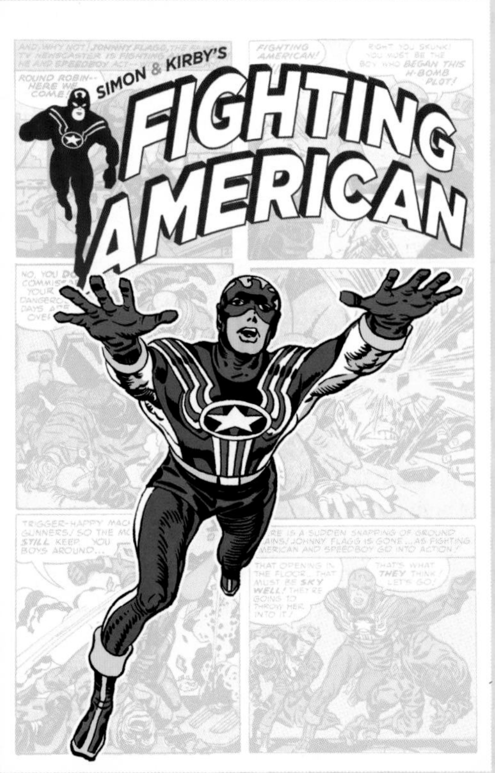
SIMON & KIRBY'S
FIGHTING AMERICAN

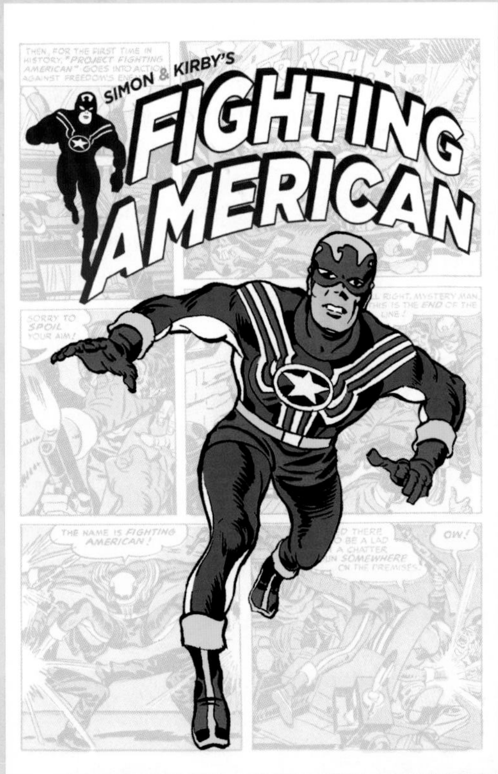
SIMON & KIRBY'S
FIGHTING AMERICAN

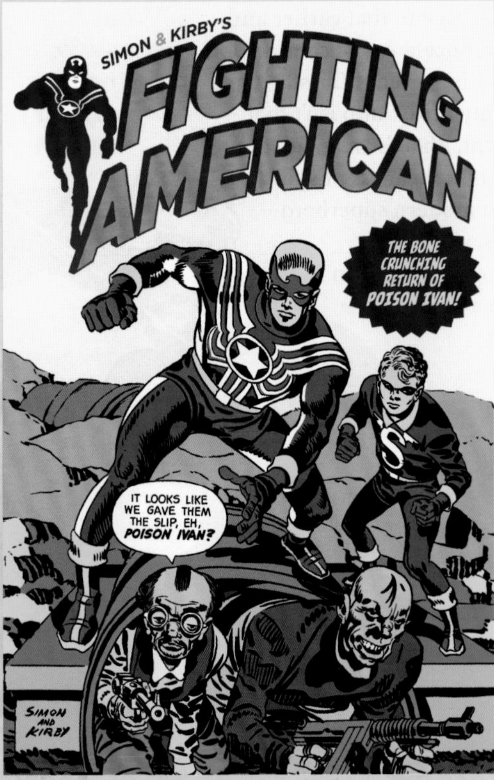
SIMON & KIRBY'S
FIGHTING AMERICAN
THE BONE CRUNCHING RETURN OF POISON IVAN!
IT LOOKS LIKE WE GAVE THEM THE SLIP, EH, POISON IVAN?
SIMON AND KIRBY

ISSUES 1-4 JACK KIRBY COVER Art by Jack Kirby. Issue #4 inked by Joe Simon

FIGHTING TALK

AN INTERVIEW WITH WRITER GORDON RENNIE AND EDITOR DAVID LEACH BY CHRIS THOMPSON

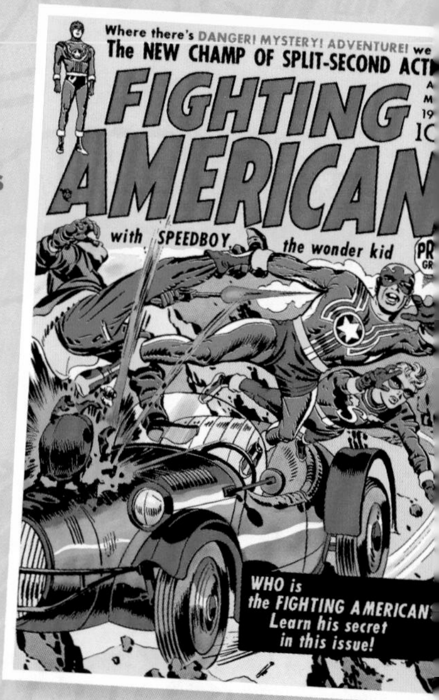

Where there's DANGER! MYSTERY! ADVENTURE! we
The NEW CHAMP OF SPLIT-SECOND ACT
FIGHTING AMERICAN
with SPEEDBOY the wonder kid
WHO is the FIGHTING AMERICAN
Learn his secret in this issue!

Aside from the obvious appeal of working on an original Simon & Kirby creation, what is the appeal of Fighting American for you? What makes him so special and what makes him the hero that the world needs now?

David Leach (DL): I think it's his gung ho attitude, his punch-first ask questions later mentality. His utter belief in his own moral superiority. He has no guile, no inner monolog and he's not crippled by self-doubt. He's from that glorious era of American history when America seemed to be at its best.

Gordon Rennie (GR): What you get with *Fighting American* is a call-back to that earlier and more innocent era of comic book storytelling, even if the story he's suddenly thrust into isn't that innocent. There's an awful lot of downright meaness of spirit stuff in modern superhero comics, so possibly we're commenting on that to a degree.

The Fighting American's origin story is pretty 'out there' – even by Simon & Kirby standards. Have you tried to contextualise that in some way or just embraced the zaniness of it all?

GR. Oh, the character's origin story is totally mental. We do revisit it in the story, without in any way trying to revise it, and one character does comment that allowing the military to transfer your consciousness into the physically superior body of your dead brother in order to carry on his anti-Red menace crusade might be considered a bit weird.

What have you done to preserve the unique flavor of the original Fighting American for modern audiences?

GR. He's the same character fr the 1950s, just suddenly brough into 2017. He doesn't try to ada himself to his new surrounding – and why should he? He think he comes from the greatest period in American history. W play a lot on the idea of differin perceptions between the 1950s now, between what was normal then and what might considered strang today. Indeed, to Fighting Americ many of our soci mores might seen equally odd.

The idea of the teenage sideki is somewhat outdated

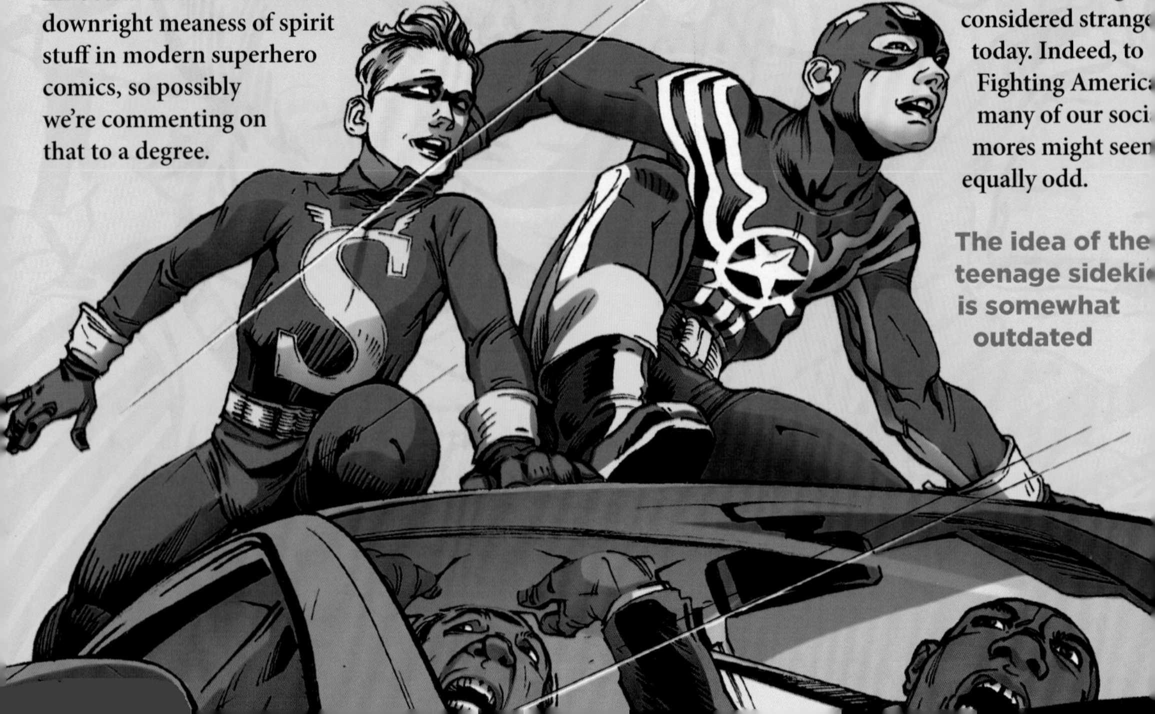

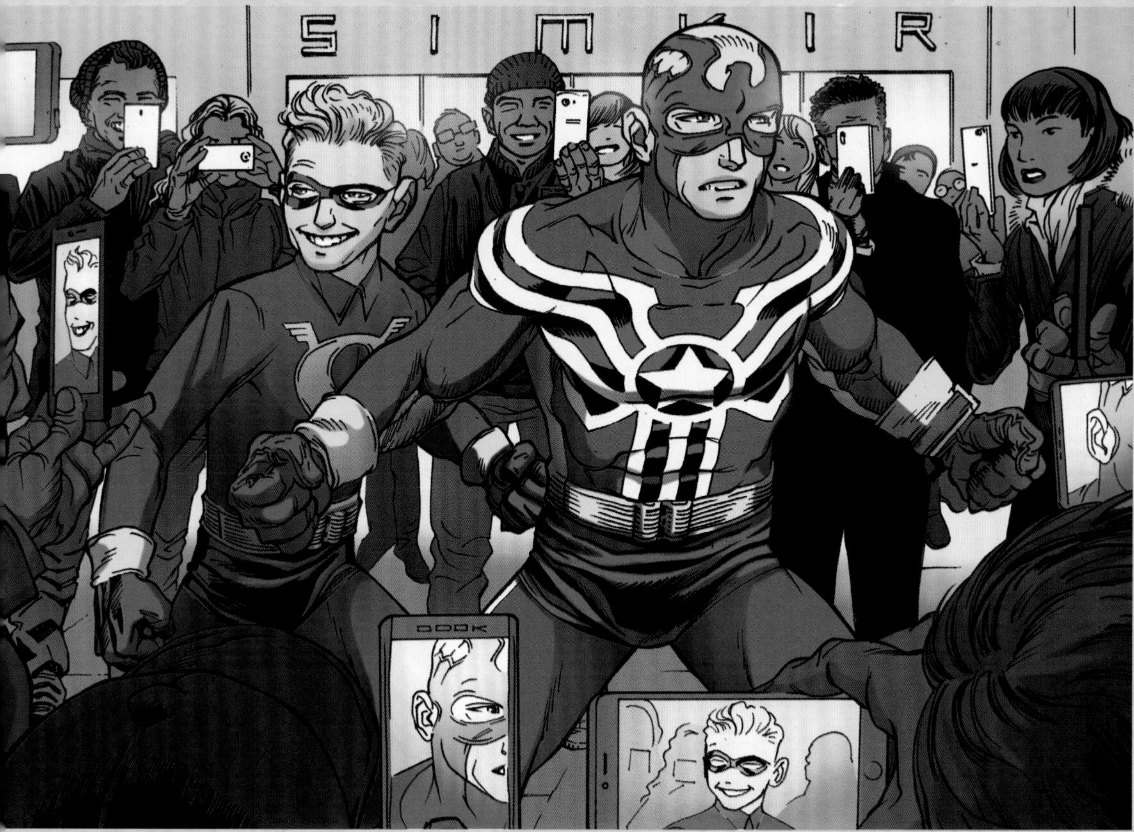

ow. How have you ldressed that with eedboy, and can we pect their relationship to ange, going forward?

R. Speedboy's a lot of fun. He's t this teenage 'Gee whizz!' 1950s nocence that might be slightly allenged by some of the ff he encounters in the odern world. Supervillains d Red plots to overthrow nerican values he can ndle, but twerking leos, building-sized gerie billboards and line adult entertainment ght be a bit tougher to il with. Speedboy is a le more susceptible to temptations of the st Century than his ardian.

e you hoping o include other elements of the series (perhaps even other Simon & Kirby creations) during the course of your run? Any hints or teases you can provide at this stage?

GR. We've got a bunch of cameos from the character's colorful rogue's gallery of villains. It would be great to dip further into the Simon & Kirby character pool in later series.

DL. Let's just say that the Simon & Kirby Universe is a wondrous place full of fantastic characters and that we see *Fighting American* as our portal into that amazing multi-dimensional universe.

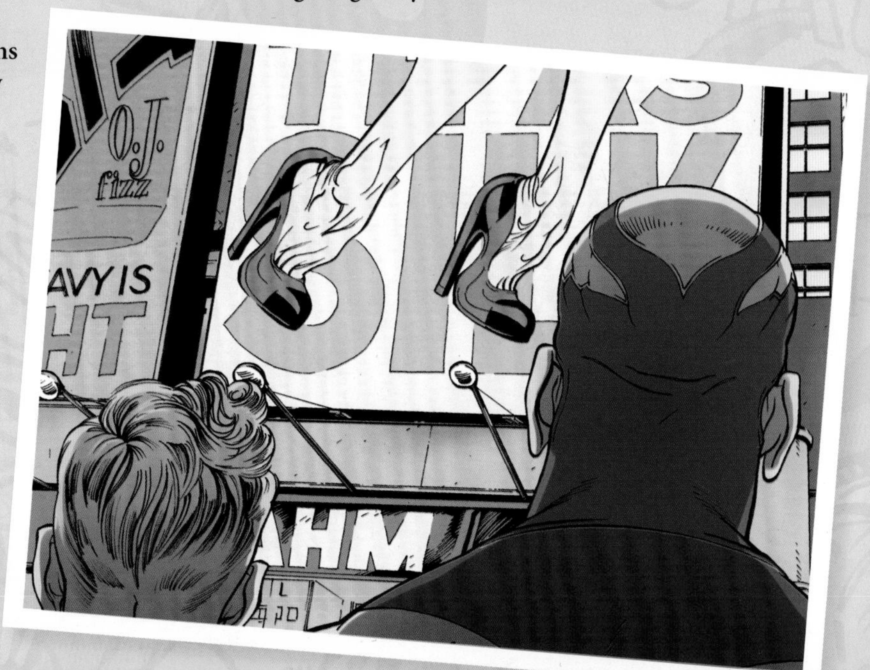
O.J. fizz

CHARACTER SKETCHES AND THUMBNAILS

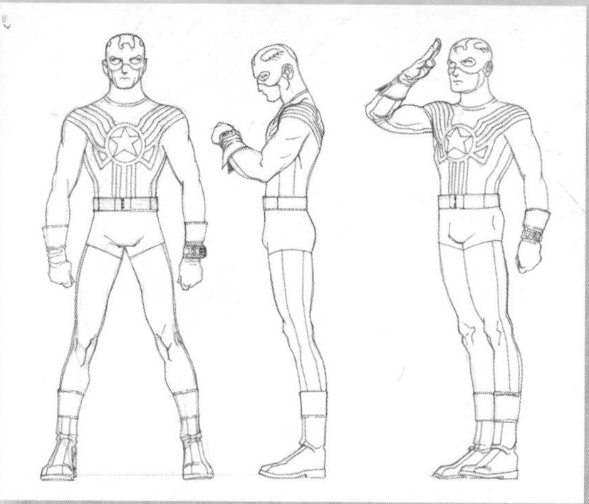

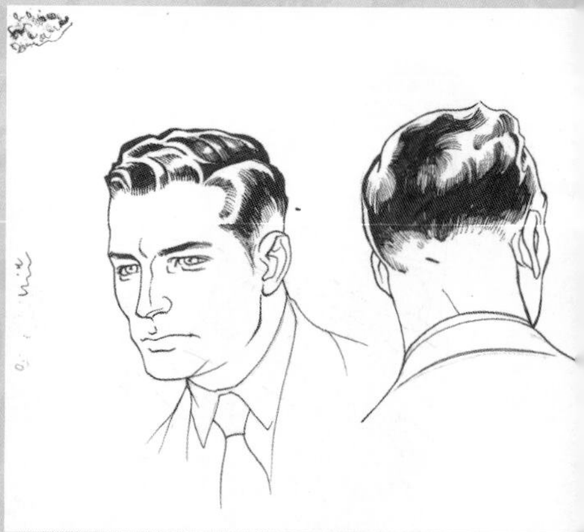

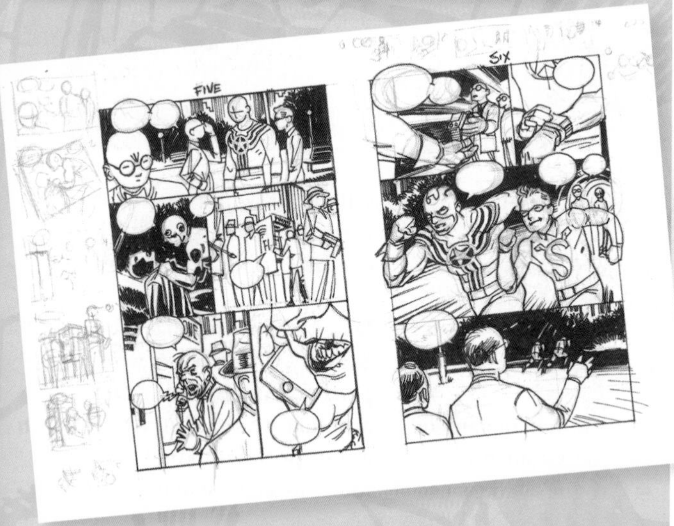
FIVE
SIX

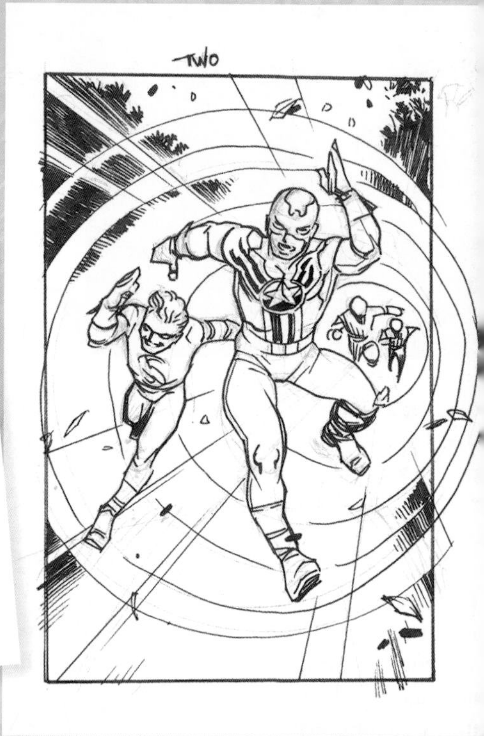
TWO

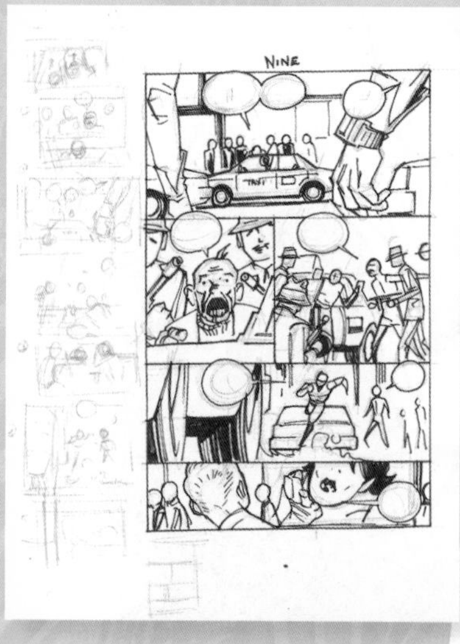
NINE

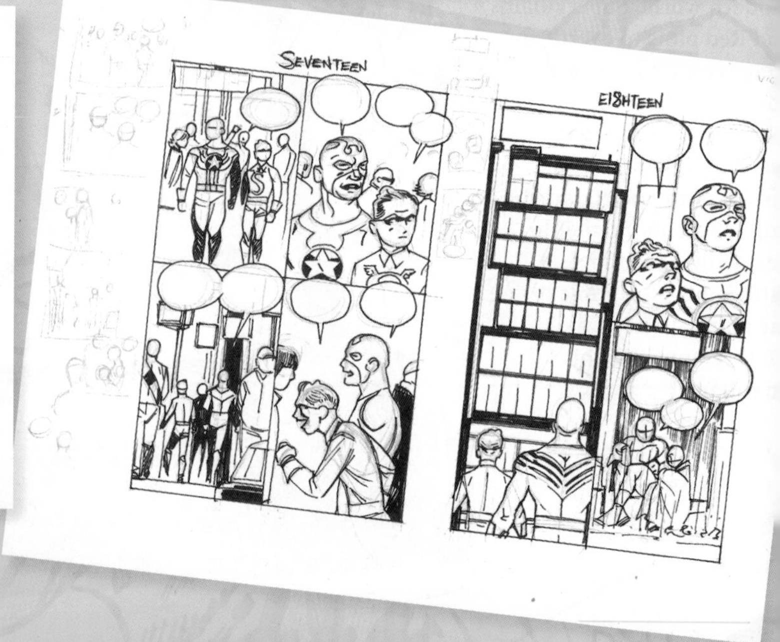
SEVENTEEN
EIGHTEEN

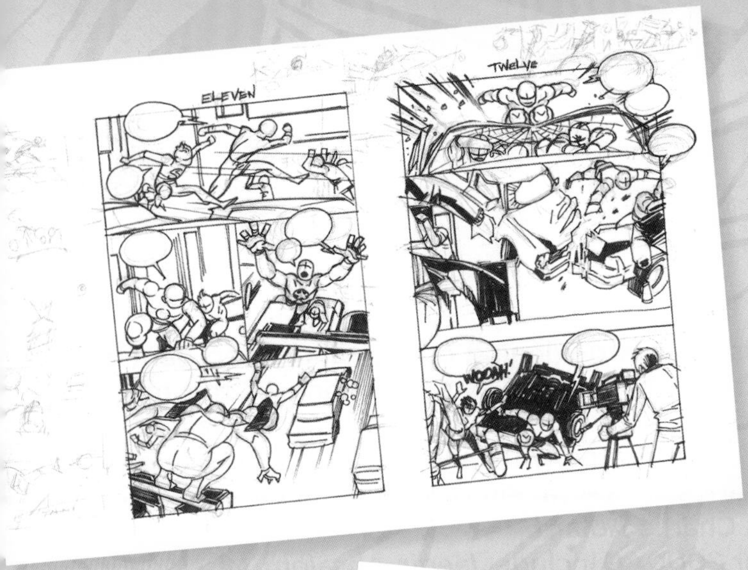
ELEVEN
TWELVE
WOOAH!

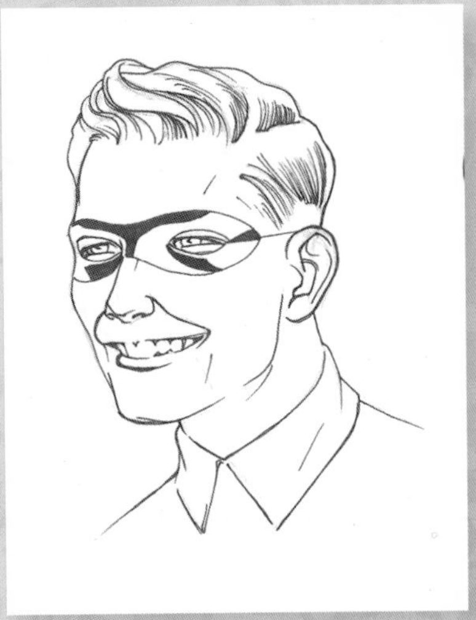

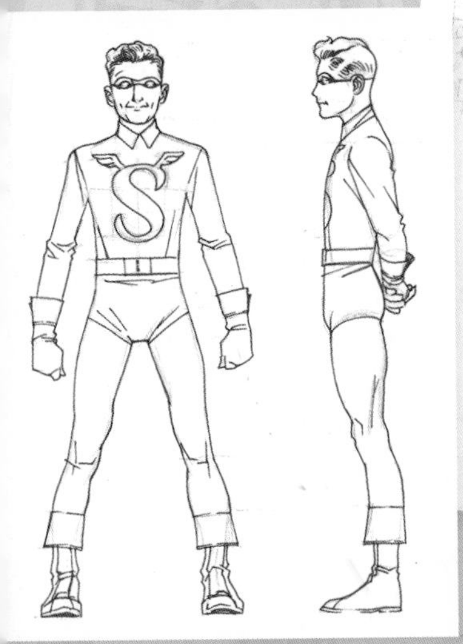

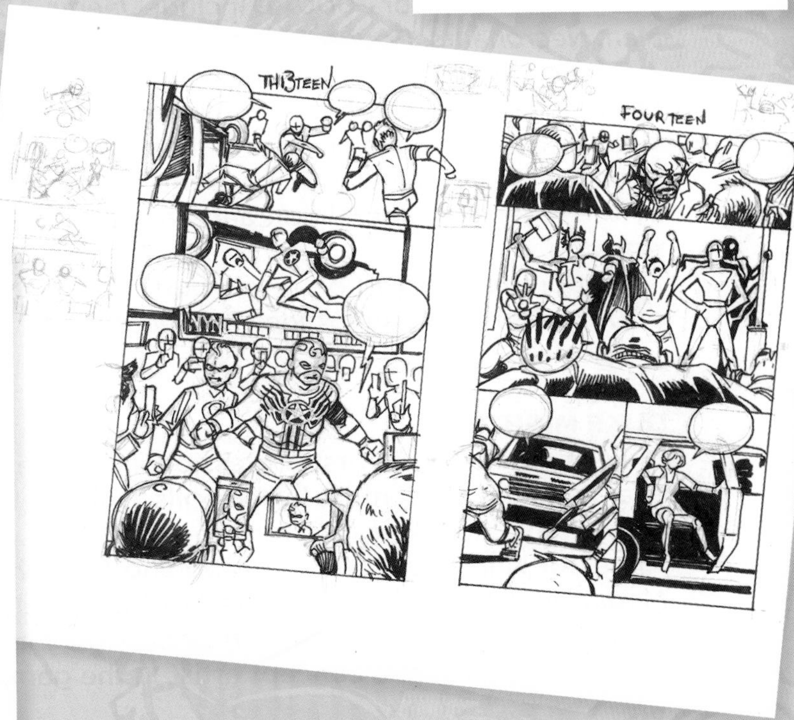
TH13TEEN
FOURTEEN

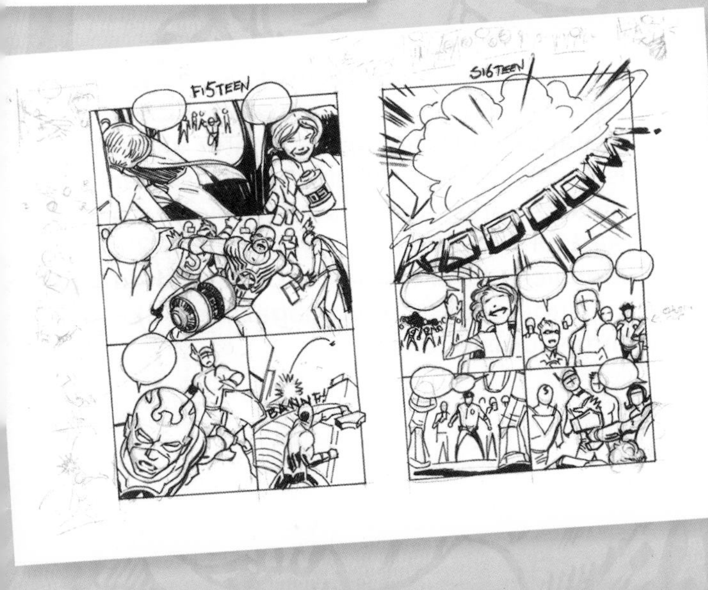
FI5TEEN
SI6TEEN

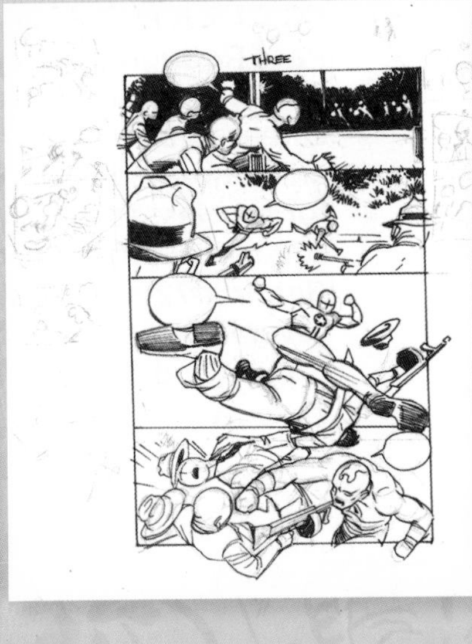
THREE

BIOS

GORDON RENNIE is an award-winning comics and video games writer. For more than 20 years, he has been one of the most prominent writers for *2000AD* and the *Judge Dredd Megazine*. On *Dredd* alone he has collaborated with legendary artists like *Judge Dredd* co-creator Carlos Ezquerra, Ian Gibson, Cam Kennedy and the *Walking Dead*'s Charlie Adlard.

His other strips for *2000AD* include *Jaegir, Absalom, Missionary Man, Necronauts, Rogue Trooper* and *Caballistics, Inc.*

Outside of *2000AD*, his work includes *Doctor Who, Department of Monsterology, Warhammer,* the award-winning *Robert Burns Witch-Hunter* graphic novel and the *Fighting American* series for *Titan Comics*, continuing the adventures of the character created by the legendary Joe Simon and Jack Kirby, creators of *Captain America.*

Gordon has worked on numerous video games, including Call of Duty, Star Wars, and *Alien Vs. Predator.*

DUKE MIGHTEN
Duke Mighten got his first professional job after being discovered at a UK comic convention by Pat Mills. Duke went on to draw *Brats Bizarre* and *Accident Man* for the cult British comic *Toxic!, Dark Angel* for Marvel UK, *Judge Dredd* and *Shimura* for *Judge Dredd Megazine,* and the *Batman: The Book of Shadows* graphic novel for DC Comics. He currently lives and works in Sydney, Australia as an art director and concept artist in the games industry.

PC DE LA FUENTE
Paco Rodriguez de la Fuente was born in the costal town of Santander, Spain. He spent his early years in Madrid and started his professional career as a storyboard artist, character designer and animator in the animation industry. He has also worked as a Production Designer for movies, as a designer for theme parks, and in advertising. As a sequential artist, Paco has worked for DC Comics, on *Robin* #123-125, *Batgirl* #72 and for IDW on *Sidechicks* #1-3. He has also worked on several European publications including *Kiss Cómic* magazine for La Cupula and *3rd World* for Tyrannosaurus books.

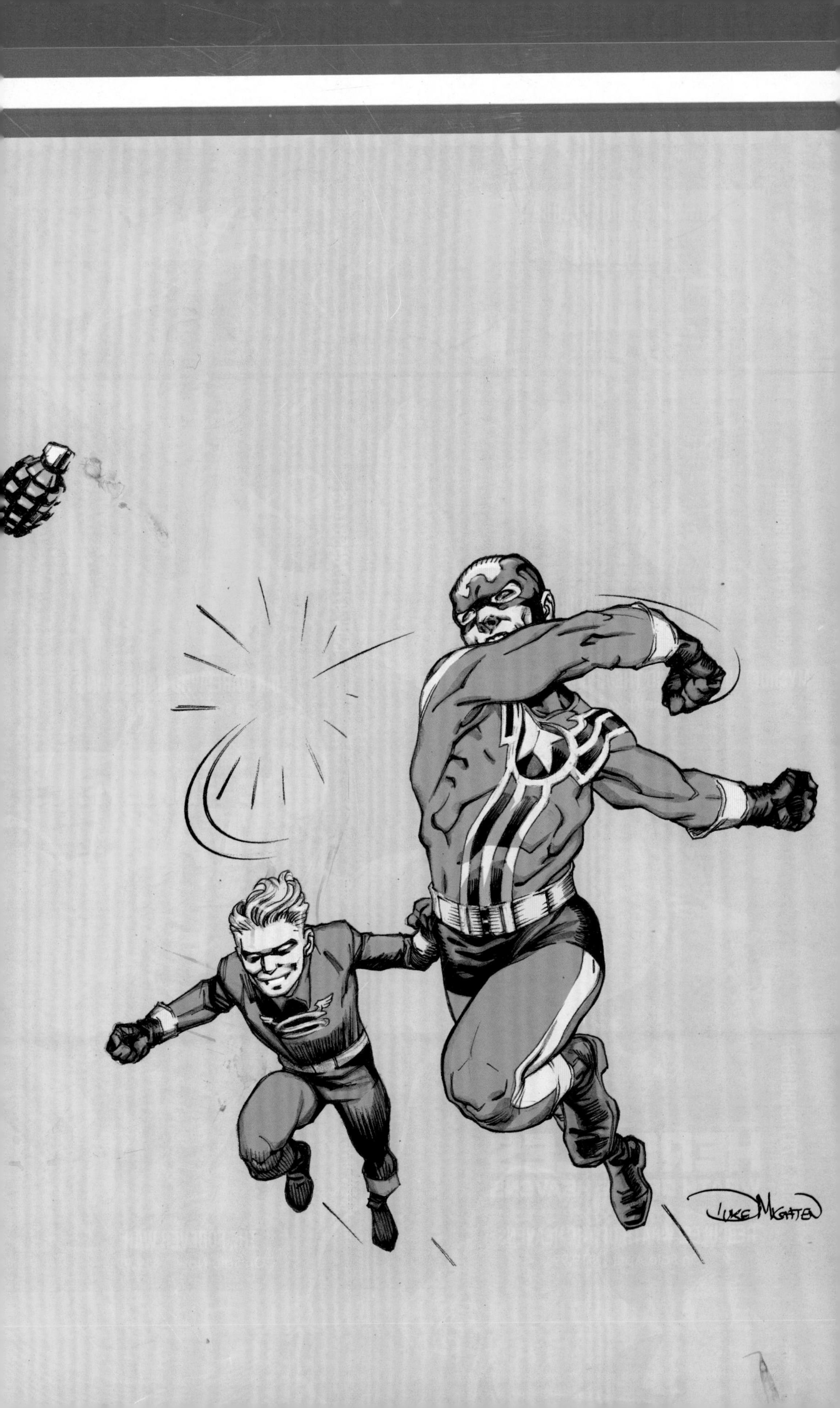

THE GREATEST HEROES - GHTING ACROSS SPACE AND TIME

KAREEM ABDUL-JABBAR
RAYMOND OBSTFELD
MYCROFT HOLMES
JOSHUA CASSARA
AND THE APOCALYPSE HANDBOOK
LUIS GUERRERO
SIMON BOWLAND

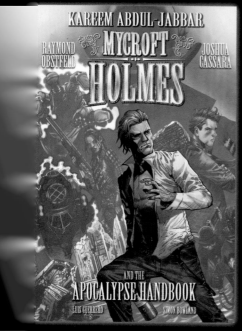

OFT HOLMES AND THE APOCALYPSE HANDBOOK
On Sale Now | $16.99

ISBN: 9781785861475

DAN DARE

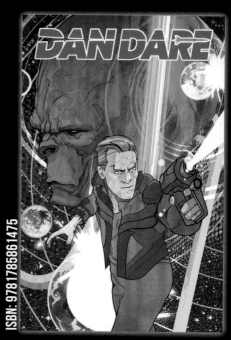

DAN DARE: WHO DARES WINS
On Sale April | $16.99

JDMORVAN
LOOKY
THILL
HERCULES
WRATH OF THE HEAVENS

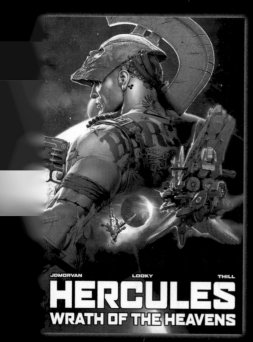

HERCULES: WRATH OF THE HEAVENS
On Sale April | $19.99

ISBN: 9781785860898

JOE HALDEMAN • MARVANO
THE FOREVER WAR
MANDELLA

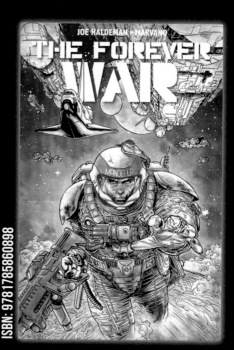

THE FOREVER WAR
On Sale Now | $19.99

AVAILABLE IN PRINT AND DIGITALLY AT TITAN-COMICS.COM

TITAN COMICS